HISTORY OF THE US MARINES

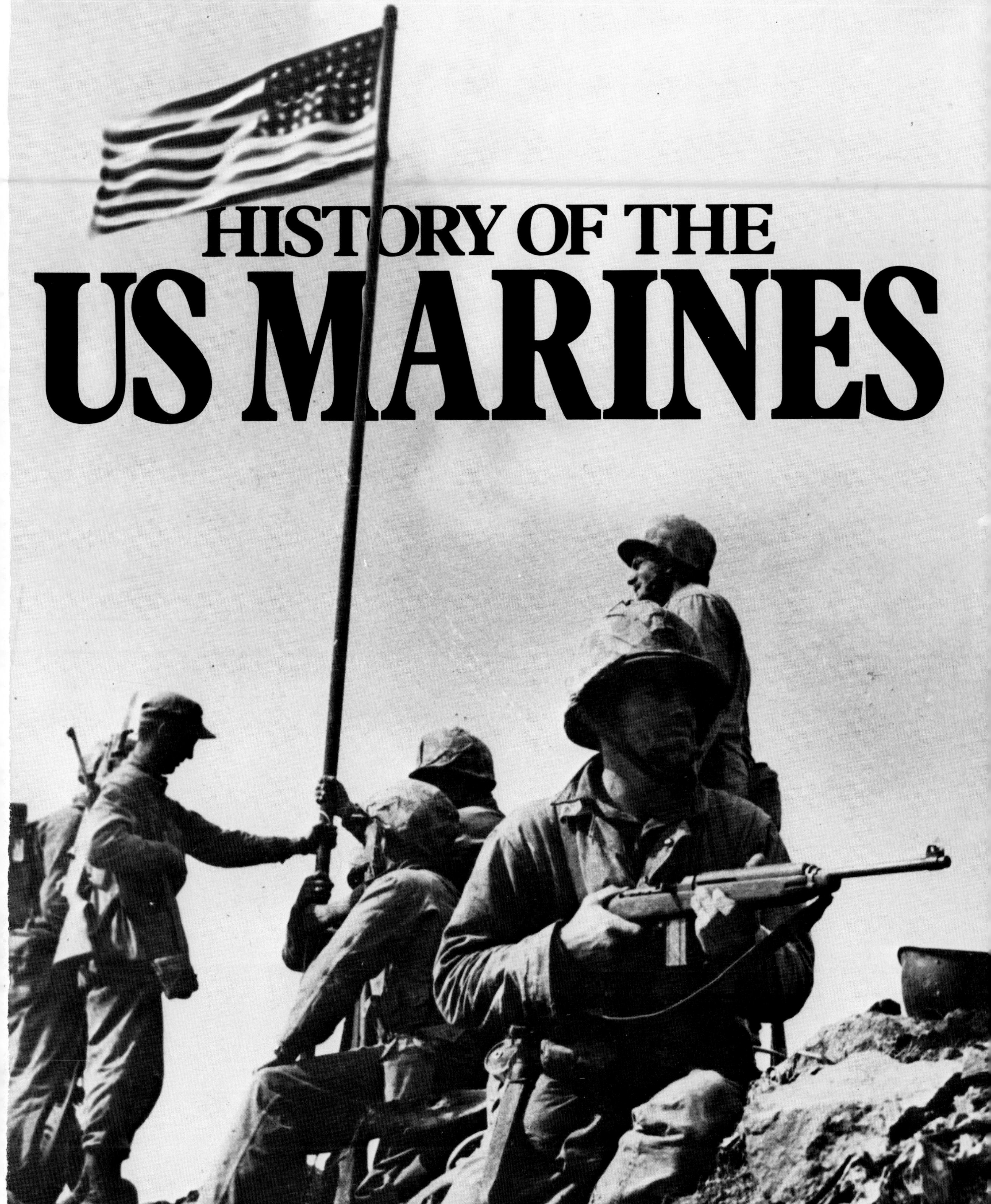

HISTORY OF THE US MARINES

Jack Murphy

NEW YORK
A Bison Book

Produced by
Bison Books Corp
17 Sherwood Place
Greenwich
CT 06830
USA

First US edition published 1984 by Exeter Books
Distributed by Bookthrift
Exeter is a trademark of Simon and Schuster
Bookthrift is a registered trademark of Simon and Schuster New York, New York.

ISBN 0-671-06982-9

Printed in Hong Kong

Page 1: Marines of the Fifth Division hoist the flag on Mount Suribachi, Iwo Jima, in February 1945.
Page 2-3: Marines debark from a UH-1 helicopter in Vietnam.
This page: A Marine detachment from the USS *Chicago* pictured in 1892.

CONTENTS

Above: Marines land ashore at Birbera, Somalia, during Operation Bright Star, the US-Egyptian exercises.

INTRODUCTION

America is in essence an island state, separated by the world's oceans from most of its allies and trading partners. Right from the start, it has had to be ready to protect its economic and political relationships in places all around the globe. The facts of geography make America a maritime nation; the necessities of geopolitics require that it not only maintain unrestricted access to the seven seas, but also remain capable of defending that access when necessary.

That is how the Corps serves the nation—as a force in readiness, always prepared to fight, anywhere, anytime.

Throughout the nearly 200 years-long history of the Marine Corps it has formed what is, compared with the other services, a tiny organization, made up—in the words of a Marine recruiting poster—of 'a few good men.' The Corps's concern for quality over quantity was foreshadowed in the document of the Continental Congress that created the Continental Marines, predecessors of the present Corps; it specified '*that particular care be taken* [to enlist] such as are good seamen, or so acquainted with maritime affairs as to be able to serve to advantage by sea, when required.'

It is no coincidence that many of the Marine Corps's more famous actions and expeditionary services have taken place in periods when the United States has not been involved in a formal state of war; the Corps works hard at maintaining a 'cutting edge' that keeps it ready to be first to fight. The key factors in achieving the Corps's constant state of readiness are those 'few good men' to which the recruiting poster refers. Though the technology of warfare changes, the need for the trained, disciplined fighting man has not changed, and will not in the foreseeable future.

There is nothing new to this—elite military forces are as old as history. The Bible tells of 300 soldiers who were 'The sword of the Lord, and of Gideon,' chosen out of 10,000 to lead an attack that defeated the army of Midian. Themistocles, leader of the Athenians, issued a decree that his navy '. . . enlist Marines, twenty to a ship

. . .;' these *Epibatas*, as they were called, helped turn back the Persian invasion. Rome, too, had special legions of *milites classiarii*, or 'soldiers of the fleet.' But the first true corps of Marines, and the ancestor of the United States Marines, was formed in 1664 when England's King Charles II decreed: *That twelve hundred land souldjers be forthwith raysed, to be in readinesse, to be distributed into his* [*Majesty's*] *Fleets prepared for Sea Service* [*which*] *twelve hundred men are to be putt into One Regiment. . . .* He gave this new group the ponderous name of 'The Duke of York and Albany's Maritime Regiment of Foot.' These were true salty soldiers, fully under the command of the Admiralty. They evolved over the next century into the British Marines; several Colonial battalions modeled on the British Marines were formed in America prior to the revolution against England.

The Marines were born to be maritime soldiers, and this definition of them is as true today as ever. The Corps consists of military specialists whose area of expertise is the beachhead where the sea touches the land. Here is where their combat training and their combat tradition are focused; the naval relationship goes bone deep. Not that this relationship hasn't been challenged—time and again during the past two centuries there have been attempts to sever the connection between the Corps and the Navy. Some of these actions originated, in fact, within the highest ranks of the Navy itself.

That the attempts failed is fortunate because, to paraphrase an old saying, 'If the Marine Corps didn't exist, it would have to be invented.' Every nation must possess the military capacity to support its international priorities, and for the United States, a world leader, this is preeminently the case. The assigned missions of the Corps provide important elements of this capacity; these missions are:

1 To keep itself ready to fight a land action anywhere in the world.
2 To maintain 'seaworthiness'—the proficient ability to coordinate with the Navy in the carrying out of amphibious operations, both during peace and war.
3 To set and maintain standards as a stable, professional combat force by which military comparisons may be made.

It is in this third area that an interesting challenge lies for the Marine Corps: to develop and perfect its proficiency in combined sea, land and air operations. Old interservice rivalries still make for difficulties in the smooth and successful carrying out of such actions, but the near future may see the Marine Corps, with its long experience in air-sea-land combat, serving as a catalyst for maximum operational cooperation among the three branches of Service.

Left: Marines of 3rd Battalion, First Marine Regiment, check a hut in Quang Tri province, Vietnam, during Operation Badger Tooth.

FROM THE REVOLUTION TO THE CIVIL WAR

'Drum, Fife and Colors'—1775–1783

In April of 1775 Governor Gage, England's man in Massachusetts, sent a strong force of British Redcoats marching toward Concord to destroy a colonist munition supply he'd learned was stored there. As the soldiers marched through the night, Paul Revere and others rode to spread the alarm, and when the British reached Lexington at dawn, grim-faced minute men were lined up to meet them. A shot rang out—fired by whom no one knows to this day—volleys were exchanged, and when the shooting ceased, eight patriots lay dead on the village green. The Redcoats pressed on to Concord where, in an incident made vivid by Ralph Waldo Emerson,

> . . . the embattled farmers stood,
> And fired the shot heard round the world.

Several weeks later, in an atmosphere of crisis, the Continental Congress convened in Philadelphia, a gathering of the most distinguished men in the colonies. Each Colony was a separate legal entity, independent of the others though answerable to the Crown, and each had its own ideas about what actions the Congress should take. Months of struggle then followed in an attempt to work out some basis for reconciliation between the Crown and the American people, and time after time these efforts were insultingly rebuffed by King George III. Gradually the conciliatory spirit of the Congress waned, to be replaced by a sterner attitude, and in November of the year this new spirit found expression in a landmark resolution in American military history.

Sitting in Tun Tavern, a popular Philadelphia inn of the day, a committee of the Congress drafted a resolution that the entire legislative body approved on 10 November 1775. It called for the creation of a new military force to be known as the Continental Marines. The owner of the Tun Tavern, Robert Mullan, a popular and energetic patriot, was named a Marine captain, and Samuel Nicholas, owner of another tavern, was designated commandant of the Continental Marines. Mullan began to actively recruit for the organization, and soon was able to report great success to his senior officer, Captain Nicholas; by early in 1776 the Continental Marines would be ready for their initial action.

Below: A more modern recruiting poster emphasizes Marine traditions.

U.S. MARINES
ARE NOW
ACCEPTING
MEN
FOR
ENLISTMENT
CALLING MARINES TO THE COLORS IN 1775

The American Revolution saw service by three types of Marines: the ones belonging to each Colony's own navy (more about these units later); the Marines aboard privateer ships authorized by Congress to attack enemy vessels for personal profit; and, most importantly, the Continental or Regular Marines. Before detailing the exploits of the Continental Marines, it will be useful to briefly trace the military origins of this organization.

Forerunners of the Corps

Experience as 'sea soldiers' was nothing new to the American colonists; their previous experience was gained, ironically, in service for, rather than against, the Crown. The colonists were British by birth or ancestry, and they gave the English kings their loyalty until George III's increasingly harsh civil and economic actions against them finally turned loyalty into rebellion.

As early as 1740, four battalions made up of 3000 Colonial men were raised for service in England's war with Spain. Designated the 43rd Regiment of Foot, they came to be known as 'Gooch's Marines,' a reference to their popular leader, Colonel William Gooch. In 1741 Gooch led his regiment in an attack on Cartagena, Spain, where he was wounded. Several months later the Marines went ashore in Cuba and secured Guantanamo Bay for the British fleet as a base.

Another name associated with the regiment, that of Admiral Edward Vernon, the British commander, later was taken by a young Marine officer in the regiment for a home he built at Little Hunting Creek, Virginia; he called it 'Mount Vernon.' The officer was Lawrence Washington, and on his death the home passed to his younger brother, the first president.

With the end of warfare with Spain, the Marines found a role for themselves in the British Navy in skirmishes against the French. During ship-to-ship actions they served as marksmen, often firing down on the other vessel from perches in the rigging, and were the main force in boarding parties. They also were the ships' security detachments, keeping the hard-worked sailors in line; this duty engendered testy feelings between sailors and Marines, feelings that persist to a degree even to this day.

'The Original Eight'

Six months before the founding of the Continental Marines, in May 1775, the Continental Congress responded to news that American forces holding Fort Ticonderoga and Crown Point were 'in a feeble state' by requesting the governor of Connecticut to reinforce these garrisons in nearby upper New York with fresh troops from his Colony's forces. By direction of the Crown, many of the colonies had long maintained their own Army, naval and Marine forces modeled on British prototypes, in addition to providing men for service in British units.

A body of troops quickly left Hartford, and with them was 'money escorted with eight Marines [from the Connecticut Navy], well spirited and equipped.' The Marines and soldiers successfully made their way through hostile Indian and British forces to relieve the beleaguered garrisons. The 'Original Eight,' as they came to be known, were representative of Marines in service before the Revolution with the navies of eight colonies: Connecticut, Massachusetts,

Rhode Island, Pennsylvania, Maryland, Virginia, North Carolina and Georgia.

'Continental risque and pay'

On 15 June 1775, with the enthusiastic sponsorship of John Adams, the selection of George Washington as Commanding General of the military forces of all the colonies was very rapidly approved by the Congress.

Washington quickly discovered, on inventorying his available materials, that the total supply of gun powder for the Army was ninety kegs—which worked out to nine rounds per man and nothing for his artillery.

Pages 10–11: George Washington reviews his ragged troops at Valley Forge.
Left: Captain Porter's Marines on the attack during the Battle of Princeton in January 1777.
Below: Captain Nicholas and Lieutenant Parke look on as the first Marines are inspected in December 1775.

Above: Captain John Paul Jones of the *Bonhomme Richard*, one of the earliest supporters of the Marine Corps.

Above: Marines raise the flag above one of the captured forts on New Providence in March 1776.

However, in October the Congress learned of two unescorted British ships sailing toward the colonies from England loaded with munitions. They ordered General Washington to obtain two armed vessels from Massachusetts and use them to capture the merchant ships, which was subsequently done. The vessels were placed on 'Continental risque and pay,' which meant that Congress would both pay the crews and be responsible for insuring the ships against loss or capture.

Congress further instructed Washington to give 'proper encouragement to the Marines and seamen' serving aboard the warships; this was penned just prior to the founding of the Continental Marines, and was the first time the Congress ever made written reference to 'Marines.'

By a masterful effort, General Washington was able to procure needed supplies and train men in time to put Colonial military forces into action early in 1776.

Operations of the Continental Marines

On 3 March 1776 the US frigate *Alfred* landed 268 Marines, under the command of Captain Samuel Nicholas, on New Providence Island in the Bahamas for their first military expedition. Within 13 days the Marine raiding party captured two forts, occupied Nassau town, took control of Government House and seized 88 guns, 16,535 shells and other supplies—an auspicious beginning for the new organization.

On the trip home the *Alfred* encountered the HMS *Glasgow*, a 20-gun British warship, off Block Island, and in a night action the ship's Marine unit experienced its first combat losses, Second Lieutenant John Fitzpatrick and six enlisted men. The *Glasgow* suffered four casualties, all caused by the muskets of Continental Marines.

Upon his return Nicholas was promoted to Major, and in December 1776 he and approximately 300 of his men joined Washington's Army in Pennsylvania just before the second battle of Trenton, in time to escape a trap set by Lord Cornwallis's forces. Soon after they fought alongside Army units in a successful strike at the enemy's flank and rear on 3 January 1777. This was the first instance recorded of Marines joining Army units in action; it would happen again many times in the Corps's history.

In the spring of that year Washington incorporated some of the Marines into artillery units of his reorganized Army, while the remainder went back to naval

Below: The Marines come ashore at New Providence in the Corps' first amphibious operation.

duties. The Marine artillerymen participated in the defense of Fort Mifflin on the Delaware River. From 22 October until 15 November 1777, a force of twelve British ships, along with Hessian artillery batteries, pounded the fort into rubble, yet the stubborn defenders were able to fire back and prevent the enemy from relieving their units holding Philadelphia.

On 10 January 1778 a small force of Marines commanded by Captain James Willing set sail down the Mississippi aboard an ancient boat renamed by Willing the *Rattletrap*, headed for New Orleans. During the next year the detachment operated in the area of that city, primarily attacking British traders, until they returned north to join in actions against hostile Indians.

Some of the subsequent Marine land actions of the war were: participation in a joint Army-Navy attempt to seize a British fort established at Penobscot Bay, Maine (though the action was unsuccessful, the Marines were commended for their 'forcible charge on the enemy'); in May 1780, a gallant but futile attempt by 200 Marines and sailors to save Charleston, South Carolina, from a superior British force; an amphibious attack by Marines from the frigate *South Carolina* on the Isle of Jersey in the English Channel during the winter of 1780–1781, the last such attack of the war.

Above : The action between the *Bonhomme Richard* and the *Serapis* was one of the most closely contested of the War of Independence.

Aboard the Bonhomme Richard

Marines figured prominently in American naval actions of the war. They took part in the attacks on English ships in European waters of the American ship *Reprisal* until its loss. In April 1778 a Marine detachment took part in two raids on the soil of Great Britain conducted from the *Ranger*, commanded by John Paul Jones; this was among

Below : The British forces retreat during the action at Penobscot Bay.

the few such landings on British soil in over 700 years. Aboard another command of Jones's, the famous *Bonhomme Richard*, the Marine unit was not American but foreign, consisting of three Irish officers and 137 French Marines from Louis XVIs *Régiment Royaux d'Infanterie et d'Artillerie de Marine.* Louis's generosity had more to do with his ongoing war with England than with sympathy for the American cause. The French Marines were valiant fighters, however, and played a major part in accomplishing Jones's renowned victory over the British frigate HMS *Serapis* off Flamborough Head on 23 September 1779. Biographers of Captain Jones say he placed great reliance on Marines, both foreign and American, and expressed his admiration for their military discipline. He tried during the Revolution to persuade the Congress to build the Continental Marines into a larger body, but without success.

The Continental Marines' last significant action at sea took place in January 1783 when the Marine detachment aboard the American warship *Hague* boarded and seized the British ship *Baille* in the West Indies. The signing of the Treaty of Paris on 11 April 1783, brought about an end of the American Revolutionary War and, before long, of the Continental Marines as well. When the sale of the *Alliance*, last of the nation's warships, was authorized on 3 June 1785, the Continental Marines—which once had numbered 124 officers and about 3000 men—went out of existence along with the Navy.

After his release from service, Major Samuel Nicholas returned to Philadelphia and his tavern business. Though the Continental Marines preceded the Marine Corps as we know it today, that early organization's military prowess helped create the new nation, and for this reason Corps historians honor Nicholas with the designation of first Marine Commandant.

'An Act for Establishing a Marine Corps'— 1798-1820

Among many concerns of the first United States Congress that met in 1789 were attacks on American merchant ships being made by Barbary pirates in the Mediterranean and by French privateers on the high seas; the privateers were unleashed by their government as a way of harassing sea commerce between America and France's enemies, the British. But so pressing were domestic matters facing the American legislators that not until 1794 did Congress get around to authorizing the reactivation of the Navy and the building of six frigates.

Another two years passed before the necessary funds were voted for constructing three ships, the *United States* the *Constellation* and the *Constitution*. All three vessels were launched the following year, 1797; by Congressional act each carried a Marine detachment consisting of five lieutenants, eight sergeants, eight corporals, three drummers, three fifers and 140 privates. Since there was then no Marine Corps as such, the Marines were considered part of the Navy crew.

The attacks on American shipping were on the mind of Alexander Hamilton when in 1798 he wrote to Secretary of War James McHenry:

> This is too much humiliation after all that has passed—Our merchants are very indignant—Our government very prostrate in the view of every man of energy.

McHenry subsequently recommended to House Naval Committee chairman Samuel Sewell of Massachusetts that an organization of Marines be formed, and before long the Committee sent to the House floor a bill calling for the creation of 'a battalion, to be called the Marine Corps.' The bill passed; the Senate changed the size of the proposed Corps to a regiment and, with House concurrence, *'An Act for Establishing and Organizing a Marine Corps'* went to President John Adams for his signature on 11 July 1798, the official 'birth date' of the Corps.

The table of organization of the fledgling

Top left: Capture of the *Sandwich* during the quasi-war with France, 11 May 1800.
Above left: Marines and seamen from Jones' *Ranger* raid the British port of Whitehaven, 22 April 1778.
Left: Replica of the Tun Tavern, birthplace of the Marines, built for the Sesquicentennial Fair in 1926.
Below: Marines and seamen aboard the *Bonhomme Richard* in action with the men of the *Serapis*.

Left: Lieutenant O'Bannon and his men raise the American flag above the citadel at Derna in Tripoli.

organization called for 33 officers and 848 'noncommissioned officers, musicians and privates.' Their uniforms were quite colorful; the shortcoats and trousers were blue edged in brilliant red, and their hats, with one turned-up side, displayed a yellow band and a cockade. Sergeants carried yellow epaulettes on their shoulders, officers wore long blue coats with red cuffs and golden epaulettes, and all the uniforms had stiff leather collars that earned the Marines their famous nickname, 'Leathernecks,' which remains to this day.

The Corps's mission was 'any . . . duty on shore as the President, at his discretion, shall direct.' The Corps was to be part of the Army or the Navy, 'according to the nature of the service in which they shall be employed,' and therefore regulated alternately by either the Articles of War or by Navy Regulations. This unwieldy proviso would create many difficulties for the Corps in the years ahead.

Scarcely a day after he signed the Act establishing the Corps, President Adams appointed William Ward Burrows of Philadelphia as its Major Commandant. Burrows, a well-reputed veteran of the Revolution, set to his recruiting job with zest and energy, and within six months had the Corps up to strength—this despite the fact that the pay for a private was only one dollar a week. Burrow's good work did not go unnoticed; he was promoted to lieutenant colonel and Congress authorized an increase in the Corps's strength of an additional eight officers and 196 men.

Two actions of Burrows worthy of particular note were his founding of the Marine Band and his decision to move Marine headquarters from his home city of Philadelphia to Washington, the new capital. On 31 March 1801, riding horseback with his friend, President Thomas Jefferson, he selected as the place for the Corps's Headquarters a location 'near the Navy Yard and within easy marching distance of the Capital,' the site at which it stands to this day. Burrows retired in 1804 for health reasons, replaced by Franklin Wharton; Burrows's commandancy would serve as a model for all those who followed him.

'To arms, especially by sea'

The leaders of the young nation, burdened with many governmental difficulties, had for years gritted their teeth and borne the attacks on American merchant ships of French privateers. The situation stung the pride of John Adams during his time as President; on 22 May 1798, he had rallied the Harvard graduating class with the patriotic cry, 'To arms, then, my young friends—to arms, especially by sea.' Six

Left: Marines are paid off at the end of the War of Independence. The permanent establishment of the Corps dates from 1798.

Above: Stephen Decatur, hero of actions against the Barbary pirates and during the War of 1812. *Right:* Decatur and his men during the action to burn the *Philadelphia* in Tripoli in 1804.

days later the President ordered an 'undeclared naval war' against France, and America's small navy went into action against one of the world's largest fleets.

Marine detachments served aboard every warship, and they participated in the many sea skirmishes that occurred. The Marines of the USS *Constitution* executed a daring attack on a French force lying in the ostensibly neutral port of Puerto Plata on the shore of Santo Domingo, then a Spanish colony. The French held a prize ship, the British vessel *Sandwich*, and in a maneuver reminiscent of the wooden horse ploy of the Trojans, 80 Marines and sailors entered the harbor hidden below-decks on the commandeered American sloop *Sally* and took the *Sandwich*. They then stormed and captured the Spanish fort, spiked its guns and sailed off with their prize. This was the first combat landing on foreign soil of the new Corps.

The USS *Constellation*, with 41 Marines aboard, engaged and severely damaged two French frigates, the *Insurgente* and *Vengeance*. The *Vengeance* limped into Dutch Curaçao seeking aid, but the neutral Dutch refused to get involved, whereupon a French unit landed, occupied part of the island and attacked the Dutch garrison in Willemstad, the capital. When the Dutch appealed to nearby American naval forces for help, the USS *Patapsco* and *Merrimack* responded, on 23 September 1800. Under covering cannon fire from the ships, Lieutenant James Middleton of the *Patapsco* and 70 Marines from both ships landed and engaged the French units laying siege to Willemstad. During that night the French broke off the action, boarded their badly-shattered ships and sailed away.

By the time peace was reached between the United States and France in February 1801, the young American war fleet had captured 85 French vessels, with the Marines contributing valiantly to this accomplishment. Within the year, however, a drive for peacetime economies and reduction of the national debt led President Jefferson to order the selling of naval vessels and the cessation of warship construction. The President also directed Secretary of the Navy Robert Smith to reduce Marine enlisted strength, an ill-advised move that brought Corps strength down to 26 officers and 453 men just at the time when the United States was entering the Tripolitan War in the Mediterranean.

Subduing the Barbary pirates

For many years the United States and European powers paid tribute to the Barbary pirates of the states of Morocco, Tunis, Algeria and Tripoli as the price for sailing their merchant ships on the Mediterranean. By 1801 the United States's payments equalled two million dollars, one-fifth of the nation's annual revenues. When the demand of Yusuf Caramanli, Pasha of Tripoli, for even larger payments from America was refused, he declared war in May 1801. Four vessels of the United States's now-tiny Navy—the USS *President, Philadelphia, Essex* and *Enterprise*—were formed into the Mediterranean Squadron and sent to protect American interests in that area. But the small force was hard-pressed to carry out its mission against the powerful Barbary pirate fleet.

On 31 October 1803 the frigate *Philadelphia* grounded on a reef off of Tripoli and was captured by pirate ships, floated free and towed into port as a prize. While negotiations went on regarding the payment of ransom for release of the crew Lieutenant Stephen Decatur, USN, and a force including Marines under the command of Sergeant Solomon Wren slipped into Tripoli Harbor, overcame the pirates aboard the *Philadelphia*, burned it to the waterline and escaped without a casualty. (The captured

Above: The battle between the American ship *Planter* and a French privateer during the quasi-war with France, 10 July 1799.

crew was subsequently released after the payment of a large ransom, another humiliation for the young nation.)

O'Bannon at Tripoli

The most extraordinary exploit of the war was that of Marine Lieutenant Presley N O'Bannon and William Eaton, American diplomatic agent and former army general. Hamet Bey, brother of Yusuf Caramanli and rightful ruler of Tripoli, was in exile in Egypt; Eaton persuaded Hamet to join in a land assault with the purpose of restoring him to his throne. To do this, Eaton and O'Bannon recruited a mercenary force in Alexandria and led them on a daring seven-week trek across 600 miles of the Libyan desert. Surviving mutiny, pilfery, religious clashes among the men and terrible thirst and hunger, the two Americans brought their motley force through the desert to the walls of Derna, Yusuf's capital, on 25 April 1805. They sent a messenger into the city with a note ordering the bey, or mayor, to surrender, to which he replied, 'Your head or mine.'

O'Bannon and Eaton informed him that they had no objection to his terms.

The Americans launched an attack supported by a bombardment of the city delivered from three warships in the harbor. O'Bannon's force, made up of Marines and mercenaries, was at the center of the attack on the walls, and quickly came under the heaviest fire. When the mercenaries began to panic, O'Bannon and Eaton led them in a charge against the enemy. Eaton fell wounded, along with three Marines and several mercenaries, but the surprise tactic worked—the startled enemy were caught off balance and began a retreat.

Pressing their advantage, O'Bannon's men soon drove the enemy from the walls. Hamet Bey then led his Arab troops in a successful attack on the bey's castle, and by 4:00 PM Lieutenant O'Bannon was able to raise the Stars and Stripes above the city, the first American flag to fly over a captured fortification in the Old World. This victory contributed to the signing of a favorable peace treaty with the Pasha of Tripoli on 4 June 1805.

In appreciation for O'Bannon's services, Hamet Bey presented him with his own sword, a handsome curved blade with ivory hilt topped by a golden eagle head. The Mameluk sword, so called after the Egyptian sect that forged it, subsequently served as the pattern for swords carried to this day by Marine officers.

War with Britain

To the great nations of Europe—England, France and Spain—the winning of independence by the United States in 1783 was of small importance, and they demonstrated this attitude by continuing to treat American merchant ships as though they belonged to a colony. Particularly flagrant in this regard was Great Britain, despite US trade with them; in the words of President James Madison to the Congress in June of 1812:

> They hover over and harass our entering and departing commerce. To the most insulting pretensions, they have added the most lawless proceedings in our very harbors, and have wantonly spilt American blood within the sanctuary of our territorial jurisdiction. . . .

The mood of the Congress was not with Madison, however; though they authorized an enlargement of the Marine Corps to 1869 officers and men, the Congress failed to vote an appropriation to make the increase possible. The Corps had not recovered from the Jefferson-imposed reductions in its size, and when war against Great Britain was declared by the Congress on 18 June 1812, the Corps consisted of 10 officers and 483 enlisted men, with less than half of them on sea duty. And though the popular slogan for the war was 'Free Trade and Sailors's Rights,' the American Navy consisted of a mere three first-line warships.

In actions on the Atlantic, this small force performed well. The USS *Constitution* destroyed HMS *Guerrière* on 19 August off Nova Scotia, the *United States* seized the *Macedonian* on 25 October and the *Constitution* sank the *Java* on 28 December off Brazil, earning for itself the now-famous accolade, 'Old Ironsides.' Marines figured in each of these engagements, delivering withering musket fire and playing a major role in boarding-party attacks.

Out of the War of 1812 came what is perhaps the most incredible saga in the history of the Marine Corps, that of a 23-year-old lieutenant named John Marshall

Below: British forces advance on Washington, as seen in a somewhat fanciful contemporary engraving.

Gamble. Gamble was in charge of a Marine detachment aboard the frigate *Essex*, commanded by Captain David Porter, when it sailed from the Delaware Capes on 28 October 1812; he would not see America again for almost three years. Off the Galapagos Islands the *Essex* encountered and captured three British whaling ships. Captain Porter placed cannon and a crew of 14 men aboard one of the ships, and used his authority to commission it as the USS *Greenwich*. He placed the vessel under the command of Lieutenant Gamble, making him the only Marine in history to captain a ship of the United States Navy.

In July of 1813 Gamble demonstrated impeccable seamanship when he closed with and captured a dreaded British raider, the *Seringapatam*. That October, Porter left Gamble on Nukuhiva in the Marquesas Islands in charge of a hastily-built fortification, three British prize ships, a number of prisoners, and supported by just 22 American officers and men. When several thousand hostile native Typees massed for an attack on his camp, Gamble promptly attacked them first with his handful of men and forced their withdrawal.

On 7 May 1814 British captives attacked the Americans, wounding Gamble in the process, but he managed to rally the Americans aboard one of the British prize ships, fight off a native attack that inflicted further casualties, then set sail without charts and with a crew of seven wounded men.

The Americans were taken captive by a British warship and, when news of peace came, set ashore in Rio de Janeiro, penniless and 5000 miles from home. Gamble finally managed to find a ship that would give passage to him and his six surviving men—three Marines and three sailors—and they arrived home in August 1815. For his heroism John Marshall Gamble soon was brevetted major.

The Battles for Washington and Baltimore

The British, along with their 'minor' war with the United States, had been engaged in a major struggle with the armies of Napoleon, and when they won a victory over the French in 1814 it released great numbers of Redcoats for action on the North American continent. The British strategy was to split the United States in two so that they might lay claim to New England during the protracted peace negotiations going on in Ghent, Belgium. They further decided that a strike against the capital, Washington, would devastate American morale; in overall charge of this operation they placed Rear-Admiral Sir George Cockburn, whose temperament can be judged by the fact that he later had his portrait painted with a flaming Washington as the background.

The British attack came on 19 August 1814, when 4000 men under Major General Robert Ross landed at Benedict, Maryland, joined up with two additional battalions and set out for Washington. American plans for the defense of the Capital were, to say the least, ill-conceived, dependent primarily on a rag-tag force of 6000 militia. The battle was joined at Bladensburg, a small town just outside Washington; at the first sound of fire from the British attackers the militia threw away their weapons and fled the field. However, the American defenders also included a battalion of 114 Marines led by Captain Samuel Miller, serving under Commodore Joshua Barney, whose force also included a few battle-experienced sailors. This group stood their ground, awaiting the British charge. As Barney later reported:

> I reserved our fire. In a few minutes the British advanced, when I ordered an 18-pounder to be fired, which completely cleared the road.

The effect of their fire was devastating, blowing away an entire British company. The Marines and sailors inflicted 249 casualties and delayed the attackers for two hours, but the British pressed forward and finally forced the defenders to fall back.

Before nightfall almost every public building in Washington had been burned, including both the White House and the Capital. The one bright note for Americans in the defeat was the performance of the small unit of sailors and Marines. A contemporary observer commented:

> No troops could have stood better; and the fire of both artillery and musketry has been described as to the last degree severe. Commodore Barney himself, and Captain Miller of the Marines in particular, gained much additional reputation.

The Marines left Washington to join other Marine units in an attempt to defend Baltimore and its bastion, Fort McHenry. The British attacked by land and sea, and for days the air was filled with 'the rockets red glare, the bombs bursting in air'; the sight inspired an American prisoner aboard one of the British ships, Francis Scott Key, to pen what later became the nation's anthem.

Defending New Orleans

As the United States's principal city on the Gulf coast, New Orleans was an important military objective of the British. Vice-Admiral Sir Alexander Cochrane was assigned to capture the port, and given 9000 seasoned soldiers to serve in carrying out the task. Ironically, the attack force approached New Orleans on the same day, 14 December 1814, that the long-negotiated peace treaty was signed in far-off Ghent.

The defensive forces of General Andrew Jackson included 300 Marines under Major Daniel Carmick, as well as many pirates from the Creole band of Jean and Pierre Lafitte, all joined against their common enemy. Carmick was shot in an American counterattack against the British on December 28, and later died of his wounds. His men quickly moved into other units where, being true professionals, they served with distinction. The British struck again

Above: Marine uniforms of 1816. Drummers of military units of this period were often dressed in colors contrasting with those worn by the rank and file.
Below: The Battle of Lundy's Lane, 25 July 1814, an important engagement during the war with Britain.

and again, but without success, and by the time news finally came of the peace treaty, 2036 of their men were dead or wounded and over 500 of them prisoners. American casualties were fewer than 100. The Congress expressed its thanks 'for the valor and good conduct of Major Daniel Carmick, of the officers, noncommissioned officers, and Marines under his command.'

Unfortunately, the history of the Corps was marked by darker episodes during the war; foremost among these was the flight of Marine Commandant Franklin Wharton from Washington just prior to the British attack. Particularly incensed at Wharton's behavior was Marine Captain Archibald Henderson, who had commanded with distinction the Marine detachment aboard the *Constitution*. Henderson brought charges against the Commandant for neglect of duty and conduct unbecoming an officer and a gentleman. Though a trial held on

Above : A Marine officer (left) displays his finest uniform for a social occasion *c.* 1830.

22 September 1817 acquitted Wharton, the blot on his reputation marked him until his death the following year. His successor, Major Anthony Gale, lasted only two years, before he was court-martialed and eventually dismissed the service, cashiered for drunkenness and a number of other disreputable offences.

Fortune smiled on the Corps that same year, however, when Archibald Henderson was selected to be fifth Commandant of Marines. He took over a Corps rocked by the scandals created by its previous two Commandants, and pulled this way and that by demands from both the Army and Navy. Henderson would prove to be more than a match for these challenges.

'Gone to Fight The Indians'—1820-1859

Following the signing of the peace treaty of 1815, the Corps was at a peak of fighting efficiency, morale and public approval, but over the next five years the combined effects of peacetime economies and the abrupt loss of two Commandants under shabby circumstances threw the Corps into a state of confusion and disarray. That was how Major Archibald Henderson found it when he assumed the commandancy in 1820.

Commandant Archibald Henderson

At age 38 Henderson was, and has remained, the youngest man ever to become Commandant of the Marines. Enlisting in 1806, the slim redhead had served with distinction during the recent war, indicated by the fact that he was brevetted Major for his heroism. The Virginia-born officer was organized, direct and forceful in his manner, characteristics that come through in a phrase he once wrote: 'Take care to be right, and then they are powerless.' The problems he would face put Henderson's axiom to a stern test, and would make him work extremely hard and long for his Commandant's modest pay and perquisites of $2636.16 a year.

Right: Death of the British General Packenham during the Battle of New Orleans, 8 January 1815.
Below: General Jackson inspires his defending forces to throw back the British attacks.

Above: The Marine barracks at Washington DC as seen in an illustration dating from *c.* 1830.

Small actions around the world

Henderson took command at a time when the political and economic interests of the United States were growing around the world, and with this expansion came much work for the Corps.

During 1821 and part of 1822, a force of 300 Marines serving with the Navy's West India Squadron took part in landings and assaults against pirates operating from strongholds on the north coast of Cuba, from which they attacked American commerce in the Caribbean in a manner reminiscent of the Barbary pirates. With cannon and muskets, the Marines put an end to this activity.

On 6 December 1831 President Andrew Jackson sent a message to Congress that presaged the military clash in 1982 between England and Argentina over Argentina's claim to the Falkland Islands. The message concerned the seizure of three American whaling ships for fishing near the Falklands and the holding of their crews on the islands 'by a band, acting, as they pretend, under the authority of the Government of Buenos Ayres.' The USS *Lexington* sailed to the rescue and evacuated 38 Americans under the protective guns of the ship's detachment of Marines.

During the same year the American merchant ship *Friendship* was attacked in the port of Kuala Batu in Sumatra by Malay pirates and several crewmen murdered. This was another of many attacks suffered by American ships in that area, and the administration in Washington decided that military action had to be taken. The warship *Potomac* commanded by Commodore John Downes was ordered to Sumatra.

The Malay pirates, 4000 in number, occupied four heavily-armed forts that overlooked the harbor of Kuala Batu. In the dim light of early morning on 7 February 1832, the *Potomac*, fitted out to look like a shabby merchant ship, dropped anchor off Kuala Batu and a landing force of Marines commanded by First Lieutenant Alvin Edson rowed ashore. Also with the detachment was Second Lieutenant George H Terrett, who would later conduct himself heroically at the San Cosme Gate of Mexico City. Edson was wounded in the assault on one of the four forts; Terrett assumed command and, after more than two hours of desperate fighting, the last fort fell to the Americans. Over 150 pirates were killed, along with their rajah leader, Po Mahomet.

For action and danger, the Marines didn't have to travel to such exotic, far-off places—some of their units found plenty of both right at home. Public safety organizations as we know them today, especially police and fire departments, were tiny in size in the early 19th century, and the Marines were regularly called on to help out.

In 1824 Marines from the Charlestown Navy Yard detachment helped put out a large fire in Boston. When arsonists set fire to the US Treasury in Washington, DC, Marines from 'Eighth and Eye'—Corps Headquarters located at Eighth and I Streets, SE—did double service as fire-fighters and as guards of the building's treasures. A great fire broke out in New York in December 1835, and Brooklyn Navy Yard sent Marines under Lieutenant Colonel John Marshal Gamble of War of 1812 fame, as well as seamen, to fight the blaze and guard against looters; the Marines were credited with blasting the firebreaks that saved Manhattan.

When inmates at Massachusetts State Prison rioted in 1824 and holed up in the mess hall with a guard as hostage, Marines from the Boston barracks came to help. Major R D Wainwright led 30 Marines into the mess hall to confront 283 armed and determined prisoners. Wainwright ordered his men to cock and level their muskets. 'You must leave this hall,' he told the inmates. 'I give you three minutes to decide.

Left: Uniforms of the 1840s. From right, a Marine lieutenant, a Marine staff officer and naval officers.

Above : A Colt revolving carbine used by the Marines during the war against the Creeks and Seminoles.
Below : Leatherneck. A leather stock of the type worn by Marines until 1875, which gave the Corps its nickname.

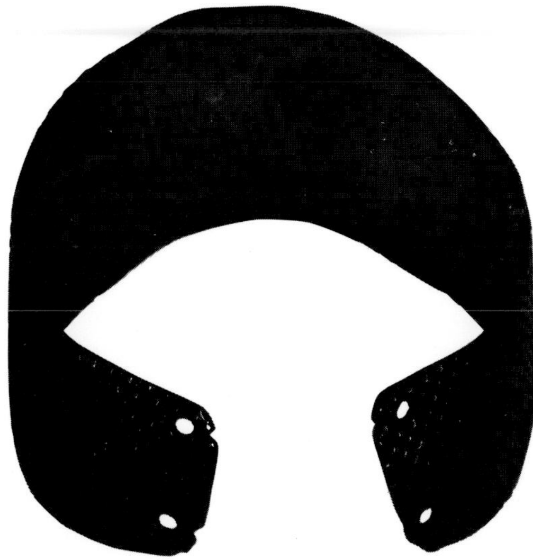

If at the end of that time a man remains, he will be shot dead. I speak no more.'

In two and a half minutes 'the hall was cleared as if by magic.'

A 'skirmish' of greater potential danger to the Marine Corps began on 8 December 1829, when President Andrew Jackson sent a message to the Congress recommending 'that the Marine Corps be merged into the artillery or infantry.' At the root of this executive assault were continuing difficulties with running the Corps under both Army and Navy regulations, financial irregularities resulting from that awkward arrangement, and the hostility of the Navy's Board of Commissioners, a group roughly equivalent to England's Admiralty.

Votes in both houses of Congress in 1830 resulted in shaky support for the Corps. But its attackers did not give up; the following year Secretary of the Navy John Branch recommended 'discontinuance of the Marine Corps . . . in its present fluctuating condition,' and its placement 'wholly under navy discipline and laws.' Commandant Henderson had no objection to such a proposal; as early as 1823 he had written: 'The Marine Corps is, and must continue to be, an appendage of the Navy, participating in its prosperity or sharing its adversity —in war braving with it the same dangers, and in peace asking nothing of it but sheer justice.'

On 30 June 1834 Henderson got his wish for justice—Congress passed 'an Act for the Better Organization of the Marine Corps,' which set the Corps's peacetime strength at 63 officers and 1224 enlisted men, made it a semi-autonomous part of the United States Navy with its own Headquarters and Commandant, and promoted Henderson to colonel. Though the Corps would come under many more political attacks, a watershed had been successfully passed.

War with the Seminoles and Creeks

Long the objects of unremitting pressures to force them off their ancestral lands, the Creek Indians of Georgia and Alabama and the Seminoles of Florida's Everglades joined in an uprising when attempts were begun to deport them to reservations west of the Mississippi River. On 23 May 1836, acting in his capacity as Commander in Chief of the Armed Forces, President Jackson detached all able-bodied Marines to service with the Army for the duration of the emergency.

Commandant Henderson was quick to respond; he reduced all Marine detachments at Navy installations to sergeants's guards, and in ten days had assembled a two-battalion regiment consisting of 38 officers and 424 enlisted men, more than half the Corps of that time. Before he strode out of Marine Headquarters gripping his gold-headed walking stick, legend has it Henderson tacked this note to his office door:

> Gone to fight the Indians. Will be back when the war is over.
>
> A. Henderson
> Col.Comdt.

By that summer's end the Creek uprising had been suppressed, and the Marines were moved south to Florida, arriving in September. When the Army commander, Major General T H Jesup, divided his forces into two brigades, Colonel Henderson was given command of one of them, a patchwork organization consisting of the Marine regiment, Creek Indian scouts, volunteers from Georgia, and infantry and artillery units from the Army. Henderson led his brigade in an action against the Seminoles northeast of Fort Brooke—now Tampa—on 27 January 1837, and won a victory, one of the few accomplished against a determined foe. For this, Henderson was brevetted brigadier general, making him the first general officer in the Corps's history.

The government forces tried with little success to pursue the Seminoles through the Everglades Swamp, and in 1842 the war dwindled to a conclusion—no treaty ever was signed—under conditions favorable to the Indians.

A Marine's Life

Life for the average American in the early part of the 19th century was stern and de-

Below : Seminole Indians watch from cover as a boatload of Marines passes by.

Above: American forces storm a Mexican fort at Churubusco in the final stages of the advance to Mexico City.

manding; for the enlisted Marine, it was even more so. The private's pay as late as 1843 still was only $6 a month, plus a $30 a year uniform allowance, with which he was expected to maintain himself in impeccable array. And discipline was severe. Drunks were made to drink several quarts of salt water, which had unpleasant and sobering effects; falling asleep on watch called for walking guard duty for several months while wearing an iron collar and dragging ankle chains-and-balls; disobeying the commands of a sentry earned twelve lashes from a cat-o'-nine-tails. Other minor violations could lose the offender his daily ration of a gill of grog, a concoction of rum and water which must have helped considerably to alleviate the harsh life.

With it all, men still signed up when the recruiter appeared, as recalled by one old Marine:

'the drummer and I would put on our red full dress tunics, with swallow tails, form a procession and down the street we'd go. The captain bought some bright colored ribbons for the drummer and me, which we tied in bows on our arms and to the buttons on the sides of our shakoes, and when the wind blew we certainly made a fine sight as we marched down Broadway to the Battery, then up the Bowery and back to the rendezvous on Chambers Street, ribbons flying and playing quick-steps all the way. Then the Captain would get up on a dry-goods box in front of the recruiting office and make a speech to the crowd, telling them what a fine place the Marine Corps was for a man and what a chance he'd have to visit foreign ports. That's the way we got recruits in those days.'

Below: General view of the fighting at Churubusco. The American success in this battle and at Chapultepec ensured the fall of the capital.

Against Mexico, ashore and afloat

Just as the push of Americans southward had precipitated hostilities with the Indians living in the area, so the expansion of the country's frontiers into the West and Southwest resulted in another war, this one with the Republic of Mexico.

The particular issues leading to it were America's desire for Mexico's territory of California and for the portion of Mexico called Texas, a name derived from the Indian word *techas*, which meant 'allies' and referred to the Caddo confederacy of tribes that lived in the area. Presidents John Adams and Andrew Jackson had pressed Mexico to sell Texas to the United States and had been refused with indignation; the continuing pressure from Washington for

such a purchase caused tension between the two governments. Curiously, however, Mexico encouraged the movement of Americans into the province in large numbers. When the Texans seceded in 1835 and took over the Alamo, a Mexican Army fortress in San Antonio, the Mexicans counterattacked and killed all the American defenders. A cry of 'Remember the Alamo!' was subsequently exploited by Presidents Tyler and Polk to move the nation toward war. When, on 28 February 1845, Congress voted to annex Texas into the United States, the stage was set for combat.

That October, President Polk sent Marine First Lieutenant Archibald H Gillespie to the West Coast with secret messages for Commodore John D Sloat, commander of the Navy's Pacific squadron; Thomas O Larkin, American consul at Monterey; and Captain John C Fremont, United States Army, engaged in a mapping expedition in California. The messages asked their aid in supporting and encouraging a secession movement in California similar to the one in Texas. Gillespie—described by a contemporary as 'an elegant, precise man with a stiff pointed beard and a temper of the same description'—memorized the President's message, disguised himself as a whisky salesman and set out.

His six month's journey took him by boat to Mexico, by stagecoach across that country to the Pacific, by warship to Honolulu—an unplanned sidetrip to deceive a watchful British admiral; England, too, coveted California—from Honolulu to Monterey, California, and finally into the Sierras by

Right: General Santa Anna commanded the Mexican forces defending the capital but misjudged the direction of the American attack. *Below:* The engagement at Cerro Gordo on 18 April 1847 during the advance from Vera Cruz to Mexico City.

Above : The last-man defense of the Alamo during the Texas War of Independence, a source of inspiration for events in the Mexican-American War.

Above : Dress (right) and working uniforms of a Marine private in 1847.

canoe and horseback to find Frémont. Gillespie's mission was a success, setting the stage for the birth of the California 'Bear Flag' republic on 14 June 1846.

On 11 May 1846 Polk asked Congress to declare war on Mexico, which it quickly did. The first military action of the war took place on May 18 when a Marine detachment fought a skirmish at Burrita, 15 miles up from the mouth of the Rio Grande River. Marines from the Navy's Gulf Coast Squadron next were involved in a series of landings at Mexican ports to establish and maintain a blockade in aid of the thrust toward Mexico City of the army of flamboyant General Zachary Taylor—'Old Rough and Ready.' When Commodore Matthew C Perry took command of the Squadron in March 1847, he initiated a series of amphibious landings, culminating in the attack on San Juan Bautista successfully carried off by 150 Marines and 60 seamen, a victory that closed the Mexicans's last remaining port of entry.

Angered over Taylor's self-promotional involvement with the press, suspecting that it represented presidential aspirations, Polk pinched off supplies to Taylor's forces and instead ordered an attack by Army Major General Winfield Scott—'Old Fuss and Feathers'—out of Vera Cruz toward Mexico City. On the way to this goal, the enlistment time of many of Scott's soldiers ran out and they left for home, bringing his march to a halt in the town of Puebla. Learning of this back in Washington, Marine Commandant Henderson—taking advantage of a 1000-man increase in Corps strength authorized by Congress on 3 March 1847—began a feverish recruiting drive, at the same time obtaining permission for Marines to join Scott to make up his losses. A battalion of Marines 357 strong joined Scott's forces at Puebla on 6 August 1847, and was attached to General John A Quitman's 4th Division, coming under the command of Marine Major Levi Twiggs, a decorated veteran of the Florida campaign.

The main defensive position before Mexico City was Chapultepec, a 200-foot-high promontory on top of which stood a stone castle surrounded by a wall that would have to be scaled. At eight in the morning on 13 September 1847 American troops in position below the walls began their attack up the rock face, including the Marines led by Major Twiggs, armed with his favorite double-barreled shotgun. Musket balls and cannon shot rained down on them; Twiggs was killed in an early volley—'the brave and lamented Twiggs,' General Quitman called him—but despite heavy casualties the assault carried to the base of the wall on top of the hill. Still under deadly fire, the Americans raised scaling ladders and swarmed up the walls, and before long the castle was theirs. Twenty-four Marines were casualties in the assault; among the wounded was Second Lieutenant C A Henderson, son of the Commandant.

Other 4th Division elements, including Marines, pressed on to Mexico City. When the Americans ran into strong enemy resistance, Marine Captain Terrett—who had distinguished himself in 1832 against Malay pirates at Kuala Batu—moved his Marine company forward on his own initiative to burst through a line of Mexican artillery and break up an attack by Mexican lancers; his company was accompanied by a small group of soldiers under Second Lieutenant Ulysses S Grant. The Americans pressed forward toward Mexico City; at dawn General Quitman was about to order an attack when a lone soldier emerged from the city under a white flag. The Mexican army, he said, had slipped away during the night; the city was theirs.

Exhausted and missing one shoe, Quitman led his ragged, bloodied force into Mexico City, where Marine Lieutenant Nicholson ran up the Stars and Stripes. 'The Capital is mine,' Quitman told Marine Captain Baker. 'My brave fellows have conquered it. . . !'

It is said that this victory inspired some unknown Marine to compose a brief lyric to a tune popular in that day, taken from the opera *Genevieve de Brabant* by Jacques Offenbach. The words went like this:

From the halls of Montezuma to the shores of Tripoli;
We fight our country's battles on land and on the sea.
First to fight for right and freedom and to keep our honor clean,
We are proud to claim the title of United States Marine.

And so the famous Marine Corps Hymn was born. In 1929 two additional stanzas were added to form the official version of the Hymn, and in 1942 a line of the first stanza was changed to read '. . . In the air, on land, and sea,' in recognition of the Corps's additional dimension of combat.

On 2 February 1848 the Treaty of Guadalupe Hidalgo brought the war to an end. The United States gained Texas, New Mexico—including what would later become Arizona—and California from San Diego north. The cost in American lives was 13,271 men killed in battle, or dead of wounds or disease—a significant number of these being Marines.

Fourteen troubled years

As has always happened following a war, the Corps's strength was cut back, in this instance to its authorized peacetime strength of 1224 enlisted men. But the workload of the Marines did not diminish during the 14-years period from the end of the War with Mexico to the Civil War, for it was a time of great expansion of America's commercial interests. Between 1846 and 1860, for example, the nation's foreign trade would grow by 300 percent, mostly transported by American ships, and Marines would be called on to protect those ships on the high seas and in ports around the world.

However, it became the Corps's duty to suppress rather than protect one part of this shipping, that of slavers sailing from the African coast. Congress had outlawed slave trade in 1808. In 1820 it declared such sea commerce by American-flag ships to be piracy. In 1842 the United States signed the Webster-Ashburton Treaty with England, specifying that the United States would station warships along the African coast to work against the slave trade. This the United States did with the Navy's African Squadron.

When the Squadron's commander, Commodore Matthew C Perry of Mexican War fame, landed in Liberia in 1843 to investigate slaver activities, he was attacked by Ben Crack-O, chief of the Berribees, a tribe involved in the slave traffic. A Marine sergeant sprang forward to Perry's defense and shot the chief, setting off a fight with the tribesmen that ended in a Marine victory. The last Marine landing in Africa against slavers took place in 1860 involving a detachment from the sloop *Marion*.

South America was another troubled area in the 1850s as the USA expanded its interests through the Southern Hemisphere. Marines from the *Congress* and the *Jamestown* landed at Buenos Aires in 1852 in response to reports of threats to American lives and property by rioting Argentines. Within days of that landing Marines from the *Albany* went to the aid of the citizens of San Juan del Sur, Nicaragua, to fight a fire that swept their city; two years later, in July 1854, Marines of the *Cyane* would land to bombard and burn the same city. Marines were in action repeatedly in Panama between 1856 and 1860 to protect the workers of an American company building a railroad across the isthmus to serve the booming California gold fields.

Above: Perry and his Marine escort during the negotiations with Liberian chiefs in 1843, shortly before violence erupted.

Battles of the Barrier Forts in China

China became inflamed during the mid-century with the bloody Taiping religious rebellion, a holocaust that would claim 20 million lives during the 15 years of its course. As this period began, attacks on foreign properties by both warring factions became more and more frequent, and Marines were called in repeatedly to provide protection. The situation came to a head in November 1856 when four so-called 'Barrier Forts' on the Pearl River near Canton—armed with 176 cannon up to ten inches in caliber, set behind granite-faced breastworks seven feet thick—opened fire on American ships.

The Navy steam frigate *San Jacinto* and the sloops-of-war *Portsmouth* and *Levant* sailed up the Pearl, and on 20 November a force of Marines commanded by Captain J D Simms—who had been brevetted for gallantry at Chapultepec—and seamen stormed ashore and splashed through rice fields toward the first of the forts. Supported by a bombardment from the ships, the force charged the walls and drove out the

Below: The US forces on the march from Puebla in early August 1847 in the final stages of the Mexican-American War.

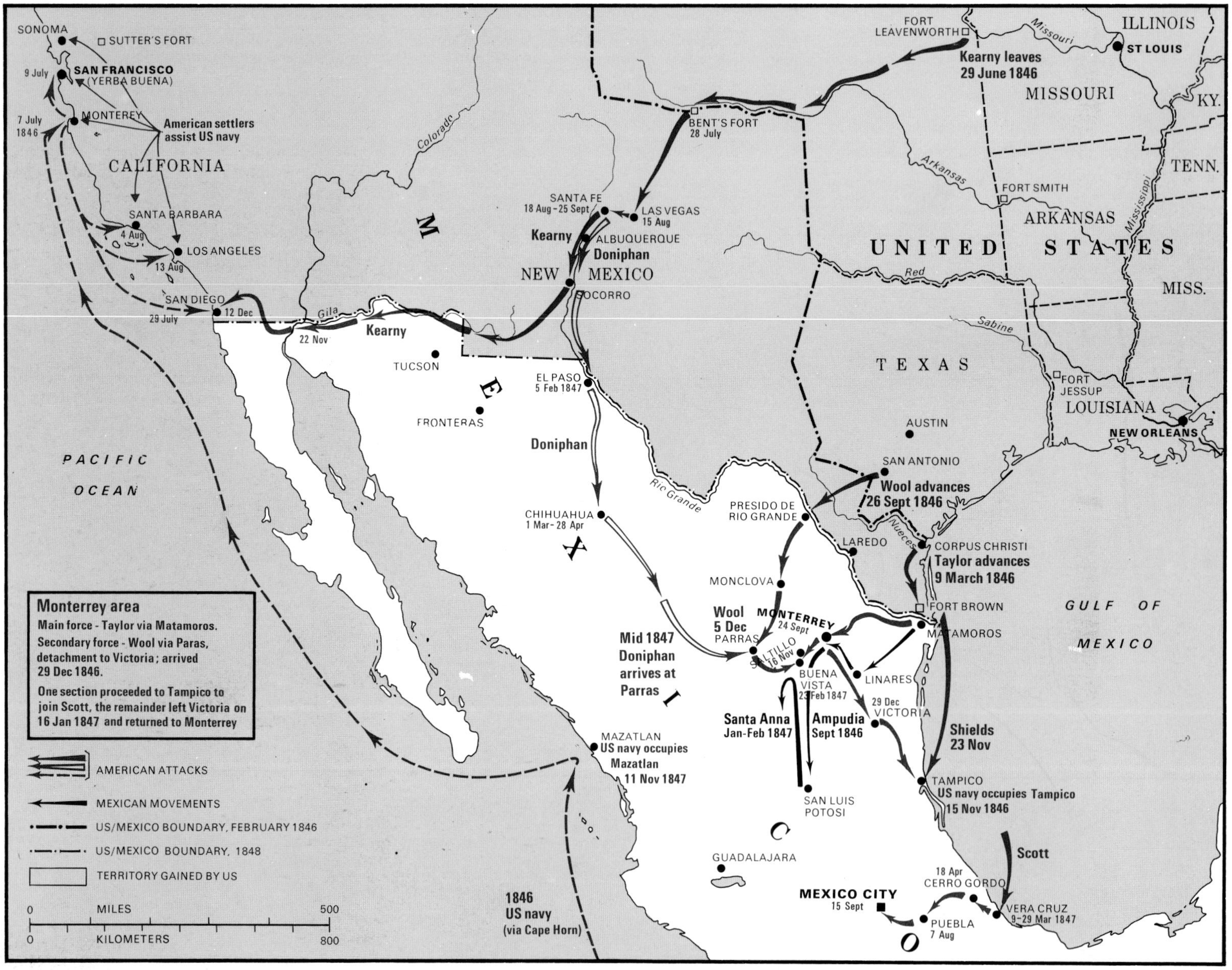

Monterrey area
Main force - Taylor via Matamoros.
Secondary force - Wool via Paras, detachment to Victoria; arrived 29 Dec 1846.
One section proceeded to Tampico to join Scott, the remainder left Victoria on 16 Jan 1847 and returned to Monterrey
AMERICAN ATTACKS
MEXICAN MOVEMENTS
US/MEXICO BOUNDARY, FEBRUARY 1846
US/MEXICO BOUNDARY, 1848
TERRITORY GAINED BY US
0 MILES 500
0 KILOMETERS 800
SONOMA
SUTTER'S FORT
9 July
SAN FRANCISCO (YERBA BUENA)
7 July 1846
MONTEREY
American settlers assist US navy
CALIFORNIA
SANTA BARBARA
4 Aug
LOS ANGELES
13 Aug
SAN DIEGO
29 July
12 Dec
Gila
22 Nov
Kearny
TUCSON
FRONTERAS
PACIFIC OCEAN
Colorado
FORT LEAVENWORTH
Kearny leaves 29 June 1846
Missouri
ST LOUIS
ILLINOIS
MISSOURI
KY.
TENN.
BENT'S FORT 28 July
Arkansas
FORT SMITH
ARKANSAS
Mississippi
SANTA FE 18 Aug - 25 Sept
LAS VEGAS 15 Aug
Kearny
ALBUQUERQUE
Doniphan
NEW MEXICO
SOCORRO
UNITED STATES
Red
MISS.
Sabine
TEXAS
FORT JESSUP
LOUISIANA
NEW ORLEANS
AUSTIN
SAN ANTONIO
Wool advances 26 Sept 1846
EL PASO 5 Feb 1847
Doniphan
Rio Grande
PRESIDO DE RIO GRANDE
Nueces
CORPUS CHRISTI
Taylor advances 9 March 1846
LAREDO
CHIHUAHUA 1 Mar - 28 Apr
M E X I C O
MONCLOVA
FORT BROWN
GULF OF MEXICO
Wool 5 Dec
MONTERREY 24 Sept
MATAMOROS
PARRAS
Mid 1847 Doniphan arrives at Parras
SALTILLO 16 Nov
BUENA VISTA 23 Feb 1847
LINARES
29 Dec VICTORIA
Santa Anna Jan-Feb 1847
Ampudia Sept 1846
Shields 23 Nov
MAZATLAN
US navy occupies Mazatlan 11 Nov 1847
TAMPICO
US navy occupies Tampico 15 Nov 1846
SAN LUIS POTOSI
Scott
GUADALAJARA
18 Apr CERRO GORDO
MEXICO CITY 15 Sept
VERA CRUZ 9-29 Mar 1847
PUEBLA 7 Aug
1846 US navy (via Cape Horn)

Left: Marines of Perry's squadron parade as the Commodore meets the Japanese Imperial Commissioner at Yokahama in March 1854.
Above: General Quitman leads his Marines and Army men into Mexico City.
Bottom: The entry into Mexico City.

fort's defenders, 'the Marines being in advance opened fire upon the fugitives with deadly effect.'

Over the following two days the Marines successively stormed and captured the remaining three forts, spiked some guns and threw others in the river, then blew up the fortifications with their own powder. Killed in the action: 500 enemy, 10 Americans.

In his report on the action, the captain of the *Portsmouth*, Commodore A H Foote, wrote this: 'It may be seen in this report how efficient our Marines are in service of this kind; and the inference is inevitable that an increase of that Corps, and of the number of officers and men attached to our ships, would tend to insure success in like expeditions.'

The 'Grand Old Man'

On 1 June 1857, the orderly process of elections in Washington, DC, was threatened by the arrival from Baltimore of a large gang of heavily-armed toughs, self-styled the 'Plug-Uglies,' who were determined to seize and control the polling places. When the city police were frightened off by the gang, Mayor Magruder sent out an emergency call for assistance from the Marines stationed at Corps Headquarters. Near Fifth and K Streets the two groups confronted one another, and the Plug-Uglies aimed a cannon at the line of Marines.

At that moment a white-whiskered man in civilian clothes and carrying a gold-headed cane stepped from the watching crowd and walked up to the line of toughs; it was Marine Commandant Brigadier General Archibald Henderson. The slim, erect 74-year-old man, standing in front of the cannon's muzzle, spoke calmly to the mob: 'Men, you had better think twice before you fire this piece at the Marines.'

A man thrust a pistol at Henderson two feet from his face; the Commandant seized the man and hauled him away to be placed under arrest. A volley of shots aimed at the Marines rang out, and 'they poured in an answering fire.' Within a few seconds the rioters fell back, then took to their heels and fled.

Two years later, on 6 January 1859, Archibald Henderson died while still in office. He had served as commandant for 39 years, under ten presidents, during the most tumultuous years of the nation's growth. Truly the 'Grand Old Man of the Corps,' as his contemporaries called him, Henderson set standards for rigorous training, professional discipline and courageous service that do honor to the Corps to this day.

Henderson also left a Corps that would shortly face an agonizing conflict of interest, one that would go beyond any previous test of the mettle of Marines—their own nation's Civil War.

FROM WAR TO BORROWED PEACE

'Rushing In Like Tigers'—1859–1865

As the decade of the 1850s drew to a close, the level of tension and confrontation in the United States between pro- and anti-slavery forces approached its climactic expression in the tragedy of the Civil War. The tension was manifest within the ranks of the Marine Corps as its members felt the pull of differing loyalties, depending mostly on the region of the country from which they came. Large numbers of Marines soon would resign to serve with the Confederacy, and this loss would leave the Corps poorly equipped to serve the Union effectively during the ensuing conflict.

Most of the resignations were by younger officers of company rank, with the result that the officer corps soon consisted heavily of elderly field-grade officers, some of whom were too feeble to serve in the field. The dash and spirit of another elderly Marine, Archibald Henderson, was nowhere to be seen in the senior ranks, and most particularly not in the person of Commandant Colonel John Harris, Henderson's successor.

As a result of these resignations, as well as of governmental pennypinching regarding the Marines, the Corps would consist in early 1861 of 1892 officers and enlisted men. And even with the subsequent increase authorized by Congress to a strength of 3167, the Corps never reached a size during the war that was adequate for carrying out the missions required of it. However, in one engagement on the eve of the Civil War the Marines did acquit themselves with honor.

Incident at Harpers Ferry

John Brown, a militant abolitionist from Kansas, was gripped by the idea of creating a refuge for runaway slaves in the rugged Southern hills, equipped with sufficient arms for the runaways to protect themselves against slave hunters. To procure the needed arms, Brown led a force of 18 armed men into the small town of Harpers Ferry, Virginia (now West Virginia) on the night of 16 October 1859, and seized the Federal arsenal located there, along with 40 hostages, one of whom was Colonel Lewis Washington, the first president's great-grandnephew.

Within the hour the new commandant of Marines, Colonel John Harris, had ordered into action from Corps headquarters First Lieutenant Israel Green and a force of 86 Marines. Green was told that Colonel Robert E Lee of the Army would be at the scene to assume overall command of the operation.

The Marine unit arrived at midnight of the same day; by the following dawn Colonel Lee had his plans made and a 24-man assault party briefed and ready to go. Lee asked the state militia unit that had arrived on the scene if they wished to conduct the attack on the heavily-fortified arsenal; they declined the offer vigorously. Colonel Lee then ordered Green and an Army cavalry lieutenant, J E B Stuart, to begin the operation.

Stuart walked to the arsenal door and read aloud an ultimatum of surrender, and when Brown would not comply, Stuart waved his cap as a signal to Lieutenant Green and his Marines. In Green's words, 'the men took hold bravely and made a tremendous assault upon the door' with heavy sledges and a battering ram, 'rushing in like tigers.' Green was first through the shattered doorway; a gun inside thundered, the round narrowly missed his head and struck the Marine behind him, Private Luke Quinn, mortally wounding him. Green saw Brown crouched and reloading a carbine; the lieutenant sprang forward and struck Brown down with a saber slash across the side of his neck. Within seconds the fight was won and John Brown's insurrection was over; he would subsequently hang for his attempt.

In a sense it might be said that the first serviceman to die in the Civil War was that unsung Marine, Private Quinn.

A time of low fortunes

This sort of cooperation between Southern and Northern members of American military units ended with the beginning of the Civil War; Colonel Lee and Lieutenant Stuart were distinguished examples of the many men who left Federal forces to join the Army of the Confederacy. Congress authorized Marine Corps expansion to 93 officers and 3074 enlisted men—President Lincoln raised this figure by 1000 more—but these increases could not make up for the losses in experienced personnel suffered by the Corps. As a result, the Marines did not play a major part in the ensuing conflict.

In the months immediately prior to the

Pages 34–35: Men of the 1st Marines pose for the photographer near Olongapo during the Philippine Insurrection.
Above: A scene during the Battle of Bull Run, one of the least creditable in the Marines' history.
Left: Marines parading outside their barracks in Washington on the eve of the Civil War in 1861.
Right: Union forces on the march across the Potomac during the Civil War.

declaration of war on 15 April 1861, Marine units were employed to reinforce Federal garrisons located in Southern states. A unit of 100 Marines sent to Norfolk Navy Yards destroyed seven Union ships as well as arms and supplies to keep them from the Confederates.

Once war began, the first major action of the Marines was at the First Battle of Bull Run [Manassas] on 21 July 1861. The 353-man Marine unit, part of a 35,000-man Union force, was under Major John G Reynolds, with Major Jacob Zeilin of Mexican War renown in command of a company. The Marine unit that entered the battle consisted primarily of inexperienced

Right : The CSS *Virginia (Merrimack)* engages the Union blockading squadron in Hampton Roads on 8 March 1862, the day before the battle with the *Monitor*.

enlisted men and junior officers. After suffering 44 casualties in the course of three assaults on their position by the riflemen of the 33rd Virginia and the cavalry forces of J E B Stuart, now a Confederate colonel, the Marines broke and ran. This was reported by their commandant, Colonel Harris, to Secretary of the Navy Gideon Welles as 'the first instance in [Marine Corps] history where any portion of its members turned their backs to the enemy,'

Amphibious action along the Southern coast

The naval and amphibious uses to which Marines were put during the balance of the war were far more appropriate to the Corps's training and mission than was their disastrous action at Bull Run. A key strategy of the Union was to blockade Southern ports so as to prevent resupply of Confederate forces, and the Marines served well in the implementation of this strategy.

A month after Bull Run, Marines undertook the first of two operations aimed at gaining naval control of Hatteras Inlet, North Carolina; Confederate privateers were operating out of Puget Sound against Union shipping, and it was an entry point for British blockade runners carrying war materials to the South. On 28 August the Marine contingent from the USS *Minnesota*, along with Army regulars, scrambled from longboats to attack and, in a four-hour-long engagement, took Fort Clark on one side of the inlet. Soon afterward Fort Hatteras on the other side of the inlet fell to the Union attackers. This double loss shook Confederate morale, and the North gained a strategic foothold it would maintain for the rest of the war.

The concept of the Marines as an amphibious fighting force was held strongly

Below : The confused fighting at Bull Run which saw the Marines break and flee for one of very few times in their history.

by Naval Flag Officer Samuel F DuPont, commander of the South Atlantic Blockading Squadron, and together with Marine Major Reynolds he organized a 300-man battalion to that end. The group's first objective was to be Port Royal, South Carolina, but unfortunately, the Marines were given an unseaworthy boat as their transport, the sidewheeler *Governor*, and it foundered in a storm on the way to Port Royal, leaving the Marines unable to join the action.

In March 1862 Reynolds's battalion sailed to seize and occupy Fernandina, Georgia, only to discover when they arrived that Union troops already were there. Next they departed for St Augustine, Florida, to take it, but learned enroute that the Confederate garrison had abandoned the city. At this point DuPont decided there were no missions remaining that called for the special talents of the Marine amphibious battalion. The unit was broken up and the men assigned to various ships' detachments.

This wasn't the end of frustration for the Corps, however. In August 1863 Major Jacob Zeilin was sent with a battalion of 300 Marines to attack the nine fortifications guarding the port of Charleston, South Carolina. Zeilin tried to expand the unit to a regiment and train them in amphibious tactics, but found himself dissatisfied with the results. He was replaced by Major Reynolds, whose first action was to reduce the unit to battalion size and to then provide the men with further training.

On 8 September 1863 a Marine unit with sailors attached attacked Fort Sumter, the most celebrated of the Confederate-held strongholds at Charleston, in a night landing from small boats. The action went badly from the start, with many of the boats getting lost in the darkness; the 150 Marines and sailors who got ashore and were part of the unsuccessful assault took deadly accurate fire from the Confederate defenders, with the result that 44 Marines were killed, wounded or captured. The battalion was taken out of combat and sent to a rear area camp for rest and rehabilitation, but a sickness swept the unit and added to their misery. In early 1864 the battalion was broken up and its members reassigned.

The problems of the Corps at this time were many and pressing, not the least of them being the bitterness that existed between many members of the 'old guard' of staff officers and the younger line officers. These arguments visibly wore down John Harris, the Corps's Commandant, and his death on 12 May 1864, was not unexpected. Secretary of the Navy Welles seized on the event as an opportunity to 'retire the Marine officers who are past the legal age, and to bring in Zeilin as Commandant of the Corps. There seems no alternative.'

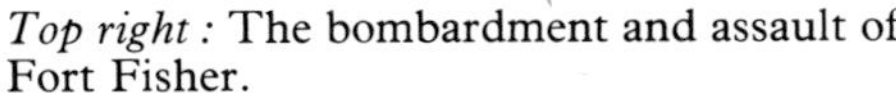

Top right: The bombardment and assault of Fort Fisher.
Right: The Marines storm ashore to take the Han River forts near Seoul in Korea in May 1871. Note the marshy terrain.

Above: Petersburg, Virginia, was an important supply base for Lee's Confederate Army of Northern Virginia.

This Welles did, with President Lincoln's approval; every Marine officer senior to Jacob Zeilin was retired, and on 10 June he was appointed as seventh Commandant of the Corps.

The Battle of Fort Fisher

By the end of 1864 Union attacks on Southern ports had neutralized all but that of Wilmington, North Carolina, which blockade runners continued to use as a point of resupply for the Confederacy. Entrance to the port was via Cape Fear River, and guarding that entrance was one of the South's more formidable fortifications, Fort Fisher, defended by 44 large-caliber cannon and more than a thousand troops.

Union action against the fort took place in two phases, the first of which resulted in embarrassment for all involved. It was commanded by an amateur soldier from Massachusetts, politician Major General Benjamin F Butler. On 24 December Butler ordered that a crewless ship filled with explosives be sailed to a point just offshore from the fort and blown up, with the hope of bringing down its walls. When the explosives went off, they did no damage whatsoever to Fort Fisher—the watching Confederates on the ramparts thought some unfortunate blockade runner had suffered an accident.

The following day, Christmas, under cover of heavy fire from Union Navy ships standing offshore, Butler's unit of 3000 men approached the huge fortification from the opposite side of the cape. They got within a few hundred yards of Fort Fisher's walls without drawing fire and apparently undetected—in fact, several daring Northerners actually scaled the walls, entered the fort and returned with trophies. Despite this, Butler showed little inclination to fight, instead ordering that the operation cease and his unit withdraw.

Union Commanding General Ulysses S Grant quickly relieved Butler of his command and replaced him with a professional soldier, Major General A H Terry, USA. Terry brought with him reinforcements of a number sufficient to swell the size of the attacking force to 8500 officers and men. Rear Admiral David D Porter, in overall command of the operation, decided that after a softening-up bombardment by his fleet, a force of 1600 seamen and 400 Marines would execute a diversionary attack from small boats against the front wall of the fort while Terry led his soldiers against the rear wall in the main assault.

The landing operation began at three o'clock in the afternoon of 15 January 1865. The idea of an attack on a fortification by seamen armed only with cutlasses and pistols was, in the words of one of Admiral Porter's own officers, 'sheer, murderous madness.' Once on the beach, the seamen were to wait until the Marines—a hastily-assembled group from the ships in Porter's command—took up positions from which they would deliver covering rifle fire. But neither the seamen nor their naval officers were experienced in land-based combat, and in the ensuing confusion the seamen launched their attack before the Marines were in place. The Confederate defenders in the fort let the attackers get within 40 yards of the walls, then cut them to ribbons with a hail of deadly gunfire. The Marines were ordered into the assault in support of the sailors, and they too were shot down in the attempt. When Porter finally gave the order to cease the attack and withdraw, 309 dead and wounded Marines and sailors were left on the beach. The diversion served its purpose, however—Terry's soldiers fought their way through the fort's defensive breastworks and over the walls to take it.

The bumbled assault on Fort Fisher loosened a storm of charges and countercharges from all the military services, with Admiral Porter at the center of the fire. Porter's defense tried to put the blame off onto the Marines: 'Had the covering party of Marines performed their duty, every one of the enemy would have been killed.' The final effect of the fiasco was to put back the cause of a separate, equal Corps of Marines, organized, trained and equipped to carry out its own unique form of military action, amphibious assaults. It would be many years before such a status would come into being.

Above: Major General Benjamin Frank Butler who led the first attack on Fort Fisher.

A few months later America's most soul-wrenching war ended, on 9 April 1865, when Lee presented his bejeweled sword to Grant in surrender at Appomattox Court House, and the United States, 'a house divided against itself,' began the long, painful process of coming back together.

As for the Corps, it had grown only slightly during the conflict, to a maximum strength of 4167 officers and men. The most telling indication of how lightly Marines had participated in the war could be seen in their casualty figures: 148 killed in combat, 312 dead as a result of other causes. The country's political and military higher authorities still had not decided on a basic mission for the Corps, and until that determination was made the Corps would continue to find its very reason-for-being under repeated assault.

'With a Blasted Muzzle-Fuzzle'—1871-1898

The Marine Corps came out of the Civil War with its reputation at a low point. Marines had not played a meaningful role in the war, most significantly not in their specialities of assaults and amphibious actions, as was obvious from the fact that only 148 Marines were killed in action during the war. Problems of low morale during the conflict had led to an inflated rate of desertions and to angry bickering between line and staff officers. But most shattering to the stability of the Corps had been the defections to the Confederacy of many Marine officers and men. These experiences combined to make the Corps vulnerable to its enemies, and on 18 June 1866 they struck: Marine Commandant Zeilin learned that the House of Representatives had just approved consideration of this resolution:

Resolved, That the Committee on Naval Affairs be directed to consider the expediency of abolishing the Marine Corps, and transferring it to the Army, and making provision for supplying such military force as may at any time be needed in the Navy, by detail from the Army.

As his predecessors had before him, Commandant Zeilin instantly counter-attacked, soliciting and receiving from the highest-ranking officers in the Navy words of total support for the Corps. A friendly House Naval Affairs Committee reported out the hostile resolution adversely on 21 February 1867, saying that 'on the contrary, the Committee recommends that [the Marine Corps'] organization as a separate Corps be preserved and strengthened . . . [and] that its commanding officer shall hold the rank of a brigadier general.'

Postwar service on many seas

With its existence once again secured, the Corps was ready to take on whatever military assignments might come its way, and in the latter half of the 19th century there would be many. In addition to a number of major actions by the Marines, they made minor landings in Formosa, Japan and Uruguay in the 1860s; Mexico, Colombia and the Hawaiian Islands in the 1870s; Egypt, Korea, Haiti, Samoa and the Hawaiian Islands in the 1880s; Argentina, Chile, Navassa Island, Nicaragua, Korea, North China, the Isthmus of Panama and Nicaragua again in the 1890s. And, too, there were many challenging events for the Corps to deal with right at home in the United States.

Assaults in Korea

In many of the above-mentioned situations the mere presence of US Marines and warships in the region made fighting unnecessary, but this was not the case with Korea in the summer of 1871.

Korea was then known as 'The Hermit Kingdom,' and with good reason, for its people manifested a strong enmity toward any foreigners who dared to enter their territory, demonstrated by their attack upon and killing of the crew of the American vessel *General Sherman* after it was shipwrecked in the Han River. Washington quickly ordered America's Minister to China, Frederick Low, to go to Korea and negotiate a treaty of amity and accord with its people. In May of 1871 Low arrived off the west coast of Korea aboard the USS *Colorado*, flagship of the Asiatic Fleet, accompanied by four other warships, all under the command of Rear Admiral John Rodgers. They dropped anchor at the mouth of the Han River and Rodgers sent off a surveying party in a small boat to find an approach to the capital city of Seoul. As the party worked its way up the channel, it was fired on from one of five forts guarding the mouth of the river.

After demanding an apology from the

Below: Fort Sumter, scene of an unsuccessful Marine attack in September 1863.

Above : General Ulysses S Grant, commander of the Union forces in the Civil War.

Koreans and waiting ten days without receiving one, Low and Rodgers decided to exact retribution. A force of bluejackets and a Marine brigade of four officers and 105 enlisted men prepared to land and attack the Korean forts. The Marine commander, Captain McLane Tilton, was apprehensive about the suitability for the mission of the breech-loading muskets then carried by his men. Tilton was an advocate of the new breech-loading repeating rifle—in fact, he had earlier written Headquarters Marine Corps as follows:

> *One man* with a breech loader is equal to 12 to 15 armed as we are and in the event of any landing, or even chasing Coreans armed with an excellent repeater, what ever could Americans do with a blasted *Muzzle Fuzzle*?

On 10 June the force landed on a mud flat south of the first fort, a small one, and the men promptly sank in the mud up to their knees; there might have been carnage had not the big guns of the warships provided covering fire until the Americans were able to extricate themselves and move forward. The naval cannonade had been too much for the defenders and they fled the fort, which the Marines and bluejackets then occupied and busied themselves with spiking its guns. The next day Tilton led his men to the second small fort and took it with as little effort as they had the first one.

Next came the major Korean fortification, 'The Citadel.' The Americans' approach path to the fort was over rugged terrain of steep hills and deep ravines, with a force of Korean riflemen firing at them from nearby ridges as they advanced. The final assault was straight up a 150-foot hillside with heavy fire raining down on the attackers, but despite these desperate conditions they finally made it to the top. During the ensuing hand-to-hand battle the Americans performed magnificently, which is obvious from the fact that six Marines received Medals of Honor for this action in which 243 Korean defenders were killed compared with just two Marine casualties. Frederick Low continued on to Seoul, and though no successful treaty came of his negotiations, hostile actions against Americans ceased.

Ashore in Alexandria

The next significant test of the Marines came in 1882. In the summer of that year the British Mediterranean Fleet bombarded Alexandria, Egypt, when an antiforeign movement in that city led to looting and murdering by *fellah* mobs. With part of Alexandria on fire and American nationals in danger, Marines from the European Squadron were dispatched to provide protection. Marine Captain H C Cochrane was chosen to head the landing force; Cochrane previously had won a small place in history when he accompanied President Lincoln on his trip to dedicate the Gettysburg cemetery. Henry Clay Cochrane was very much his own man, described by a fellow officer as

> '. . . distinctly a gentleman and always extremely courteous in his social contacts, but "ornery" and meaner than hell on duty. . . . A man of no sympathy and no affection, but efficient to an unusual degree. A magnificent barracks and mess officer. Cordially hated by officers and men alike.'

On 14 July Cochrane led ashore a unit consisting of 73 Marines and 60 bluejackets, a tiny force compared with the city's great mobs. He marched them directly to the Grand Square of Mehemet Ali where the American Consulate was located and immediately set up a protective cordon around the building. This done, Cochrane sent units out in all directions with orders to work from street to street and gradually create a zone of order around the square. When reinforcements for the antiforeign rioters marched toward the city, Cochrane said he would 'stick by the British and take

Below : Contemporary sketch map of the American operations in Korea in 1871, showing the positions taken by the Marines.

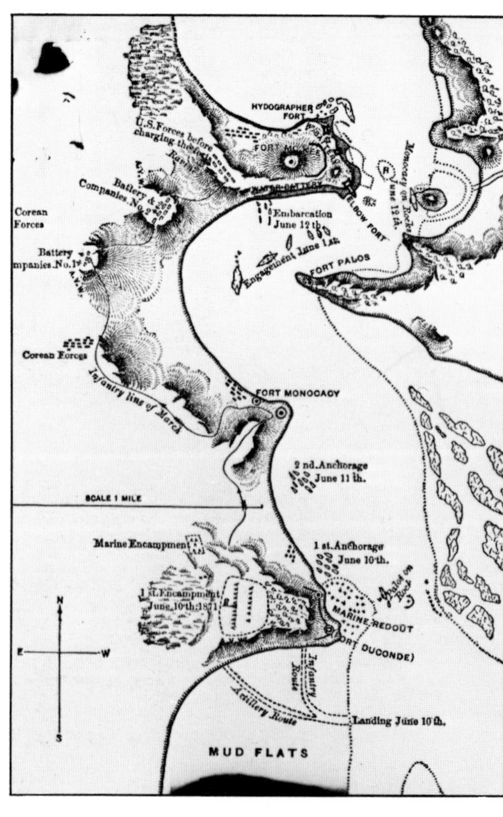

their chances.' Some 4000 British troops soon arrived to relieve the situation, and they and their political leaders were quick in expressing their appreciation for Cochrane's steadiness; the local British commander, Lord Charles Beresford, sent this message: 'To your smart, faithful force, great credit is due. . . . I have represented these facts to my government.'

Hot times in Panama

The year 1885 saw fighting explode on the Isthmus of Panama as its residents revolted against Colombia, which then ruled the area; the combat brought travel across the isthmus to a halt. Such traffic was of great importance to America's economic and military interests, and Washington quickly reacted to the stoppage. On 2 April 1885, Marine Commandant Zeilin received orders to organize and dispatch a battalion of Marines to Aspinwall (now Colón, a large city of Panama). Within 24 hours the force sailed out of New York Harbor, under the command of Brevet Lieutenant Colonel Charles Heywood, known as the 'boy

Above: Parade ground and, right, commandant's house at the Marine barracks during the Civil War. *Left:* Hats *c.* 1878. Clockwise from top left: field officer, full dress; company officer, fatigues; all officers, undress pattern; full dress, enlisted men; fatigue, enlisted men; undress, bandsmen; full dress, company officer.

colonel' because of his rapid rise through the officer ranks.

Five days later a second battalion of Marines, along with a battalion of rifle-armed bluejackets under Commander Bowman H McCalla, departed from the United States for Panama; McCalla was designated by the Navy Department to be the commander of all American forces once they went ashore in Panama. The Marines were led by Captain J H Higbee; Captain Robert W Huntington, who would win fame at Guantanamo Bay, headed one company and a future Commandant, First Lieutenant George F Elliott, served with him.

The ship carrying the battalion headed by Colonel Heywood arrived off Panama while McCalla's force still was at sea. Heywood promptly ordered his unit ashore, and by sundown of the same day, 12 April, they had marched across the 47-mile wide isthmus, set up a camp outside Panama City, and Marine guards were aboard each train of the trans-Isthmus Panama Railroad. When Commander McCalla arrived three days later, a large degree of control already was established outside the city. Probably in recognition of this well-done piece of work, when another Marine battalion arrived from the United States, the three battalions were formed into a brigade and Colonel Heywood made its commander; this was the first organization of a Marine brigade.

By 20 April the military situation within Panama City had deteriorated badly, with the anti-government forces threatening to burn the city in a fight to the death. Hey-

Above: The Stars and Stripes flies above part of the Allied encampment at Alexandria during the expedition in 1882.

wood's Marines marched into the beleagured city, destroyed all the street fortifications thrown up by the protestors and quickly gained military control of the city. The Marines maintained this control in the face of a numerically superior opposing force until 30 April, when Colombian regular army troops arrived in Panama City to take over the situation.

The sterling performance of the Marines affirmed the by-then widely held admiration of them; the captain of a British warship in the city's harbor, upon learning that a Marine unit was joining the action, had said, 'Tranquility is then assured.' But newspaper correspondent Richard Harding Davis provided the most memorable description of the episode: 'The Marines have landed and have the situation well in hand.'

Moonshine raids in Brooklyn

With the exception of such overseas expeditions, peacetime duty for the Corps was not very exciting, which is why the buoyant-spirited Marines appreciated the occasional stateside assignments that came their way, as unmilitary as some of these duties were. For example, after President Lincoln's assassination, Marines had been given the tension-filled job of providing detention security for the members of the murder plot as, one by one, they were captured and held for trial.

An even more unlikely assignment was that of performing as prohibition agents, which Marines did repeatedly between 1867 and 1871. Operators of illegal stills in the area of Brooklyn, New York, then known as 'Irishtown,' gave an inhospitable reception to federal revenue agents who attempted to shut down their bootlegging operations, and neither the city's police nor units of the Army's 8th Infantry had been able to provide the agents with sufficient protection. The local army commander, Major General Israel Vogdes, who had respectful memories of the Marines from his Civil War service, urged that the Leatherneck unit from the Brooklyn Navy Yard be assigned the task. This was done, and soon members of the Corps with bayonets fixed were marching through the area's streets, guarding revenue officers who searched out and smashed illegal stills. The Marines subsequently were thanked for the steadfastness of their service by everyone involved—everyone, that is, except the bootleggers.

Right and *above right:* The Marine guard from the USS *Boston* pictured in 1888 in full dress (right) and undress uniforms.
Below: Marine racing crew from the USS *Olympia.*

The railroad 'insurrection'

On the scorching summer afternoon of 21 July 1877, a trying episode began for the Marines. Orders came down from the highest level to Corps Headquarters in Washington for a battalion to hurry to Baltimore to restore order; striking railroad workers in nine states were tearing up rails, burning rolling stock and even attacking local authorities who attempted to control them. Army and Marine units under the overall command of Major General W S Hancock, USA, were ordered to aid police in what would prove to be one of the more tumultuous labor disputes in American history.

Under the command of Colonel Charles Heywood, of Panama fame, the Marine battalion proceeded to Baltimore's Camden Station by train, after some difficulty with finding an engineer courageous enough to operate the locomotive during the strike. It was night when the troop train arrived in Baltimore, a night lighted by the flames of blazing tank cars in the railroad yard; the Marines could see the running figures of the arsonists silhouetted against the flames. Throughout that chaotic night the Marines guarded Camden and Mount Clare Stations against violence; in the morning Heywood marched his small force, drums beating and colors flying, to Baltimore's prestigious Eutaw House for breakfast.

Heywood was awakened from sleep the following night by a Duty Officer holding a telegram; it contained urgent orders from the Secretary of the Navy for Heywood to move his battalion to Philadelphia, where striker violence had created a state of lawlessness similar to the situation in Baltimore.

This time the trip was slowed by torn-up track, but at mid-day of 23 July the Marines were in action on Philadelphia's streets, and by nightfall a condition of orderliness had been imposed. The Marines were disconcerted when they were then ordered to stand inspection by General Hancock, since they had not been out of their uniforms for three days, but they need not have been concerned; Hancock, a seasoned combat soldier, conveyed his warm feelings regarding their performance in his General Order 46, which said:

> The major-general commanding desires to express his high appreciation of the excellent conduct and soldierly qualities of the Marines. . . .

During this same period, another battalion was assembled with Marines from Norfolk and Washington Marine Barracks as well as from ships' detachments, placed under the command of Brevet Lieutenant Colonel James Forney and given the mission of keeping open the railroad right-of-way between Washington and Martinsburg, West Virginia. Other Marine units were sent to Watervliet, New York, and Frankford, Pennsylvania, to guard the local arsenals against raids by striker gangs. In each of these instances, the Marine units carried out their assignments with quiet efficiency. In 1894 the Corps again sent men to restore peace in a railroad strike, this time involving the Central Pacific Railroad. Once again they demonstrated their efficiency and discipline.

Three innovative commandants
Fate smiled on the Marine Corps during the years between the Civil War and the Spanish-American War. The Marines had emerged from the earlier conflict torn both in organization and in morale, but they had the good fortune to get Jacob Zeilin as their leader following the dramatic forced retirement of every Marine officer senior to him. Zeilin brought the Corps back together both in body and spirit with his incisive leadership, as well as with such measures as the creation of a new standardized drill and tactics, and by the introduction of the annual inspection of every Marine station.

When Zeilin voluntarily retired himself on 1 November 1876, he had, with typical efficiency, seen to it that his successor was well prepared to take over as the eighth Commandant. Charles Grymes McCawley, who had served alongside Jacob Zeilin during the Civil War, had been ordered to Washington some time earlier so that he could learn first-hand what was involved in running the Corps. McCawley learned well, for among his administrative accomplishments were a number that would permanently improve the quality of the Marine Corps.

He vigorously led a four-year successful drive in the halls of Congress and with the Navy Department to have Marine Corps officers come from the ranks of Naval Academy graduates, with the result that all 50 officers who entered the Marine Corps between 1881 and 1897 were Academy graduates. McCawley supervised the creation of the first standard table of organization for the Corps; ordered the first factory mass production of uniforms to achieve standardization in sizes and appearance; brought about a thorough reorganization of the Headquarters Marine Corps cadre with the goals of improving soldierly skills and divesting junior commanders of independent authority; instituted a variety of promotion- and retirement-related measures for noncommissioned officers and enlisted men designed to make a career in the Corps a more attractive consideration.

Ironically, McCawley's most memorable contribution to the history of the Corps was not military but was, rather, a musical one involving the Marine band. Some time after he began his service as Commandant, McCawley was reported to have complained, 'The Band gives me more trouble than all the rest of the Corps put together.' When it became necessary in 1880 for him to dismiss Louis Schneider as the band's director following the report by an investigative board that Schneider was unfit for duty, McCawley appointed in his place, with wages of $23.50 a week, a musician by the name of John Philip Sousa. During his 12 years as leader of the Marine band, Sousa converted it into one of the world's finer musical groups.

McCawley, a teetotaler, did not win the hearts of some Marines, however, with his measures relating to intoxicating beverages; he forbade the sale of beer in Marine canteens, and he permitted the use of the Marine Band Hall for meetings by a group with the unlikely name of the Marines Temperance Union.

When McCawley stepped down on 30 January 1891, the 'boy colonel,' Charles Heywood, was selected to take his place and become the Corps's ninth Commandant. Heywood quickly instituted an important step toward the further professionalization of the Corps: he created the School of Application in Washington, forerunner of the Marine Basic School system. During his tour as Commandant the number of Marine bases increased from 12 to 21, one of them being a barracks at Port Royal, South Carolina, that would one day become the Corps' largest training area in the Eastern United States, Parris Island. Heywood instituted mandatory promotion examinations for officers and created a system of officers' schools. Finally, his stringent insistence on the fundamentals—physical fitness, marksmanship, field service and modern tactics—would serve the Corps well when America entered the Spanish-American War.

Below: Aboard the USS *Essex* in 1888, Marines and seamen drawn up for inspection.

Above: Marines at bayonet drill around 1890. Moored to the dock in the background is the receiving ship USS *New Hampshire*.

Navy-versus-Marines tension

By 1890 the Corps had never been more fit and ready, yet at that very moment plans were in the making by a group of junior Naval officers calculated to eliminate the Corps *per se* and convert it into an artillery adjunct of the Army. Behind this plot of the Naval officers was their frustration with the lack of meaningful duty for deck officers in the 'new Navy' of steam engines and other machinery. The spokesman for the Naval group was a brilliant young lieutenant, William F Fullam, USN, who in 1890 presented a paper to the United States Naval Institute in Annapolis in which he proposed the transfer of the Corps to the Army and the creation in its place of an amphibious infantry organization consisting of Naval officers and bluejackets. As in the past, this anti-Corps movement soon found sponsors in the Congress, and on 24 August 1894 a bill was introduced in the Senate that would have combined the Marine Corps with the Army's five regiments of artillery.

The bill died in the Military Affairs Committee, due largely to the testimony of the president of the Naval War College, Captain Henry C Taylor, USN, who made this telling point about the proposed Naval replacement organization for the Marine Corps:

> . . . I do not doubt that those seamen, and the officers [who] command them, would evolve . . . into a new Corps, identical to the present Marines.

The enemies of the Marine Corps in the Navy were not about to be dissuaded from their hostile purposes, however; between 1895 and 1897, three separate attempts were made to restrict or eliminate the role of the Corps within the United States Navy, with each of the attacks being defeated or turned aside. The Corps was secure—at least until the next assault.

Below: The wreck of the USS *Maine* in the harbor of Havana, Cuba. 28 Marines died in the explosion which is now believed to have been caused by spontaneous detonation of unstable ammunition.

Below: Commodore George Dewey, hero of the Battle of Manila Bay.

'Brave Hearts and Bright Weapons—1898-1917

Brave Hearts

The angry interservice arguments with the Navy regarding the value of the Marine Corps were still taking place in 1898 when dramatic events brought the discussion to a temporary halt.

War with Spain: Manila, Guantanamo and Cuzco Valley

The evening of 15 February was pleasantly comfortable in Havana, Cuba. In the harbor the American battleship USS *Maine* lay at anchor; Charles D Sigsbee, the battleship's captain, sat at a table in his quarters composing a letter to his wife, and First Lieutenant A W Catlin, commander of the ship's Marine detachment, was busy with an inspection of extra sentry posts he had established on the captain's orders. The *Maine* had arrived in Havana several weeks previously, ostensibly for a routine courtesy call on the local Spanish authorities; however, anyone who followed current events knew that the visit was in fact the result of an emotional campaign against Spain being conducted in the newspapers of William Randolph Hearst. A revolution had been going on in Cuba for three years, and the headlines in Hearst newspapers regularly featured horrendous stories alleging atrocities committed by the Spanish against Cuban militants and civilians, with suggestions that Americans working on the island might be the next to be attacked. The United States had no meaningful stake in the Cuban events, but the emotional newspaper coverage finally had made the people at the State Department sufficiently uneasy that they arranged for the *Maine* to visit Havana to 'show the colors.'

Below right: Marine riflemen prepare to engage the enemy shortly after the landing at Guantanamo Bay.
Below: Marines entrenching on McCalla Hill near Guantanamo, Cuba in June 1898.

The provocation worked all too well; 20 minutes after Taps that evening the mighty warship was lifted by a gigantic explosion and its hull split open like a torn paper bag. The calm words of Marine Private William Anthony to Captain Sigsbee would make him a national hero: 'Sir, I beg to report that the Captain's ship is sinking.' Within a brief time the *Maine* went to the bottom by the bow, carrying 28 Marines and 238 bluejackets with it.

Given the hostile atmosphere of the time, the next events were predictable; on 21 April 1898, despite earnest attempts by President William McKinley to pacify the public, Congress passed a declaration of war against Spain, and three days later Spain declared war on the United States. By Congressional act the authorized strength of the Corps was increased to 4713 enlisted men and 119 officers, a new high, and Commandant Heywood's rank was raised to that of brigadier general.

While McKinley apparently was a reluctant participant in the war, his assistant secretary of the Navy, Theodore Roosevelt, was not. As early as 25 February Roosevelt had cabled orders to his protege, Commodore George Dewey, commander of the Asiatic Squadron of the US Navy fleet. The cable read as follows:

> Secret and confidential. Order the Squadron . . . to Hong Kong. Keep full of coal. In the event of declaration of war [with] Spain, your duty will be to see that the Spanish squadron does not leave the Asiatic coast and then offensive operations in Philippine Islands. . . . Roosevelt.

Dewey's temperament was perfectly suited to the assignment. Early in the morning of 1 May 1898, following a leisurely breakfast, he sent his seven ships into Manila Bay to attack the fleet of Admiral Montojo. After eight hours of furious fighting the Spanish admiral struck his colors, giving Dewey the most brilliantly-won naval victory until then in the age of steam-driven warships. Two days later Dewey sent ashore a contingent of Marines from the USS *Baltimore* under First Lieutenant Dion Williams to secure the Spaniards' Cavite Navy Yard on Manila Bay. The Marines accomplished the assignment with little difficulty, and soon were settled into their combat post. Williams remembered the situation thus:

> In the barracks storerooms were supplies of clothing and rations which reminded us of our own barracks at home, one feature which greatly interested our men being several barrels of red wine as this formed an important part of the Spanish ration. Cavite was evidently an old-time 'navy yard town' as shown by the number of liquor shops and other places of amusement for sailors, and some of our Marines said 'it was just like Vallejo,' the *Baltimore* having gone into commission at Mares Island.

Dewey's Marines had to wait in the Cavite Navy Yard for over two months

until Army troops arrived, much to Commodore Dewey's exasperation; in a later communication he complained, 'If there had been 5000 Marines under my command at Manila Bay, the city would have surrendered to me on May 1.'

Another American military officer to receive sealed orders even before hostilities erupted with the Spanish was Marine Corps Commandant Colonel Heywood. He was told to organize a battalion of crack Marines at the Brooklyn Navy Yard against the possibility of war, and hold them in readiness for action in Cuba. Heywood selected Lieutenant Colonel Robert W Huntington to head the new battalion. While Huntington, a full-bearded veteran of the Civil War, organized his 647 men into five infantry companies and one artillery battery, Heywood arrived in Brooklyn from Headquarters Marine Corps to personally see to it that:

> . . . [the battalion] was supplied with all the equipment and necessities for field service under conditions prevailing in Cuba, including mosquito netting, woolen and linen clothing, heavy and light weight underwear, three months' supply of provisions, wheelbarrows, pushcarts, pick-axes, shovels, barbed-wire cutters, wall and shelter tents, and a full supply of medical stores.

A merchant ship, the USS *Panther*, was fitted out as a transport for the Marine battalion, and it was ready for action when war came. The Marine battalion paraded through Brooklyn's streets to the blare of band music and the enthusiastic cries of spectators, boarded their transport and sailed for Key West. But the old rivalry between Navy and Marine Corps rose to haunt them; the *Panther*'s captain, Commander G C Reiter, saw the Marines as being under his command, and he put them ashore at night into a disease-ridden swamp at Key West. Making the most of a bad situation, Huntington set his battalion to practicing marksmanship and tactical maneuvering.

For a time the Marines feared they might spend the war in that hellish place, but when Commodore Schley's Flying Squadron needed a shore base to support a blockade of the Spanish fleet in Santiago Harbor, Navy Secretary Long asked Rear Admiral Sampson, the Atlantic Fleet commander, 'Can you not take possession of Guantanamo, occupy as a coaling station?' In response, Sampson ordered Huntington's Marines into action.

Guantanamo Bay lay about forty miles to the east of Santiago. On 7 June the USS

Right: Marines ready for inspection aboard the USS *Portsmouth* in 1885.

Above: The Battle of Manila Bay was a most one-sided engagement with almost the whole Spanish fleet destroyed at a cost of only eight Americans wounded.

Marblehead, a small cruiser accompanying the Marine's transport ship *Panther*, commenced shelling the Spanish defenses inshore, consisting of a gunboat, a few marine mines in the harbor and some 8000 Spanish troops. Three days later, with the additional covering fire of the newly-arrived battleship *Oregon*, the Marines waded ashore at Guantanamo into an eerie quiet. For unknown reasons, the Spanish defenders were nowhere to be seen; not a shot was fired against the Americans.

Below: The first ever photograph taken of US Marines on Guam in October 1899.

Then a difficulty arose; Reiter, the *Panther*'s captain, refused to send ashore the Marine's small-arms ammunitions, claiming he needed it as ballast for his ship. Huntington appealed to the senior Navy officer in the area, the *Marblehead*'s captain, who chanced to be Commander Bowman McCalla, a veteran of the Panama campaign. McCalla, who had fond memories of the Marines' performance in the Isthmus campaign, wired the *Panther*'s skipper in cold anger:

Sir, Break out immediately and land with the crew of the *Panther*, 50,000 rounds [small arms] ammunition. In future, do not require Colonel Huntington to break out or land his stores with members of his command. Use your own officers and men for this purpose, and supply the Commanding Officer of Marines promptly with anything he may desire.

The Marines ashore promptly named their bivouac area Camp McCalla. Within 24 hours of the landing, the Spanish defenders suddenly came alive, pouring deadly fire into the Marine encampment. To deprive the attackers of a vital supply, Huntington sent out two rifle companies together with friendly Cuban guerrillas to find and destroy the Spaniards' only water source at Cuzco, about six miles from the Marines' position. This well was located inside a heavily-defended blockhouse, and the Marine unit's commander, Captain George F Elliott, saw that he would need the support of fire from the heavy guns of a Navy ship, the USS *Dolphin*, then waiting offshore. When the fire came in, however, it began falling dangerously close to Elliott's own men. As the captain looked about for a signalman, Marine Sergeant John H Quick jumped to his feet with an improvised semaphore flag; with Spanish bullets and shells from the *Dolphin*'s cannons flying all about him, Quick calmly signalled the Navy vessel to redirect its fire onto the enemy, and the Marines soon moved in to take their objective. For his action Sergeant Quick received the Congressional Medal of

Honor. Stephen Crane, author of the classic war novel '*Red Badge of Courage*,' was at Cuzco as a correspondent and reported this about the heroic sergeant:

. . . I saw Quick betray only one sign of emotion. As he swung his clumsy flag to and fro, an end of it once caught on a cactus plant. He looked annoyed.

The success of Cuzco broke the back of enemy action at Guantanamo, and for the remainder of the Marines' stay in the area their patrols made little contact with Spanish forces. While Huntington's men dug in their defensive positions, Americans were active elsewhere in Cuba. The Army's Fifth Corps came ashore at Daiquiri and began a march toward Santiago, 20 miles to the east. Subsequently, a group of horsemen serving under the enthusiastic but amateur leadership of Colonel Theodore Roosevelt rode into fame and history with their wild charge up San Juan Hill. At dawn of 3 July the Spanish Navy, in a desperate bid for freedom, steamed out of Santiago Harbor with cannon blazing, but they were hopelessly and tragically outgunned and outclassed; the larger and heavier-gunned American ships cut the Spanish vessels to pieces and sent every one of them to the bottom. Within a month the war was over.

The superb performance of the Marines in the conflict was not lost on the American public. Where other services had experienced time-consuming delays in moving from peacetime slackness to combat readiness, the Marines had been capable of responding almost instantly and carried the war to the enemy, winning both time and territory. In combat fitness, too, the comparison was striking. The Marines were vastly better prepared for tropical warfare; whereas 50 percent of Army soldiers contracted yellow fever, malaria or enteric disease, only 2 percent of Marines suffered enteric disease and not one of them contracted yellow fever.

Recognition and reward for the Corps' fine performance came in a practical and meaningful form: on 3 March 1899 Congress passed a bill calling for a permanent Marine Corps consisting of 201 officers and 6062 men, which was a better than 100 percent increase in strength over just three years earlier.

Guam, Samoa, the Philippine Insurrection

While the country's attention was fixed on events in Cuba, other Marines were fighting battles on other islands. Guam was controlled by Spain at that time, which made it a target for the attentions of the United States Navy. A Marine contingent from the USS *Charleston* headed by First Lieutenant John Twiggs Myers—dubbed 'Handsome Jack' by his friends—landed and secured the island on 21 June 1898, after a preliminary bombardment by the American ship that the Spanish garrison at first took to be a courteous gun salute. Then, on 28 July the Marine detachment of the battleship USS *Massachusetts* went ashore at Ponce, Puerto Rico, and wrested control of the city from the Spanish garrison with virtually no effort.

Above: A group of officers from the 1st Marines in camp near the Portsmouth, New Hampshire, Navy Yard.

Samoa in the far-off South Pacific flared into violence in 1899 over an internal argument about the chieftancy of the island. Since Samoa then was a joint protectorate of Britain and the United States, the flare-up brought two British ships and an American cruiser to the scene. A landing party consisting of British and American Marines and sailors went ashore on 1 April to subdue the more violent of the contending factions, and the results were tragic. The joint force was ambushed near the village of Apia, and in the subsequent fire fight US Navy Lieutenant P V H Lansdale and Ensign John Monahagn were wounded. While the main Anglo-American force retreated, Marine Private H L Hulbert stayed with the wounded officers until both were dead, then he made his way to safety through heavy hostile fire. Marine First Lieutenant C M Perkins, who took over and led the withdrawal, said of Hulbert that 'His behavior throughout was worthy of all praise and honor.' The British and Americans responded to the defeat promptly with heavy reprisals against the factions involved, and within three weeks the Samoan uprising was terminated.

However, an uprising in another part of the Pacific was not nearly so easy to deal with. Commodore Dewey's desire for a sufficient number of Marines to finish the job in the Philippines soon turned out to be grimly appropriate; when the newly-liberated Filipinos saw that the Americans did not appear ready to give them their indepen-

Below: A sentry under the palms at Guantanamo Bay, Cuba. A picture taken shortly before World War II and symbolic of the continuing existence of the US base.

Above: A Marine firing line advances against insurgent positions in the fighting in the Philippines in 1901.
Left: Supposedly an action picture from the same campaign but more probably a scene specially composed for the camera.

dence, their cheers for the small Marine garrison at Cavite Navy Yard quickly turned into angry cries and then became rifle fire.

In March 1899 Dewey sent through an urgent request for a battalion of Marines to reinforce his hard-pressed detachment at Cavite. Within weeks a battalion consisting of 15 officers and 260 enlisted men sailed from the New York Naval Shipyard under the command of Colonel P C Pope, who had served Huntington at Guantanamo as his executive officer. A meaningful footnote to this expedition—one that presaged an end to the romantic era of warfare—was an item in the unit's orders that instructed officers, for the first time in Corps history, to leave their swords behind and take only their service pistols.

That September a second Marine battalion under Major G F Elliott departed hurriedly in response to messages from Dewey that the Philippine situation was worsening. Just three months later yet another battalion sailed for the Pacific, this one led by Major L W T Waller. By the end of 1900 a total of six Marine battalions would be in the Philippines, forming what subsequently would be designated the 1st Marine Brigade, consisting of two rifle regiments and two artillery companies with a total of 58 officers and 1547 enlisted men. Included in the unit were a number of officers who in later years would be Corps commandants.

The work of the Marines during the three years they spent in the Philippines consisted of long periods of boredom interspersed with episodes of the most harrowing and deadly sort of combat. Their first action took place on the main island of Luzon at Olongapo, on Subic Bay, on 23 September 1899, when a force of 70 Marines under Captain John T ('Handsome Jack') Myers landed under covering fire from Navy ships to seize and destroy formerly Spanish coast defense guns that had been captured by the insurgents and were in use against American vessels. Myers' group quickly overran the insurgents' positions and blew up the offending cannon.

The following month the regiment of Lieutenant Colonel G F Elliott was given the difficult assignment of attacking and driving from cover the insurgents of Novaleta, an inaccessible coastal area between Cavite and Manila; this was the same Elliott who only a year before had been a captain at Guantanamo Bay. His attack was to be so coordinated with a move by an Army column that it would deliver the fleeing enemy into the gunsights of the soldiers. On 8 October Elliott's 376 men approached Novaleta in two columns, struggling through a marshy tidal lagoon choked almost impenetrably by mangrove shrubs, and at that moment the waiting insurgents opened up with a hail of deadly fire from the Marine's front and left flank. Pressing forward through sometimes shoulder-deep water, the Marines managed to join up with the Army column, and by midday the combined forces had captured the fortified town. Reporting later to the Commander in Chief, Asiatic Station, Elliott wrote, 'A great deal of personal bravery among officers and men was shown'; but then he added with a combat veteran's wisdom, 'I respectfully request that the Admiral will admonish these young officers for bravado which might have caused a failure in carrying the fort provided these officers had been killed or wounded.'

'Stand, gentlemen, he served on Samar'

There were many instances of courage and resoluteness during the Philippine campaign, but none burned its way so deeply into Corps legend as did the expedition to Samar.

By 1901 peace had been brought to all of the scattered islands of the Philippine

group with the exception of Samar, far down in the southeast. There, legendary fighters known as Moros held the island and terrified the local farming people. On 28 September the Moros attacked an Army company's garrison as the soldiers sat at dinner and killed them almost to a man, many by means of unspeakable torture. A Marine battalion was ordered to hurry to Samar to stabilize the situation until the Army could reestablish its presence on the island. Commanding the battalion was Major Littleton Walter Tazewell Waller, a diminutive redhead who as a young lieutenant had served under Cochrane in the action at Alexandria, Egypt. 'A most excellent officer,' a colleague later said about him, 'who talked a lot about himself but who could always deliver the goods. The Marine Corps was his god. He never let you forget it.'

When Waller arrived off Samar the local US Army commander, Brigadier General 'Hell-Roaring Jake' Smith, to whose force Waller's battalion was attached, told him in no uncertain terms exactly what he wanted to see accomplished: 'I want no prisoners. I wish you to burn and kill; the more you burn and kill, the better it will please me.'

Waller set to his assignment with enthusiasm, and in less than three weeks his battalion had driven the Moros deep into the jungle and into their heavily-fortified stronghold in the cliffs of the Basey River, an area the Spanish Army had never dared penetrate. Approaching in three columns the Marines scaled a 200-foot cliff and, catching the Moros totally by surprise, captured their fortress. Two of the officers involved, Captains Porter and Bearss, earned Medals of Honor for extraordinary bravery.

This mission accomplished, Waller next was ordered by General Smith to determine the best route across Samar for a military telegraph line. Waller assembled a company-sized party and set out on 28 December 1901. Almost immediately the group began experiencing one disaster after another; boats swamped in jungle river, mutiny by bearers, illness and even madness suffered by the men. Finally Waller divided the expedition into two groups, with the weaker members to proceed at a slower pace. When all survivors finally emerged from the jungle on 15 January 1902, at Basey, site of the former Moros stronghold, Waller discovered that ten of his men had perished from fever or exhaustion. Still imperiled by the plotting of guides and bearers against the party, Waller conducted a drumhead court at Basey, sentenced 11 of the Filipinos to death, and had the sentences carried out on the spot. The events that followed caught Waller by surprise. In his words:

> Leaving Samar . . . we reached Cavite. . . . we expected a warm welcome home. . . . This welcome we received . . . cheer after cheer went up for us. . . . [then] I went to my Commander In Chief and was met with the charge of murder.

Incredibly, to Waller and his officers and men, it was true. A political decision had been made by a line of senior Army and civilian authorities reaching all the way back to Washington, and on 17 March Waller and one of his officers were tried by court-martial in Manila on 11 counts of murder. The Army's performance in the matter did it little credit; when the Marine officers were acquitted, the local commanding general, Adna R Chaffee, probably under pressure from Washington, disapproved the verdict. But then the Army Judge Advocate General's office threw out the entire case on the grounds that the Marines had never been detached for service with the Army by presidential order.

Though Waller's name was legally cleared, it is thought by Marine historians that the shadow of the case hung over his otherwise brilliant career, and quite possibly was the single reason why he never became Corps commandant. Within Waller's own brigade, however, a custom came into being that gave witness to the respect and affection in which he and the other members of the legendary expedition were held. Whenever one of them was present at brigade mess, this toast would be raised:

> 'Stand, gentlemen, he served on Samar.'

'The Fist of Righteous Amity': the Boxer Rebellion

The winds of social change that blew across the Pacific at the beginning of the twentieth century reached all the way to China. Disraeli had said, 'Let China sleep; when she awakes, the world will regret it.' The wild actions of *Yao* mobs seemed to affirm the wisdom of those words.

The *Yao* were groups scattered throughout China that shared a belief in magic and incantations; these spells, they believed, would shield them from harm in battle. The

Below : Marines hike into the jungle near Olongapo in 1900. Note the typical jungle terrain of the Bataan peninsula.

Above: A battalion of Marines on parade in the Forbidden City of Peking after the recapture of the city by the Allied expedition.

initial purpose of the groups was to oppose the dynasty of the Dowager Empress, but the ruling Manchus cleverly diverted the anger of the *Yao* onto the many foreigners in the country, and soon cities throughout China were literally aflame as angry mobs roamed the streets seeking to kill any Westerner they could find. The most militant of the *Yao* groups had a name that translated into English as the 'Fist of Righteous Amity'; this soon was shortened by Americans and British into the 'Boxers.'

As the spring of 1900 warmed into the heat of summer, so did the emotional temperature in China rise. On 27 May mobs of Boxers went on a destructive rampage, burning a number of railroad stations on the Belgian-built line between Peking and Paotingfu. The following day they put to the torch the Imperial Railway shops in Fengtai near Peking. At this point the legations of various Western nations became alarmed for their physical safety, and they wired their governments requesting military protection.

The American Minister, anticipating the violence, had asked for help even earlier, and on 24 May a force under Captain John T ('Handsome Jack') Myers of 48 Marines, one junior officer and an assistant surgeon had left the USS *Newark* at Taku and set off up the Heiho River in commandeered junks. Among those who greeted the Marines' arrival in Tientsin was a young engineer named Herbert Hoover who later recalled that, 'I do not remember a more satisfying musical performance than the bugles of the American Marines entering the settlement playing "There'll Be a Hot Time in the Old Town Tonight".' Overcoming the resistance of railroad officials, the US Marines and the military forces of Britain, Austria, Germany, France, Italy, Japan and Russia assembled a train and set off on 31 May for Peking. Arriving that night, the Marines marched to the American Legation building through huge mobs of angry but silent *Yao* members. 'The dense mass. . .,' reported Myers, 'seemed more ominous than a demonstration of hostility would have been.'

By 10 June the Boxers had torn up the track below Peking; the city was cut off. At this point the captain of the *Newark*, Captain Bowman H McCalla, the Marines' 'friend in need' in the Spanish-American War, declared 'I'll be damned if I sit here . . . and just wait.' McCalla and 112 bluejackets, joined by 2017 soldiers and Marines of the other nations, set off up the rail line toward Peking under the command of Vice Admiral Sir Edward Seymour, RN. But the Seymour party never reached its destination; unrelenting fire coming night and day from bands of Boxers so weakened the expedition that, though only 25 miles from their destination, they had to turn back and hole up at the Hsi-ku arsenal six miles north of Tientsin and await relief. Thirty-two of McCalla's 112-man force had been killed or wounded, and the captain himself was wounded three times.

This was on 22 June; two days later an international relief force that included 131 Marines and seven officers headed by Major Waller lifted the seige at the arsenal. Writing in his report afterwards, Waller said this:

> Our men . . . have gained the highest praise from all present, and have earned my love and confidence. They are like Falstaff's army in appearance, but with brave hearts and bright weapons. . . .

Back at Taku, warships of the Western Nations were arriving constantly with fresh troops. On 13 July these forces launched an attack to capture Tientsin which, after 24 hours of hard fighting, proved successful. By 3 August a new regiment of Marines was in Tientsin under the command of Major William P Biddle; a wounded 19-year old lieutenant named Smedley D Butler talked his way out of the hospital in time to join the regiment as it set off for Peking. The international force launched its final attack on 14 August; Smedley Butler scaled a wall and forced open the main gate of the British compound (in the process suffering a grazing wound that erased the map of South America from a Marine emblem tattooed above his heart). By nightfall the city was secured, the Americans having taken 17 killed or wounded. The fall of the Forbidden City took the last fight out of the Boxers, and by 10 October the 1st Marine Regiment was able to board ships for its base at Cavite in the Philippines.

From Panama to Addis Ababa

Upon General Charles Heywood's retirement as commandant in October 1903, George F Elliott came into the office. Elliott was a West Pointer, the last to become a Marine officer for almost one hundred years, and he had the astounding

Below: A section of the wall of the British Legation in Peking showing how it was reinforced by stone and timber. This was so effective that no shot penetrated the walls.

Above: A dramatic contemporary illustration showing street fighting in Peking between well-armed Marines and the Boxer forces.

record of having gone from company officer to commandant in just five years—after having been a lieutenant for 22 years! Hardly had Elliott assumed office when trouble for the Corps came his way. Negotiations between the United States and Colombia for the right to dig a canal across the Isthmus of Panama had broken down—Colombia then held Panama as a province—and on 3 November the Panamanian people, who very much wanted the canal, began wild rioting in Panama City, attacking in particular installations of the occupying Colombian authorities. Their actual objective was nothing less than full independence from Colombia.

President Theodore Roosevelt ordered the Marines into action. The gunboat USS *Nashville* raced to the scene and put ashore a small landing party with orders to 'prevent landing of any armed forces with hostile intent,' which meant the Colombians. When a group of 474 Colombian soldiers arrived and sought train passage to get to the scene of major rebel activity, the railway superintendent managed to delay them with bureaucratic red tape long enough for a battalion of Marines under Major Lejeune to arrive. When the Colombians saw the battle-hardened veterans march, bayonets fixed, down the gangplank of their transport, they quietly boarded a friendly merchant ship and sailed away.

President Roosevelt had the final word on the events: 'I took the Canal Zone and let Congress debate, and while the debate goes on, the Canal does also.'

Almost halfway around the world at about the same time, another Marine group under Captain G C Thorpe was escorting an American diplomatic mission on its way to Addis Ababa, capital of the ancient African nation of Ethiopia, for the purpose of negotiating a treaty with Emperor Menelik II. The march took the party across 300 miles of wild mountain country traveling by camel train. When the camel master took strong exception to the route selected by Thorpe and tried to lead them another way, the captain had him bound hand and foot and tied behind a camel. The officer

Below: Defending the American legation in Peking during the Boxer Rebellion, one of a series of photographs taken by Mrs Anna Woodward, a guest of the US Minister.

Above: President Teddy Roosevelt, despite his active foreign policy, fought to limit the Marine Corps.
Below: Marines on parade near the harbor at Vera Cruz during the intervention in 1914.

then informed the camel master he'd either lead them by the route he'd been told to or he'd travel the rest of the way dragged behind the camel. Faced with such clear logic, the *haban* quickly agreed to take them by Thorpe's route.

Outside Addis Ababa, Thorpe had his men put on special dress uniforms of blue blouses topped with scarlet collars, and a cap with a scarlet band, then they marched into the capital in dress parade style flanked by Abyssinian warriors wearing magnificent leopard skins. The Marines were put up in a royal palace, reviewed by the Emperor and each awarded the Menelik Medal; when the time for departure came, they set off on camels bearing with them a present for President Roosevelt of two live lions.

Trouble in Cuba

When the United States aided the Cubans in obtaining their independence from Spain and then established a protectorate relationship with the new country, the Washington administration didn't realize what a volatile 'foster child' it was taking on. But they soon found out.

In August 1906 the followers of Cuba's Liberal Party erupted into mob violence when a rigged election denied them office. President Tomas Estrada Palma, leader of the incumbent Moderate Party, beseeched President Roosevelt for aid, and Roosevelt agreed, though with reluctance. A battalion-strength group of Marines and sailors was hurried to Cuba and, on landing, set up their encampment directly in front of the Presidential palace. Shortly thereafter other Marine units arrived and took control of 24 towns across the island, protected ports and plantations, and rode as guards on every train in the country's rail system. Order was restored, but when the feuding political parties showed that they could not resolve their problems, Roosevelt ordered in a US Army of Cuban Pacification, set up a provisional government and named William Howard Taft, then Secretary of War, to be governor of the island.

There was a ridiculous footnote to the Cuban action: the *Ferrocarril Nacional de Cuba* sent the Navy Department a bill for tickets for every one of the Marines who had ridden 'shotgun' on their trains!

Under Presidential attack

Marines had suffered political attacks throughout their history, most of them by officers of the United States Navy, but as the Corps celebrated its 131st birthday on 10 November 1906, the first event in the most dangerous attack yet on their existence took place. Rear Admiral G A Converse, USN,

Above : Marines set to work to prepare their camp shortly after landing in Vera Cruz.

Above: Marines prepare their rations in the countryside outside Vera Cruz.

told the House Naval Affairs Committee that Marines should be taken off sea duty. Shortly thereafter the Corps' old enemy, William F Fullam, now a commander, endorsed Converse's views in a letter to the Secretary of the Navy. Over the next several years other persons in positions of power put forth similar ideas, all with the same goal: to obliterate the Corps as it had existed up to then.

In 1908 a stunning blow was struck: President Roosevelt ordered that Marine detachments be forthwith removed from all navy ships, and shortly thereafter he issued Executive Order 969 which, if carried out, would have had the effect of turning Marines into nothing more than night watchmen for naval stations, and eliminated their usefulness as amphibious infantry. The Marines promptly mounted a counterattack, an important element of which was the fact that one of the Corps' great heroes, Smedley Butler, was the son of the Chairman of the House Naval Affairs Committee, Congressman Thomas Butler. When the president's men and other enemies of the Marine Corps came before the Committee, they were stopped cold in their tracks: on 3 March 1909, a rider to the annual Naval Appropriations Bill bluntly told Roosevelt that he would receive no money for the Marines unless the men of that body continued to serve on warships as they always had in the past. Roosevelt roared with anger, but Congress's will prevailed.

The Marines had little chance to celebrate, for Roosevelt's successor in office, William Howard Taft, had no more love for the Corps than his predecessor had, and he made this clear in a private conversation with a Naval officer in which he alluded to 'the Government's . . . plans for the Corps.' Throughout his time in office he demonstrated that the 'plans' he had in mind involved the reduction of the Marine Corps into a meaningless non-entity.

Despite these harassments, Marine planning for continuing improvements in their organization went on. In 1901 General Heywood's Annual Report described a military exercise the Corps had conducted in small-unit beach landings and amphibious strategies and warfare. As a result of many such experimental exercises over the next 15 years under commandants Elliott, Biddle and Barnett, a vision gradually emerged of floating battalions aboard their own high-speed, heavily-armed transports, ready instantly to sail into combat with aviation support. Though these ideas, known as the Advance Base Force concept, were put into effect only loosely at that time, they would reappear and come fully into their own in warfare almost half a century later.

Double trouble in Hispaniola

The early years of the twentieth century, compared with the combat-ridden decades immediately preceding them, were relatively quiet ones for the Marine Corps.

In a flareup between political factions in Nicaragua, the United States took the side of the Catholic moderates, and in May 1910 a Marine force of 15 officers and 450 men under Major Smedley Butler landed from the gunboat USS *Paducah* to give witness to America's point of view. Another Marine force went into Veracruz, Mexico, in April 1914, this one commanded by a tough colonel, John Archer Lejeune. Washington had learned that a German ship soon was to deliver a cargo of arms to Victoriana Huerta, a general who had assassinated the elected president and seized power. The Marines landed and, after heavy house-to-house fighting over a three day period, secured the city. Huerta was persuaded to leave the country and a duly-elected government took over.

Trouble of a horrendously uglier nature followed in 1915 on the island of Hispaniola in the Caribbean, an island divided into the two countries of Haiti and Santo Domingo. Haiti, black and French-speaking, had a bloody political history; in the 29 years since 1886 it had run through 10 presidents, four of whom were killed in office and the others driven out in fear of their lives by rivals. In addition, the country's finances, never very good, had reached a state of total collapse. When, in March of 1915, a strongman named Vilbrun Guillaume Sam seized control in Port-au-Prince, the capital, another revolutionary named Dr Rosalvo Bobo began organizing an opposition force in the hills to the north. This instability caught the attention of Germany and France, and they began maneuvering for positions of power in the country; at this point the Washington administration became concerned about the growing possibility of a violation of the Monroe Doctrine if it did not take action.

In the dark morning hours of 27 July in Port-au-Prince, an attack began on the Presidential palace where President Sam lay sleeping; at the sound of gunfire the governor of the city personally began executing 167 political prisoners held in the local penitentiary; when his guns ran out of ammunition he continued the blood-bath with a machete. The mob finally broke in, seized the governor and killed him; they then discovered President Sam hiding in the French legation. The American *chargé d'affaires* described what happened next:

> I could see that somebody or something was on the ground in the center of the crowd . . . a man disentangled himself from the crowd and rushed howling by me with a severed hand from which the blood was dripping, the thumb of which he had stuck in his mouth. Behind him came other men with the feet, the other hand, the head, and other parts of the body displayed on poles, each one followed by a mob of screaming men and women.

The following day a hastily-assembled regiment made up of sailors and ships-detachments Marines landed and won control of Port-au-Prince. They were followed in the ensuing months by the 2nd Marine Regiment under Colonel Eli K Cole and by the 1st Marine Regiment and Headquarters, 1st Marine Brigade, under Colonel Waller, hero of Samar. This American force, though somewhat patched together, represented a workable version of the Advance Base Force concept in action. Major Smedley Butler was one of Waller's officers, and serving under him was a fresh-cheeked

Right: Marines on an inland patrol after the fighting in Vera Cruz had died down.
Below, main picture: Men of the Marine Expeditionary Force land supplies on the beach at Carracao in the Philippine Islands in 1911.

Above: Marines come ashore at Port-au-Prince in the early stages of the long and controversial involvement in Haiti.

lieutenant named Alexander A Vandegrift.

The fighting that followed over the next three months was violent and dramatic as the Marines pursued and defeated the major troublemakers in Haiti, a criminal-*cum*-military group known as the *Cacos*; their name was taken from a local bird of prey. Butler's sterling performance earned him a second Medal of Honor to add to the one he had won at Veracruz. Once stability had been brought about and a government installed, elements of the 1st Marines stayed on in Haiti to see to it that things remained that way; in fact, it would not be until 21 August 1934 that the last Marine would depart the country.

As Haiti suffered its own violence, events on the eastern side of Hispaniola in Spanish-speaking Santo Domingo were coming to a head. The United States had exercised a financial receivership over the country since 1904 when Roosevelt had acted to block Santo Domingo's European creditors from closing in on it. But relationships between the two countries gradually had deteriorated, and in April 1916 civil war broke out in the capital, Ciudad Santo Domingo. Units of the Advanced Base Force were detached from duty in Haiti and sent to Santo Domingo to restore order. The two companies of Marines, along with 225 bluejackets, were commanded by Major Newt Hall, and his executive officer was Captain F M ('Dopey') Wise. The unit entered the city at dawn on 15 May and were greeted by an eerie silence; not a shot was fired and, when they searched the houses, not a weapon was to be found. Arias, the rebel leader, and his followers had slipped away during the night to their stronghold in Santiago, a city in the central mountains.

Sailing aboard the USS *Louisiana*, Wise circled the island to the north coast and on 26 May came ashore at Monte Cristo, seizing and holding the town against rebel attacks. When a combined force of Marines and sailors captured the nearby town of Puerta Plata on 1 June, this put the north coast of Santo Domingo into American hands and sent the last of the rebels into mountain hiding. For the moment at least, the situation was stabilized.

The Corps spent the next five years in Santo Domingo in operations against bandits, meanwhile working on public health and development projects. Beginning in 1919, the Marines' efforts incorporated six 'Jennies' of the 1st Air Squadron, whose pilots experimented with dive-bombing techniques when not occupied with bandits. A decision near the end of 1920 to end the occupation of Santo Domingo brought about a busy and successful roundup of bandits, followed by a period of amnesty. With the country in the process of settling down, the Marines began pulling out in 1922, but it would be September 1925 before the last company of US Marines left Santo Domingo.

But long before this, the United States and the rest of the Western world had slid into the abyss of World War I, by which time the Marine Corps had reached a high level of professionalism and military competency because of its varied experiences in the engagements of the past two decades. Ironically, while some recognition of these achievements was at least tacitly manifested by the US Navy, signs of future trouble for the Corps were revealed in comments and criticisms expressed by officers of the Army. But the Marines felt competent enough to take on and weather such assaults; combat, both on foreign fields and in the halls of Congress, had made the Corps tough, skilled, resilient, and ready for battle.

Right: Mounted Marines on patrol during the troubles in Santo Domingo.

Right: Marine 3-inch field gun at full recoil during fighting near Santiago in 1916.

Below: Marines of the 8th Company form a skirmish line during fighting in the area between Monte Cristi and Santiago in June 1916.

THE GREAT WAR AND ITS AFTERMATH

'Retreat, Hell! We Just Got Here!'—1917-1918

In November of 1916 Woodrow Wilson was reelected President on the campaign slogan, 'He kept us out of war.' By then war had been raging in Europe since the summer of 1914, when a Serbian student assassinated the Archduke of Austria-Hungary and his wife. This precipitated a Serbo-Austrian brawl that, because of various intricate military alliances as well as long-standing trade rivalries, quickly swept through Europe and other parts of the world.

The Germans began in the autumn of 1914 with a massive wheel through Belgium that was finally halted by the Allies. The conflict then settled down on the Western Front into a debilitating static trench warfare across a front some 600 miles long in Belgium and France. This was not an entirely new development in warfare; it had been a feature of several campaigns in the American Civil War, most notably the siege of Petersburg. But the military leaders of Europe had by no means addressed the demands of trench warfare; instead, their devotion to outmoded ideas—an obsession with the offensive, a reliance on the bayonet and on horse cavalry, among others—raised casualty lists to unprecedented numbers. It was to be some time before the generals learned that modern firepower—including the machine gun—had made trenches virtually invulnerable.

Previous page: Marines advance cautiously through a wood shattered by shellfire during the Meuse-Argonne campaign in France in 1918. *Below:* General Pershing is mobbed by enthusiastic French crowds.

Growth of the Corps

Wilson hoped to stay out of the war not only to avoid its ravages on the country but also to reserve for America a peacemaking role, which would be impossible if America became a belligerent. He wanted to keep America 'neutral in fact as well as in name.' But events in Europe as well as American public opinion made entry into the war steadily more likely. Thus, preparations had to be made.

The 1916 Naval Personnel Bill enlarged the US Marine Corps by almost 50 percent. It also recreated the rank of Brigadier General and made a number of promotions, most notably that of John A Lejeune, who was later to succeed Major General George Barnett as Commandant of the Corps. Further enlargements were soon instituted. Just before America's entry into the war, the Corps stood at 17,400 enlisted men and 693 officers, hardly enough to make a dent in a real conflict. Nonetheless, this Corps was larger, better trained and better led than any in the 142-year history of the Marines. They formed an ideal foundation for the rapid growth that was to come during wartime.

America enters the war

In 1915 a German submarine torpedoed the *Lusitania*, killing 128 Americans. After that, Germany, seeing the wisdom of not antagonizing America, made some pacifying agreements. Having weathered that crisis, Washington nonetheless instituted a program of preparedness. In addition to enlarging all the services in 1916, Congress allotted $7,000,000,000 for defense, the largest military budget in American history till then.

In 1917 Germany stepped up its submarine warfare, sinking a number of American merchantmen. Also that year it was learned that Germany had made overtures to Mexico to join the Central Powers if the United States entered the war, and had promised to pay them off for that service with American territory.

These actions of Germany, along with a rising tide of American public opinion in favor of the war and the declining fortunes of the Allies, brought about American entry into the conflict in April 1917. In his declaration, Wilson said to Congress, 'The

world must be made safe for democracy.' Significantly, the United States declared itself in support of the Allies but did not make a formal treaty with them. This perhaps reflected the determination of General John J Pershing, leader of the American Expeditionary Forces, that American troops would function essentially as an independent body, not merely as a reserve to be absorbed into British and French Forces.

The Marine enlistment slogan was the stirring, 'First to Fight!' It produced a wave of enlistments into the Corps, totalling some 46,000 by the end of the war. The training camps at Mare Island (California) and Parris Island (South Carolina) were swamped with recruits; accordingly, new centers were developed at Quantico, Virginia, and elsewhere.

For years Marines had been engaged primarily in chasing bandits around various jungles, but now the Corps had to face the exigencies of a new kind of war—and one that so far was imperfectly understood by the highest levels of command both in Europe and America. The Navy still saw the Marines only in light of their usual functions—ship's guards, security forces and advance base forces. No one but the Corps itself seemed to have great faith in its ability as an infantry force. It would take some hard fighting to prove that point.

As for training, the Marines between 1915 and 1917 had developed the institution of Boot Camp. Deciding that it did not want to tie up its officers running training camps, the position of non-commissioned Drill Instructor (DI) evolved, and these implacable men wielded an authority second only to that of the Almighty. The training program was designed to build the toughest fighters and best marksmen in the world, and to weed out anyone not up to the Marine standard. The camps became a legendary part of American military history, frequently criticized as brutal and sadistic, but nonetheless a vital element of the unique Marine *esprit de corps* as well as its fighting prowess.

Right: A Marine recruiting poster of the First World War.
Below: Applicants arriving at the recruit depot Paris Island SC in 1917. (The spelling was later changed to Parris Island).

Trouble with Pershing

It was decided by military authorities that the final training of all elements of the American Expeditionary Forces had best be in Europe, with the experienced trench fighters of Britain and France. In his dealings with the Marines, General Pershing quickly showed a discouraging attitude that was to persist throughout the war and after. To begin with, Pershing was not convinced that the Marines, despite their recruiting posters, would be 'First to Fight' among the American Forces in Europe. Commandant Barnett, trying to make good on that pledge, was repeatedly rebuffed by

Pershing and the War Department, who claimed that Marine weapons and tactics were incompatible with those of the Army. Having successfully put that notion to rest, Barnett secured an agreement from President Wilson that the Marines would go over in the first convoy. To make sure, Barnett rounded up the ships for their transportation himself. The Marines sailed on 14 June 1917, arriving in St Nazaire, France just under two weeks later.

This was the 5th Marine Regiment, which had been put together from men in service all around the globe. Later was to follow the 6th Marines, made up of new recruits added to a cadre of regulars, and a machine gun battalion. Eventually the 5th and 6th regiments were joined to form the 4th Marine Brigade, the largest tactical unit in Corps history.

Once in France, Marine leadership had to cope with further political barriers. The 5th Marines were scattered throughout France in support of the Army and used mainly for tasks behind the lines. As the irrepressible General Smedley Butler later wrote, Marines in this position were expected:

> . . . to sit in the rear and run this filthy mudhole [a camp near Brest]. Although 97 percent of my men were expert riflemen or sharpshooters, troops

Left: A privately-taken photograph of Marines resting near the front line during the Battle of Belleau Wood.
Below: Heavily-laden Marines pause in a French village while en route to join the fighting at at Belleau Wood.

that hardly knew which end of the gun to shoot were sent to the trenches. My crack regiment was broken up to do manual labor and guard duty.

Besides the recalcitrance of Pershing, there were also troubles with General Ferdinand Foch, French Commander-in-Chief of the Allied forces. Though the Allies desperately needed American manpower, they were not at all disposed to give Americans a position of strength in running the war or a unified command in fighting it. Not convinced of the fighting abilities of these fresh and over-enthusiastic new arrivals from a junior member of the coalition, Foch wanted to sprinkle the AEF among his own forces.

Pershing fought a tough and eventually successful battle to preserve the status of the Americans, insisting that they be an integrated component of the Allied command. Pershing's efforts were soon to be aided by the fighting performance of his men, most notably in the first major engagement of the Marines.

Belleau Wood: a turning point in Marine history

In March 1918 the Marines finally went into the Western Front, though they were considered to be only completing their training in the trenches. Thus a quiet sector was chosen at Toulon, just south of Verdun on the Meuse River. The first casualty of the fighting was the 5th Regiment Band's bass drum, punctured by a shell (the drummer, fortunately, was untouched). The Marines settled restlessly into the life of the trenches, becoming familiar with mud, gas alarms, rats and the regular rain of enemy shells, which accounted for 872 casualties before the Marines were pulled out, after 53 days for additional training. The French and British command soon began to realize that these newcomers were full of fight and fast learners—as compared to the warworn and often cynical French and British veterans.

In late May German commander Ludendorff unleashed a major offensive that created three large salients in the German line—one near Neuve-Chapelle in the north, one near Amiens in the middle of the front, the other along the Marne to the south. The latter salient threatened Paris itself; the French government prepared to flee. Now Foch had to use American troops. They were the only reserve he had. As the most battle-ready of the American units, the 4th Marine Brigade was ordered into the sector at Belleau Wood.

As the Marines tramped down the road to their goal on 5 June, they first met a stream of civilian refugees. One of the men remembered the sight:

> Everything that a terrified peasantry would be likely to think of bringing from among their humble treasures was to be seen on that congested highway. Men, women, children, hurrying to the

Above: German positions in Belleau Wood after their capture by the Marines.
Bottom: The Battle of Belleau Wood.

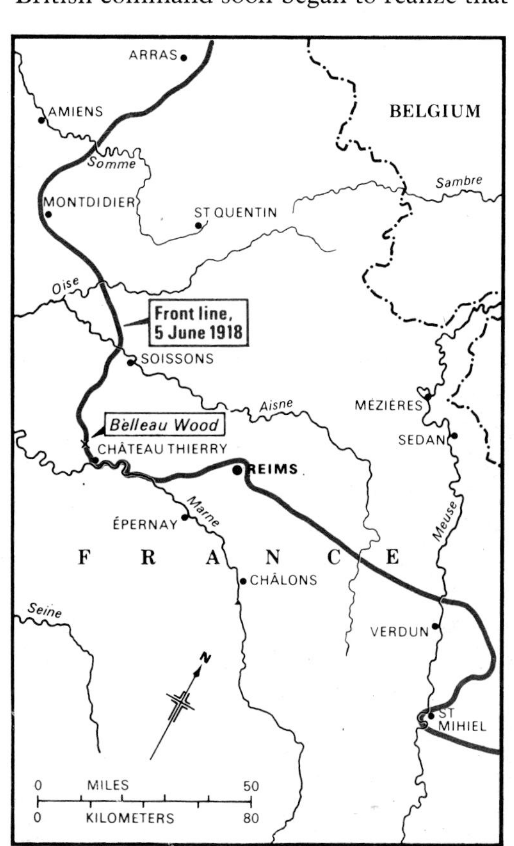

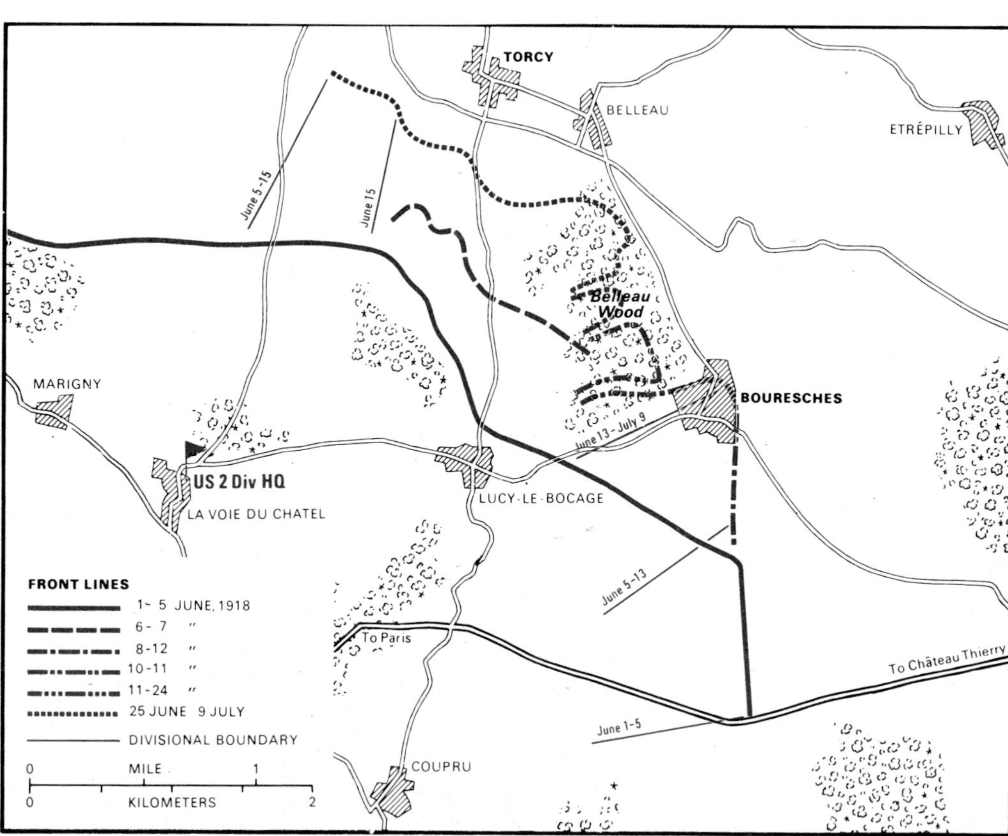

Above: Scenes of devastation in the woods near Chateau Thierry following a heavy German bombardment of Marine positions.

rear; tired and worn, with stark terror on their faces. Many were walking, an occasional woman wheeled a perambulator with the baby in it. Sick people were lying exhausted beside the road. Some were driving carts piled high with their worldly goods. . . . Little flocks of sheep, a led cow, crates of chicken on carts.

Soon they also encountered a bedraggled column of beaten French soldiers, retreating as fast as their exhaustion would allow. One Captain Lloyd W Williams, when advised by a French officer to join the retreat, replied with one of the great ripostes of the war: 'Retreat, hell! We just got here!'

Heading for the sound of gunfire, the Marines soon arrived on the outskirts of Belleau Wood, where the German advance had halted and erected a formidable defensive position in the square mile of woods and rocks, manned by 1200 of the veteran 461st Imperial German Infantry.

The Marines opened fire on advanced German units at 800 yards, to the amazement of the Germans, who considered fire at over 200 yards to be ineffective. The Corps' marksmanship had made its first impression on the enemy. As the 9444 men of the 4th Brigade advanced, firing steadily and accurately, the Germans began to wonder if the Americans were charging them with machine guns. They dug in to await developments.

In the morning of 6 June the 1st Battalion, 5th Marines, led the attack west of Belleau Wood. They moved out into a vicious machine-gun crossfire that drove them back and claimed 410 casualties. A second try gained a toehold in the edge of the woods and 1087 more casualties. In the day's fighting the losses were the worst the Marines would suffer until 1943, at Betio Island, Tarawa Atoll. The Marines had confidently expected to sweep through the woods in a few hours. Now they were about to learn the hard way that this war did not work that way. But Marine pluck was not diminished; Sergeant Dan Daly led a charge with the immortal exhortation, 'Come on, you sons of bitches! Do you want to live forever?'

Pulling in reinforcements to the edge of the wood, the Marines began a process of close, bloody fighting in brushy terrain against the well-armed and experienced foe. It was tough going indeed. And it took 20 days. Units from the 5th and 6th Marines pushed up through the woods from the south, slowly driving the Germans back until the third defense line had retreated and the enemy was all but gone from the woods. Then on 13 June the German infantry counterattacked, led by a storm of shell and gas. In spite of deadly accurate long-range American rifle fire, the Germans advanced steadily, until the village of Bouresches, within the wood, was about to be abandoned by the Marines. However, the 1st Battalion, 6th Marines, under Major John A Hughes, was not inclined to give up the town. They held on, taking 450 casualties, until the Germans gave up. On 15 June an Army regiment relieved the exhausted 5th Marines, who returned to action on the 22nd and once again took up the gruelling job of dislodging the enemy.

After a failed American assault on the evening of the 23rd, the following day saw an artillery barrage that softened up the German positions. Then the 3rd Battalion, 5th Marines, charged into the last German holdouts and emerged from the other side of the woods at last. The commander of the unit, Major Maurice Shearer, telegraphed AEF headquarters, 'Woods now US Marine Corps' entirely.'

Repercussions of the battle of Belleau Wood were significant both for the progress of the war and for the future of the Marine Corps. Above all, Paris was now out of danger. The action received its proper testimonials from the Allies—future President (then Assistant Secretary of the Navy) Franklin Delano Roosevelt cabled his enthusiasm to Washington in August, and the

Below: An artist's impression of the Marines storming into German machine gun nests during the fighting at Belleau Wood.

grateful French renamed the wood 'Bois de la Brigade de Marine.' But perhaps the most eloquent testimonial to the fighting prowess of the Americans at Belleau Wood came from German intelligence:

> The 2nd American Division must be considered a very good one, and may perhaps even be reckoned as storm troops. The different attacks on Belleau Wood were carried out with bravery and dash. The moral effect of our gunfire cannot seriously impede the advance of the American riflemen.

The battle of Belleau Wood was also to change the future thrust of the Marine Corps. Traditionally, the Corps had seen action largely in small campaigns against insurgents or guerrillas in various parts of the world. It was this tradition that had made the Army dubious about using them on the Western Front. Now the Marines had proven themselves against seasoned infantry using the latest arms and tactics. And they had shown a cutting edge possible only to an elite unit of high *esprit* and courage. Their effectiveness in this kind of warfare was not to go unnoticed in American military planning of the future.

Finally, there was one other gift to history from the action in Belleau Wood. As the Marines scraped out rifle pits in the lines, they took to calling them 'foxholes.'

Soissons, St Mihiel and Blanc Mont

After the German offensives in the spring of 1918, General Ludendorff had gained valuable territory, punching three huge salients into the Allied lines in the first major shift of positions since 1914. He had also lost 600,000 men in the process, and these were troops he sorely missed. In July Foch decided it was time to counterattack on those bothersome salients.

Along the Marne the Allied attack, called the Aisne-Marne offensive, was made with a mixture of French, British, Italian and American troops. The French used 300 tanks in the action. A British invention, tanks were to be one of the deciding factors in the war, especially in the coming Allied offensive at Amiens—the iron monsters could roll with impunity into enemy trenches, and thus, along with airplanes, were chiefly responsible for breaking the stalemate of trench warfare. (Failing to develop their own tanks was one of the biggest German mistakes of the war.) The Aisne-Marne offensive was the place where the American soldiers came of age, establishing themselves once and for all as reliable fighters and finally gaining Pershing's goal of maintaining the unity of his forces.

In mid-July the 5th Marines and US Army forces were on the march with a polyglot collection of forces in the French XX Corps. The troops staggered along in

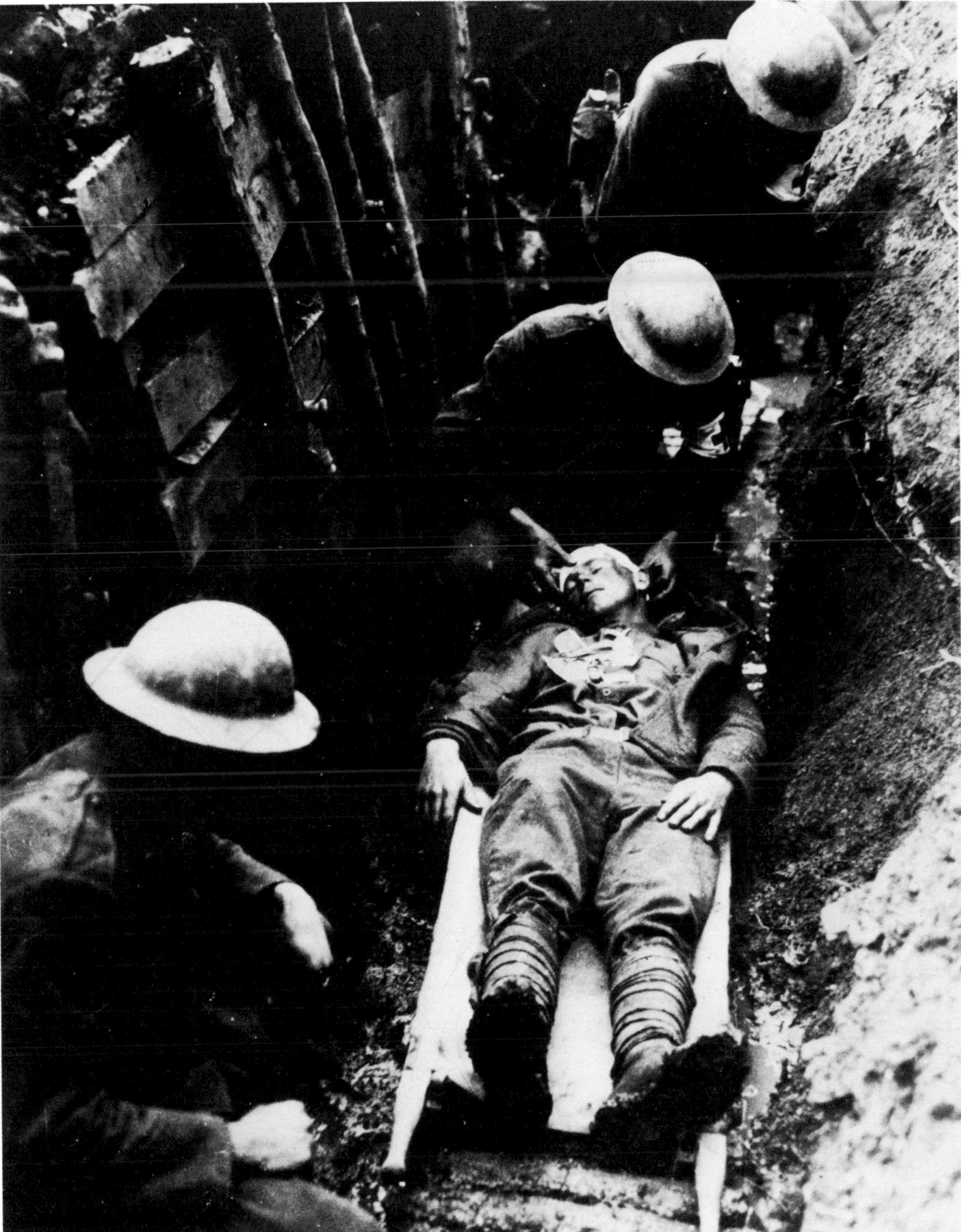

Above: A wounded Marine is given first aid in a front line trench.
Left: General Lejeune examines a battle plan at his command post.

Above: American troops pause by the roadside as a French cavalry unit passes by during the Meuse Argonne offensive.

heavy rains and mud, cannons sticking and slowing in the road, men falling into ditches and breaking limbs. One Marine remembered that march:

Cold, hungry, and wet, on we marched, hour after hour, each man bearing a pack weighing about 45 pounds, consisting of two blankets, a supply of underclothes, a pair of trousers, emergency rations of hardtack and 'monkey meat' (canned corn beef), besides a heavy belt with 100 rounds of ammunition, a canteen, wire cutters, gas mask, helmet, rifle and bayonet. Yes, and each man had around his neck, next to his body, two identification tags, one of which would mark his grave and the other his body.

On 18 July came the attack near Soissons, prepared by the customary artillery barrage. The Marines pressed out, sweeping over open ground against German entrenchments, but nonetheless gaining two miles by noon and another three by evening. Casualties were severe, the 2nd Battalion, 6th Marines, losing over 50 percent in 30 minutes. Next day they came afoul of a German counterattack, but still managed to make nearly two miles. A field message from Lieutenant C B Cates gives some idea of the severity of the action:

I am in an old abandoned French trench bordering on road leading out from your CP and 350 yards from an old mill. I have only two men left out of my company and 20 out of other companies. We need support but it is almost suicide to try to get it here as we are swept by machine gun fire and a constant artillery barrage is upon us. I have no one on my left and only a few on my right. I will hold.

Finally the regimental casualties passed 50 percent and the Americans dug in, the Marines overlooking the Soissons–Château Thierry road, a major German supply route. They had taken 1972 casualties in the fighting, but the salient had been pinched out as ordered. Just after the action, General John A Lejeune, future Commandant of the Corps, took command of the 2nd Division. It was to be the only time in history that a Marine was to command an Army division.

Another part of Foch's Allied offensive was in the Meuse–Argonne region. The St Mihiel operation was directed at a German salient to the southeast, along the Meuse, that had existed since 1914. General Pershing had had his eye on that salient for some time, seeing that it would be a good training ground for his forces and, if broken through, allow the Allies to penetrate deep into German territory. Foch scuttled the latter idea, but agreed that the Americans would lead the fighting, pinching in the sides of the salient while the French held the point. It was to be the first mainly-American show of the war.

The attack was led by two Army corps with the Marine 4th Brigade (under General Wendell C Neville) following up as divisional reserve. On 12 September the Army corps strode out to the attack. The Germans were, as it happened, already in the process of abandoning the salient; that fact, combined with a heavy fog and the freshness of the American troops, made for some confusion in the advance. Still the Army men pressed forward gallantly, gaining territory and capturing 3300 prisoners by nightfall. A number of these prisoners were rounded up by German-born Marine Major William Ulrich, who single-handedly chased them down, shouting vociferously in German, and returned to his lines leading 40 of them, explaining, 'They were willing to listen to reason.'

On the second day the Marines took over the task of reducing the fortifications that screened the Hindenburg Line, the German fallback position and a dreaded strongpoint. The strength of the German pillboxes was recalled by a participant:

These were strong fortifications built of concrete with walls about two feet thick ranging in size from about five feet to 20 feet square. They were about five feet underground with about two feet extending above the surface, were well camouflaged and the larger ones were designed for four or more compartments. We also came upon many large dugouts, some of them 50 feet underground, into which we entered with great caution.

Nonetheless, the Marines reduced the forts as ordered. Overhead during the battle flew an Allied air force commanded by American Colonel Billy Mitchell—planes were now joined with tanks to break the war out of the trenches. Meanwhile in the Bois de la Montagne, ostensibly unoccupied, the 2nd Battalion, 6th Marines, had to rout a substantial enemy force and then deal with four counterattacks, including artillery and gas. On 15 September the enemy gave up in the woods. The St Mihiel salient had been wiped out. But to their great surprise and

Below: Marines at rest alongside a light railway of the type often used during the First World War to bring ammunition and supplies close to the front; near Verdun 1918.

Above : Marines man 3-inch guns aboard the battleship *Pennsylvania* during World War I. *Right :* Marine machine gunners on maneuvers in France in the winter of 1917–18.

relief, the Germans found that the Americans were not going to push in further. In the four days of fighting the Marines had been comparatively lightly engaged, but still lost 132 in killed and 574 wounded. Their next engagement would not let them off so lightly.

Now the Allies entered the next phase of the Meuse–Argonne offensive, the objective being to drive the Germans back across their railroad communications. The 2nd Division, under General Lejeune, joined Foch's Frenchmen in the operation. Since losing that area would be fatal to the German fallback position—the Hindenburg Line—they were prepared to mount maximum resistance. The result was to be the hardest fighting of the war for the Americans.

To the east of the Allied offensive the American attack was to fall on the Heights of the Meuse, a series of hills which had seen terrible fighting two years previously and from whence the German July offensive had begun. The hills were a forbidding natural

Above: Fully-armed Marines dismount from their trucks and march off during training maneuvers in France in 1917, before American forces were fully committed to the front line.

defensive line. The key feature of the hills was Blanc Mont Ridge, held by the enemy since 1914. By the end of September the French had fought their way to the village of Somme–Py, at the foot of Blanc Mont Ridge and right on the Hindenburg Line. The French command considered breaking up the American 2nd Division to replace the exhausted fighters in the line, but Lejeune proposed instead that the Yanks be given a crack at the ridge. The French agreed.

On the morning of 3 October the American attack kicked off after a short artillery barrage, the 6th Marines, followed by the 5th, aiming for the left side of the ridge. The right side was to be assaulted by the 3rd Infantry Brigade. Together they were to bypass a German strongpoint and pinch it off, a tricky maneuver that was much liked by commanders on both sides and little liked by soldiers.

After three hours of heavy fighting the Marines had broken through the Hindenburg Line and gained their objective. Meanwhile, a company of the 5th Regiment had fallen off to the left side of the ridge to help the French take a nest of German machine guns; this enemy position was taken by the Marines, then lost by the French, then retaken by the Marines. During the advance two Marines earned the Medal of Honor. Private John Kelley singlehandedly charged a machine-gun emplacement, killed two, and brought back eight prisoners, all done in the middle of an American artillery barrage. Corporal J H Pruitt accounted for two enemy machine guns and 40 prisoners before being killed.

Finally reaching the crest of Blanc Mont Ridge to the left, the 6th Marines found themselves weak on the left flank due to French slowness on the western slope. Following close behind, the 5th Marines fell into a flanking position at right angles to the 6th. Thus protected, the men waited for the next day. On 4 October the two regiments changed places, the 5th pressing forward some three miles while the 6th protected the flank, picking away at the German machine guns on the western slope.

In sight of the village of St Etienne, the 5th was struck hard by an enemy assault on the left flank. A thousand men of the 1st Battalion swung and charged into the on-rushing enemy. A participant remembered those moments:

All along the extended line the saffron shrapnel flowered, flinging death and mutilation down. Singing balls and jagged bits of steel spattered on the hard ground like sheets of hail; the line writhed and staggered, steadied and went on, closing toward the center as the shells bit into it. High explosive shells came with the shrapnel, and where they fell geysers of torn earth and black smoke roared up to mingle with the devilish yellow in the air. A foul murky cloud of dust and smoke formed and went with the thinning companies, a cloud lit with red flashes and full of howling death.

Nearly 900 Marines fell in that barrage, but the remainder charged into the Germans and drove them back to St Etienne.

The next days saw incessant and severe fighting, the 5th and 6th Regiments joining with French troops to drive the Germans from the village while the rest of the ridge fell to the 2nd Division. On 8 October Marines finally marched into St Etienne. After another determined German counterattack, the Marines were relieved from the front. They had helped break through the line the Germans had built to be impregnable, and done their part in breaking the back of the Central Powers. It had cost 2538 casualties; in one company only 23 remained of 230 that had begun the battle.

Thereafter the Marines received their third citation from the French Army, earning the right to carry the Croix de Guerre on their colors. And they earned this commendation from a Marshal of France: 'The taking of Blanc Mont Ridge is the greatest single achievement of the 1918 campaign.'

The development of Marine aviation

In July 1918 the first contingent of the 1st Marine Aviation Air Force arrived in Brest. The unit had grown from a modest stateside beginning in the summer of 1917. A year later they were in action over France and bombing German submarine bases in the English Channel.

One of the earliest missions was an odd 'bombing' raid on 1 October 1918. Flying borrowed French de Havillands, the bombers dropped a payload of French bread and canned goods onto a stranded French regiment. Despite heavy fire, this and four later runs supported the beleagured Allies.

By the end of the war the Marine Air Unit had 2500 men and 340 airplanes, had inflicted 330 enemy casualties and shot down 12 planes, and dropped 52,000 pounds of bombs on 57 raids. It was a vigorous Marine entry into the air age, which would flower in the next war.

Above right: Marines board their transport during the Allied advance in 1918.
Right: Heavy machine gun and Marine aboard a patrol boat during the Allied occupation of the Rhineland in the immediate aftermath of World War I.

The final battle

As the Central Powers began to fall apart, Lejeune's 2nd Division, with some difficulty, joined the First Army in late October 1918, for final operations in the northern end of the Argonne Forest. The American forces in the area were given the task of punching through the Hindenburg Line and reducing two major fortifications—'Brünhilde' and 'Freya Stellung.'

On All Saints' Day the Marines of the 4th Brigade set out and pushed the demoralized Germans toward the Meuse, battalions leapfrogging one another to keep the attack moving steadily. German desertions increased, the retreating soldiers shouting at the incoming reserves that they were prolonging the war. Nonetheless, resistance remained stiff.

As was often the case, the Marines made faster progress than their Army compatriots; by mid-afternoon, units of the 4th Brigade were entrenching on high ground and waiting for the Army to catch up before resuming the advance. Some 1700 of the enemy had been captured. Then on 1 November the Marines outdid themselves, racing across the landscape at a rate that elicited this praise from an Army general:

> It was a brilliant advance of more than nine kilometers, destroying the last stronghold in the Hindenburg Line, capturing the Freya Stellung, one of the most remarkable achievements made by any troops in this war . . . These results must be

attributed to the great dash and speed of the troops, and to the irresistible force with which they struck and overcame the enemy.

After further rapid Allied advances, the Germans by 9 November had retreated over the Meuse and the 4th Brigade was ready to spearhead attacks across the river at Mouzon and Villemontry. On the night of the 10th, assault units crossed under heavy enemy fire on new Army footbridges. Next morning, as the Marines prepared to renew the advance, the artillery fire suddenly sank to a strange silence a little before 11 o'clock. That silence signaled the end of the war.

Action away from the Western Front

While the 4th Brigade was fighting in France, other segments of the Corps maintained their duties all around the world—in Haiti, Santo Domingo, and Cuba. Elsewhere, numbers of Marines served on Navy ships patroling the Atlantic. In the Azores, Marines guarded Navy antisubmarine bases; although no enemy submarine showed up in the area, this operation, involving artillery and planes, was a prototype of the kind of air-ground island operations which would be critical in World War II.

In June of 1918 Marines were sent to Vladivostok, helping to protect the United States Consulate in the wake of the Russian Revolution. Though most of the forces there gave way to Army Units in late August, a guard of Marines remained until 1922 at a Navy radio station in Vladivostok Bay.

A new Commandant

With the tour of command of George Barnett running out in early 1918, it was assumed as a matter of course that he would be reappointed. His men, everyone agreed, had done outstandingly well in their action. Navy Secretary Josephus Daniels indeed made the reappointment in February; but at the same time, to Barnett's surprise, Daniels prodded the Commandant to retire. Barnett refused and the Secretary backed down. But a few months later Barnett was astonished to hear himself denounced in the House of Representatives as a 'rocking-chair warrior.' (The Representative doing so happened to be the father of Marine General Smedley D Butler, no admirer of Barnett due partly to the fact that the Commandant himself had seen little combat action.)

Despite Barnett's stated outrage, the matter rested for two years, at which point Secretary Daniels summarily cashiered him and put General John A Lejeune in his place. The irregular nature of the affair was duly noted, but the respect and popularity commanded by Lejeune at length made it a moot question. General Lejeune became the 12th Commandant of the Corps on 30 June, 1920.

Right: A Marine Corps seaplane equipped for mapping work in the late 1920s.
Below: Marine infantry make a cautious advance on a German position in late 1918.
Bottom: Aerial mapping plane of the Cuban Aerial Survey takes off.

Above: Marines man a rudimentary air defense position in France in 1918.
Below: A Marine cameraman is caught at work filming captured German guns in 1919.

Peace: military lessons of World War I

The nature of war had changed. It had changed by the beginning of the war, when the tactics and imaginations of military leaders had not shown themselves up to the new demands of trench warfare, and it had changed again by the end of the war.

At the outset the spade and the bullet ruled the battlefield; traditional offensive tactics were all but impotent against that combination. This impasse had been broken at last by a new element of technology—the internal combustion engine, which made possible the tanks that drove through the trenches and the planes that assaulted them from the air. Added to these were wireless telegraphy, which speeded battlefield communications, and the new effectiveness of

Above: American forces march through the streets of Vladivostok during the Allied intervention in Russia after the Revolution. *Left:* Marines at ease in Santo Domingo in the World War I period.

submarines. Because of the new technology, war was to become a contest of machines as much as of men, of numbers of factories as much as numbers of soldiers. Battle in the future would move at a vastly increased tempo, and with considerably enhanced destructive power.

The leaders of the US Marine Corps pondered these changes, knowing that the new ways of war would still require an elite group of fighting men. The aviation branch had gotten its start; developing from that would be the techniques of close-air support which would be vital in the next conflict. Still to come were the important concepts and developments that would lead to modern Marine amphibious warfare.

'Peace is Hell'—1918-1941

After the experience of the First World War, Commandant Lejeune began to take stock and to set in motion a good deal of thinking about the future function and tactics of the Corps. In this effort he was guided, as it turned out, by a mixture of planning, prophecy, and happenstance that would unite to transform the whole nature and mission of the Corps, turning it away from its traditional function as a colonial infantry and toward an integrated and vital role within the United States services. But before that could happen, there were still a few adventures in the 'colonies.'

Cuba, Haiti, and Santo Domingo

Early in 1917 unrest flared around the sugar-cane fields at Guacanayabo Bay, Cuba. Since sugar was considered necessary to the Allied war effort, the US Consul in Santiago called in the Marines to restore order. Thus came about the 'Sugar Intervention.'

In late February a fleet of US ships converged around the island and the Marines seized the north coast and Santiago in the east. The general idea was to protect the American-owned sugar mills while allowing the Cuban Army to round up dissidents. This strategy worked well enough, and things quickly cooled down around the countryside to the extent that a number of Marines were sent back stateside in May, to prepare for action in Europe.

But the relative tranquility proved short-lived. Encouraged, it was said, by German agents, rebels began a program of sabotage against the sugar plantations. In late 1917 two regiments of Marines were sent to the Oriente Province, again protecting the sugar plantations while the Cuban Army operated against the rebels. And once again things quickly calmed down. The Marines stayed on in Cuba as a visible but not particularly active force until 1919.

In Haiti things were not so easy. After a couple of years of relative peace, the Cacos took arms again in 1918. Their immediate grievance was the resurrection, by American authorities, of the practice of *corvée*, an old French dictate which required peasants to work unpaid on public roads. Not surprisingly, the peasants were enraged at this enforced peonage.

Into this unsettled situation stepped one Charlemagne Péralte, a dynamic leader who had been active with Cacos in central Haiti. He began recruiting peasants for organized revolt, and by 1918 had an army of some 5000 men and an active revolution in progress.

The American commandant of the Haitian Gendarmerie, realizing this was beyond their capabilities, called for the Marines in spring 1919. The 1st Brigade arrived and over the spring and summer engaged in some 131 engagements with Charlemagne's band of Cacos—without, however, making much of a dent in their operations.

The frustration of the campaign led Marine Sergeant Herman H Hanneken to decide on some rather under-the-table tactics to reach the elusive Caco chief. In August 1919 Hanneken set up his own bandit leader, a prominent local citizen who took to the field with a small band and began a series of phony 'battles' with Hanneken's men (the sergeant at one point sported a wound, also ersatz, from one of these mock battles). Slowly Hanneken's stooge, Conzé, earned the attention and the trust of Charlemagne.

Conzé then urged Charlemagne to join him in a raid on the town of Grande Rivière du Nord. This agreed to, Hanneken was duly informed; he made plans to defend the town and also to meet Charlemagne personally. On the day of the scheduled attack, Hanneken and Lieutenant William R Button, darkened with burnt cork and disguised as Cacos, led a group of similarly-disguised gendarmes into rebel territory. Guided by an informer, they made it through several near-exposures to Charlemagne's camp, which was manned by some 200 Cacos.

Charlemagne was pointed out by the informer, and Hanneken stepped up to him. As Charlemagne turned to address the stranger, he was greeted by two .45 slugs in the chest, which killed him instantly. The gendarme band immediately emptied their rifles into the crowd and settled down to repel several counterattacks during the night. Next day they made it back to Grande Rivière du Nord (which had successfully weathered the Caco attack) with the body of Charlemagne.

Though bandit activity continued for some time, its force had been broken. Hanneken and Button received the Congressional Medal of Honor. By mid-1920

Left: Marines on sentry duty in Santo Domingo, a deceptively peaceful view of an often violent intervention.

In midmorning two Marine planes happened to fly over the town on reconnaissance. Seeing the situation, they strafed the rebels, returned to base and came back loaded with bombs. They began dive-bombing Sandino's men, sending the rebels into a panic and accounting for considerable casualties. Though British and American pilots had previously experimented with dive-bombing, this was the world's first use of the technique in actual combat. Its effectiveness was dramatic, and it ended the rebel attack on Ocotal forthwith.

Thus began a new era of air-ground support that would be invaluable in World War II. This tactic would undergo considerable refinement from its first use in Nicaragua, but in Ocotal the principle had been firmly established. Other occasions soon followed. In January 1928, Marines besieged in Quilali were aided by 10 landings under fire onto an airstrip cut through the center of the town. The flights brought in supplies and took out wounded, and earned their pilot a Medal of Honor. As operations in Nicaragua went on—without managing to round up Sandino—it became regular practice to use planes in support of patrols and garrisons.

the last strongholds of Caco operations had been suppressed (some of it accomplished by a policy of amnesty). In 1924 the Marine force in Haiti was reduced to 500 men; these were finally withdrawn ten years later.

Nicaragua

The Marines had been in Nicaragua since 1913, helping that habitually troubled country to keep a lid on various internal problems. But in 1925 a Conservative faction took over the government by force. The Liberals took to arms, headed for the hills, and the ensuing conflict escalated steadily, finally threatening American business and property. The Marines appeared in 1926 their operations gradually took on the weight of an expedition.

Then there was a surprising and hopeful development. American political efforts, backed up by the presence of the Marines, led to talks between Conservative and Liberal leaders that in mid-1927 resulted in the Liberals laying down their arms and a general pacification agreement, with a promise of free elections. But this agreement, made under the shadow of American power, was not satisfactory to one of the Liberal leaders, Augusto Sandino. Refusing to accept the accord, Sandino slipped to the mountain jungles to carry on the guerrilla war.

A highly articulate man with a reported cruel streak, Sandino had a flair for publicity and the ability to cultivate connections all over the world (throughout his rebellion he had numbers of supporters in the United States). He also had considerable skill in building an army and maintaining them by appeals to ideology and patriotism. However, though he was able to elude capture for four years in spite of the best efforts of the Marines and Guardia Nacional, he was not able to lead his forces to a decisive victory.

Above: Red Cross ladies greet men of the 2nd Marines parading in New York in 1919 on their return from France.
Right: Marines in the hills of Haiti.

In 1927 the Marines began setting up numbers of garrisons in the jungle, trying to contain Sandino in the highlands. All efforts to run him aground came to naught, however, frustrated by local sympathizers and the rebels' superior knowledge of the country. Nonetheless, instead of a successful campaign in its intended direction, the Marine experience in Nicaragua was to bear unexpected fruits: it became a major laboratory in the techniques of jungle warfare, which was to prove most valuable in the future.

This fact was not lost on Marine Captain Merrit A Edson, who divined that learning methodically to fight guerrillas in the bush might come in very handy (as he himself was later to prove in the Pacific). He developed new approaches, tactics and formations for ground fighting in rough territory. And most importantly, prodded by necessity, he stumbled on the beginnings of modern air-ground coordination.

It happened first in the village of Ocotal on 16 July 1927. In a surprise offensive against that fortified town, which was manned by 62 Marines and 48 of the new, poorly-trained Guardia Nacional, Sandino sent 600 men whooping to the attack just after midnight. When his initial assault was repulsed after two hours of hard fighting, Sandino turned to a tactic of attrition, trying to force the defenders to use up their ammunition.

Right : Recruits being sworn in at the receiving station at Parris Island, a picture taken in 1919. The presiding officer is Captain Benjamin Fogg, USMC.

Despite frustrations regarding Sandino, the Marines did materially contribute to realizing the country's first free election in 1928, which placed the Liberals in power. The next year Sandino fled to Mexico for a year, where he successfully generated international support for his cause against his old Liberal compatriots (some, but by no means all, of this support came from Communist quarters—though Sandino himself was not a Communist). On his return the guerrilla war resumed; it ended only in 1934, when Sandino was lured into Managua and killed by the Guardia Nacional under Colonel Anastasio Somoza, later dictator of Nicaragua.

It had been a long and frustrating campaign for the Marines, and for the US as well. Though the tactics of jungle fighting and close-air support were to prove quite fruitful in the future, recognition of their real value also lay in the future. Meanwhile the government of the United States was beginning to rethink its paternal-interventionist policies in areas that would later be known as the Third World. The ramifications of traditional American policy were becoming increasingly complex and international, the effect on future American foreign relations increasingly unpredictable. The Marines left Nicaragua in 1933, after the third national election. It was to be the last of the 'banana wars.' But America was still to be haunted, in the 1980s, by the spirit of Augusto Sandino, when the anti-American ruling party of Nicaragua named themselves 'Sandianistas.'

Guns and letters

The early 1920s Stateside saw a nationwide crime wave that involved a series of robberies of US mail. The problem at length became serious enough that the Marines were assigned to try and do something about it. They proceeded to do so with customary directness. Secretary of the Navy Edwin Denby, a former Marine, sent a letter to Corps officers directing them to station their men, armed, alongside postmen, and included the exortation, '. . . if attacked, shoot and shoot to kill . . . When our men go in as guards over mail, that mail must be delivered or there must be a Marine dead at the post of duty.' Problems with mail robberies disappeared with notable promptness. A recurrence of robberies in 1926 was handled likewise, and with the same results.

Marines in China

In the middle 1920s China was in the grip of a civil war, with Cantonese and Northern Armies fighting it out all over the countryside. Under the leadership of Chiang Kai-shek, the Soviet-supported Cantonese threatened Shanghai early in 1927. To protect the International Settlement in the city, Marines were sent in February under the command of Smedley Butler. They spent two years troubleshooting effectively there and in other areas. By 1929 things had relaxed enough that much of the detachment was pulled out, leaving behind a force of 'China Marines' to protect American interests. They remained there until the outbreak of World War II.

Above: Marines search native huts on Santo Domingo for arms. The American involvement in Santo Domingo left a persistent legacy of bitterness and anti-American feeling on the island. *Main picture:* Marines on Santo Domingo.

Inset, below: Marines on Santo Domingo find time to relax at a field day.

The 'Orange Plan'

Between the wars Commandant Lejeune directed a good deal of hard thinking about the implications of new wars, new kinds of terrain, new machines and the new tactics that would have to accompany them. As often happens, technology had advanced faster than the understanding of how to use it; and in the case of war, this can have most unpleasant results.

The process of rethinking was started by a strange, visionary, and ultimately tragic US Marine Corps staff officer named Earl Hancock ('Pete') Ellis. In 1913, well before the First World War, Ellis had given a series of highly classified lectures at the Naval War College. There he prophesied that America would someday fight a war with Japan, and that this conflict would involve the islands and atolls of the trans-Pacific (most of which, except for US-held Guam, became Japanese after the First World War). To deal with this eventuality, Ellis proposed a far-reaching development of amphibious warfare techniques. His predictions and concepts were so revolutionary that they were hardly noticed at the time.

Then the war intervened. After service in Europe, Ellis returned to his labors. His ideas, reinforced by the reality of Japanese gains after the war, found support among the leaders of the Corps, most notably in the person of Lejeune. The ensuing conceptual work came to be known under the heading of the 'Orange Plan.' These studies led in 1921 to a publication, mostly written by Ellis, called 'Advanced Base Operations in Micronesia,' which predicted with astonishing prescience the coming war in the Pacific and outlined the operations necessary to pursue it. In spite of much dubiousness in the other services, Lejeune approved the plan and proceeded to formulate the Marines' response to its challenge.

Meanwhile, Pete Ellis, obsessed with the Japanese threat to the point of neurosis, and drinking heavily, essayed an unofficial one-man reconnaissance of Japanese-held islands in the Pacific. During this journey he died, under mysterious circumstances, on the island of Koror. The Corps learned of his death through the Japanese authorities who meanwhile had cremated his body. The exact nature of his death was never cleared up, but the work he began went on.

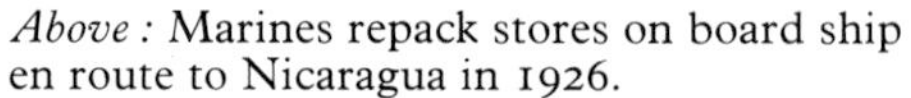

Above: Marines repack stores on board ship en route to Nicaragua in 1926.

Left: 1st Lieutenant Rogus and 1st Sergeant Belcher prepare their DH-4 aircraft for take off on a long-distance flight from Santo Domingo to Washington DC and San Francisco. The round trip took from 19 September to 9 November 1923. *Right:* F4B aircraft of VF10, part of the West Coast Expeditionary Force, around 1930.

In light of Ellis's advocacy of amphibious warfare, Colonel Robert H Dunlap began an exhaustive study of the most elaborate amphibious operation of the First World War—the Allied debacle at Gallipoli. It was finally concluded, to the Marines' satisfaction if not that of the other services, that the operation had failed not because it was impossible (as current military doctrine had it) but because it was handled with utter ineptitude. History has amply confirmed this conclusion.

Now committed to developing its amphibious capabilities, the Corps held a series of exercises in Cuba and elsewhere during the years 1922 to 1925. These landing exercises served mainly to show that current tactics and landing craft—wooden navy launches—were spectacularly inadequate to the proposed tasks. Much work had to be done, then, in the planning and development of new technology.

After 1925 expeditionary duties were to divert the Corps from these studies for some years. But during that time there did appear a significant pamphlet called *Joint Action, Army and Navy*, which was another big step in the evolution of modern joint operations.

In March 1929 Lejeune stepped down as Commandant, leaving behind the most remarkable record of leadership since the days of Archibald Henderson. His tenure had seen the extraordinarily prescient development of amphibious capability, the strengthening of Marine officer education and procurement, a system of correspondence training, enhanced coordination with other services, and a resulting rise in the readiness and *esprit* of the Corps. Lejeune's immediate successor, General Wendell C Neville, died within a year of his appointment. From 1930 to 1936 the command was filled by two old colleagues, Ben H Fuller and then John H Russell, who continued the planning and modernization begun so ably by Lejeune.

Below: Marines huddle in the bottom of their landing craft during a training exercise in World War II.

Replaying the Civil War

While most of Lejeune's efforts had taken place within the confines of the Corps, a highly publicised series of exercises kept the Marines busy during the early 1920s. They recreated several Civil War battles—Gettysburg, Antietam, and New Market—on the actual battlefields. Besides entertaining politicians and reporters, these exercises were, or were claimed to be, useful workouts in ground operations. And they kept the Marines in the nation's mind as well.

Birth of the Fleet Marine Force

Under Ben Fuller and his Assistant—later Commandant—John Russell, the Marines again addressed the issue of amphibious warfare in the early 1930s. The developments that ensued were to constitute the most dramatic turning point in Corps history.

In 1932 was published the first American military text specifically dealing with doctrines of amphibious warfare—*Marine Corps Landing Operations*. In the same era there was a complete reevaluation of the functions of the Expeditionary Force concept, which at length concluded that the Marines needed more personnel, more stability of duty, more training and new concepts along the lines pioneered by Pete Ellis.

As a result of these conclusions, Russell stabilized the Expeditionary Force and staff as an integral part of the US Fleet, in the process changing its title to the Fleet Marine Force (FMF). Then he went ahead. The doctrines of amphibious warfare had been formed; now they had to be fleshed out with appropriate field tactics.

In 1934 came a small booklet entitled *Tentative Manual for Landing Operations*. It has been called by one historian a 'pioneer work of the most daring and imaginative sort,' and by another, the 'Pentateuch and Four Gospels' of modern amphibious warfare. In revised and perfected form, the manual's tenets were to be followed by all the services of the US and her allies in World War II. It dealt briefly but succinctly with every aspect of operations—command relations, ship-to-shore movement and communications, the relations of air and naval gunfire support, the basics of disembarking and of shore party organization.

The refining of this revolutionary document took place in the schoolroom, on the drawing board, and on the beach in a number of exercises. Once the tactics were stated on paper, however, there had to be created the technology to actualize it. In contrast to the situation before the First World War, theory had outstripped technology.

Above all there had to be some kind of new landing craft. After many false starts, this requirement finally came to rest with two people. One was ship designer Andrew Higgens, whose prototypes led to the World War II 'Landing Craft Vehicle and Personnel' (LCVP) and 'Landing Craft Mechanized' (LCM). Both featured a hinged bow that dropped to disgorge soldiers and equipment on the beach; they would become familiar from endless photos of the war. And there was Donald Roebling of Florida, whose amphibious 'Alligator,' developed for rescue work in the Everglades, became the familiar Amtrack, capable of sailing up to and then over the beaches on its finned tracks.

The clouds of war gather

These developments of the 1930s capped the history of what came to be known as the 'old Marine Corps.' They arrived none too soon, because the storm clouds were building in Europe and in the Pacific. Germany, demoralized by a dictated and vindictive peace agreement in the Treaty of Versailles, fell under the spell of Adolf Hitler. (When he first saw the treaty, Marshal Foch of France had exclaimed, 'This isn't peace! This is a truce for 20 years!' He was to be quite precisely correct.) And Japan was zeroing in on the Pacific as its dreams of conquest grew. There it was to be exactly as Pete Ellis had prophesied, and exactly as the Marines had marshaled all their powers, transforming the Corps in the process, to resist and finally to help defeat the Japanese.

Right: Marine Women Reserves pass a column of Leathernecks at Camp Lejeune in 1943, a token of the many changes that World War II was to bring to the Marine Corps.

330
330

WORLD WAR II

'Remember Pearl Harbor'—1941-1945

The decline of Rome in the 5th century. The discovery of the New World at the end of the 15th century. The Reformation in the 16th. The French Revolution of 1789–1799. World War I, the cataclysmic conflict of blood and futility that pitted the world-dominating European nations against one another between 1914 and 1918 only to weaken the system upon which they were built and lead to more conflict two decades later. All were events that shook and re-formed the entire world. Nothing was the same thereafter. Each event ushered in a new world where the powers of nations and the thinking of people were dramatically changed so that what had gone before seemed to be but fading memories of a simpler and less dangerous era in the history of mankind. Each demanded a fundamental readjustment of man's perception of him-self, his life, and his destiny upon this earth. And added to this list of time-shaping events in our age was the epic conflict of nations between 1939 and 1945 we call World War II.

World War II: The Event that Cut History in Two

By this war, the United States and the Soviet Union were catapulted into pre-eminence to stand astride the globe with weapons and powers of decision-making unthinkable in earlier times. Former great nations were weakened and lost their colonies. These colonies—taking advantage of the enfeebled political and economic conditions in the countries that had recently dominated them—now demanded their share of political freedom and material largess. War-induced technological changes not only in weaponry—crowned by the over-whelming destructive force of the atomic bomb—but also in transportation, com-puterization and miniaturization, to say nothing of new medicines and their life-saving and life-prolonging benefits, brought about problems undreamed of in former times. Problems of once all-but-unknown nations became problems of the world, and it was clear that they could draw into the jaws of limited or unlimited warfare even peace-loving peoples half a world away.

Taking part in, and in many ways the chief beneficiary of, all of these changes coming out of World War II was the United States. Having abandoned its essen-tially 'Fortress America' mentality early in the twentieth century to stand beside its European allies in World War I—only largely to retreat to its own shores in a fit of isolationism arising out of its disappoint-ment with the outcome of that war—it found after the final defeat of the Axis powers in 1945 that such comfortable retreat was no longer possible. America was now a world power and the chief defender of the heritage of the Western World whether it welcomed this responsibility or not. Its friends and its interests encircled the globe. It could either stand up to those who would destroy its ideals and those of its friends or it could surrender itself to its ideological and political enemies. The stakes had been raised significantly by World War II; the dangers of miscalculation were even greater; the price of defeat was more and more un-thinkable. Playing a major role in World War II from beginning to end by standing at the fore to defend the nation, and pre-pared to continue its service in the crisis-filled years that followed, was the United States Marine Corps.

Pearl Harbor

The Marines, like the other US military services, were in the process of preparing but hardly ready when war came in De-cember 1941. As part of the mobilization program belatedly begun by the nation in the late 1930s, the Corps was anxious to move to a 50,000-man level at a minimum, but President Franklin D Roosevelt refused to make such a commitment until after the presidential election campaign of 1940. Accordingly, that level of manpower was reached only in mid-1941 (it would expand to almost 460,000 before the war was over). Nevertheless, vital steps were meanwhile being taken within the limitations imposed by political realities to prepare the Marines for action if events drew the United States into the conflicts already blazing in Europe, the Middle East and the Far East.

By late 1940 the Marine Aviation Wings (MAWs) were being expanded from their almost miniscule numbers of 452 officers and 3000 enlisted personnel. The call-up of reserve officers and enlisted men had added 5000 men to the Fleet Marine Force. On the Atlantic coast the 1st Marine Division was continuing its training exercises in am-phibious operations, and a new training camp had been established in the pine barrens of North Carolina near the new port of Morehead City (it would later be named Camp Lejeune) to further the Corps' train-ing missions and supplement Parris Island. And Cherry Point Marine Corps Air Station was under construction nearby. On the West Coast, Camp Elliot had recently been established at Kearney Mesa 12 miles out-side San Diego for the training of recruits. (In 1942 the Corps purchased the 132,000-acre site some 48 miles outside San Diego that became Camp Pendleton. These two facilities were destined to become the Corps' primary West Coast training camps.) On the West Coast, too, amphibious war-fare tactics were being developed. As in the East, these training exercises were con-ducted with the Army, but a lack of success in these dual-service operations led the Army to recommend that the Fleet Marine Force (FMF) look to the Pacific for possible areas of amphibious operations while the Army concentrated on possible European landings.

But despite its growing strength and newly-found concentration on amphibious landings for the FMF, US Marine per-sonnel as of late 1941 were still spread far and wide across the globe at various duty stations. Of its 65,000 men, 18,000 were deployed overseas from Iceland to and beyond the Philippines, including China, Guam, Wake, Midway and various other locations. Another 4000 Marines were stationed on Navy ships or at naval stations, 20,000 were in training at land bases, and the remainder were at various other installations and duties. Although few if any of them sus-pected it would come so soon, the Marines' test of battle was about to descend upon

Previous page: Unloading ammunition from landing craft during the New Georgia campaign. *Left:* Burned out fighter plane at Wheeler Field Hawaii in the aftermath of the Pearl Harbor attack. *Right:* The destroyers *Cassin* and *Downes* and the battleship *Pennsylvania* at Pearl Harbor.

Above: Close up of the damage on the *Downes* in the drydock at Pearl Harbor. Remarkably she was repaired and returned to service in the later stages of the fighting in the Pacific.

them in the form of over 300 Imperial Japanese Navy bombers, torpedo planes, and fighters that lifted from the flight decks of their carriers in the clear morning air of 7 December 1941 while 200 miles north of Pearl Harbor on the island of Oahu in the Hawaiian Islands. Within hours the greatest surprise attack in history was carried out. America soon entered World War II, and the United States Marine Corps was forced to fight its way back from heartbreaking initial defeats to attain the greatest victories in its history.

At 7:55 AM that Sunday morning the Japanese planes struck. Before the air raids were over two hours later, the 4500 Marines stationed at Pearl Harbor had fought with unparalleled bravery with whatever weapons they could get their hands on, including machine guns salvaged from what was left of the 48 planes of Marine Air Group 21 (MAG-21), almost all having been destroyed on the ground in the first attacks by the diving Japanese Zeroes and Val dive bombers. In all, 112 Marines paid with their lives for their gallant if futile defensive efforts against the Japanese attackers. American casualties totaled more than 4000. And like their counterparts in the other services, the Marines stood bloody but unbowed in the aftermath of the Pearl Harbor attack and vowed that the Japanese —and their allies—would pay dearly for their treachery. For the Marines, the final payment for Pearl Harbor was never considered paid until the last Leatherneck put down his weapon in victory on Okinawa three-and-a-half years later and learned that the final assault on the Japanese home islands was no longer necessary. The price of vindication was high and bloodstained, but the Marines were prepared to pay that price in the months and years that followed until the stain of Pearl Harbor had been removed from the American flag.

Initial Defeats

Within hours of the attack on Pearl Harbor, Marines in China and on the American outposts of Guam, Wake and Midway were feeling the fury of Japanese attacks. The small garrison of less than 200 Marines scattered on the Chinese mainland was determined to fight back, but obeyed orders from their commanders to surrender to overwhelming power rather than sacrifice themselves to American honor as they desired to do. Guam was virtually defenseless. The Marines there, numbering only 153 officers and men, were reinforced by an Insular Guard of native Guamanians, but it numbered only 80 men. The heaviest weapons available to the Marines were a few .30-caliber machine guns. The small American naval detachment, consisting of a minesweeper, an old tanker, and two patrol boats, was sunk the first day by Japanese air attacks. Then, after two days of bombing, almost 6000 Japanese soldiers landed in three locations on Guam. After a futile defense near the capital of Agana, the naval governor of the island bowed to the inevitable and surrendered his forces to the Japanese invaders on 10 December. Four Marines and 15 Guamanians had died in the defense of the island.

Although the Marine garrisons at Midway, Johnston, and Palmyra islands in the Central Pacific were only lightly attacked by Japanese naval and air units in the first few days of the war, Wake Island, located about halfway between Hawaii and the Philippines and being prepared as a base for naval patrol planes, was subjected to direct invasion within days of Pearl Harbor. The Japanese had no intention of allowing Wake to remain in American hands. On the three small islands making up Wake Atoll there were only 449 Marines and a Marine fighter squadron, lately reinforced with a dozen new Grumman F4F Wildcats as a defense force. The only other persons on the islands were some 50 Army and Navy specialists and 1200 civilian construction personnel. The Japanese attacks on Wake began on 7 December with an initial attack on the small island defenses by 36 Japanese bombers. Seven of the new Wildcats, caught on the ground while refueling, were blasted into wreckage, and the aviation gasoline tank went up in flames. Twenty-three Marines were dead or dying after the attack. For the next two days the Japanese returned to bomb the garrison, only to be met by accurate anti-aircraft fire from the ground and gallant air attacks by the remaining Wildcat pilots. Although the Marine defenders were clearly acquitting themselves well against the enemy bombers, everyone on Wake Island waited for the amphibious attack that was sure to follow. It came on 10 December in the form of nine cruisers and destroyers escorting four transports. These were met by withering fire from Marine shore batteries and skillful air attacks by the four remaining Wildcats. The furious fighting that day ended with the Japanese invasion fleet limping away in disarray, having lost 700 troops and having had two ships sunk and eight damaged.

The Americans had won the first round at Wake, but the Japanese were determined that the tiny atoll would fall into their hands. Back they came, and from 12 December until 23 December the battle for Wake Island continued. Gradually the daily Japanese bombing—one raid at mid-day and another at dusk—began to take its toll, and soon the Marine aviators and their ground crews (decimated by injuries and unable to salvage any more spare parts) could no longer put even one airplane into the air to defend the island. Yet the Marines held on because a relief expedition consisting of the carrier *Saratoga*, three heavy cruisers, nine destroyers, a tanker and the USS *Tangier* loaded with Marine reinforcements and the supplies the defenders needed to hold out was on the way. Unfortunately, its progress was dilatory and it was fated to arrive too late. The powerful task force was only 425 miles from Wake when the Japanese began an amphibious landing in force covered by 12 cruisers and destroyers on 23 December. The order went out to the task force from Pearl Harbor to retire from the scene, and the convoy turned away. The Marines and civilians remaining on Wake resisted the 1500-man invasion force as best they could, but after 11 hours of embattled resistance the Navy officer commanding decided to surrender to the Japanese to save the lives of those who remained. Those Marines who survived the attacks on Wake Island joined their comrades from China and Guam in Japanese captivity, but not before they fought with everything possible to uphold the honor and territory of their country on the tiny mid-Pacific atoll.

Meanwhile the Marines and their Army and Navy comrades in the Philippines were writing their own tale of courage in the face of overwhelming odds in the first weeks of the war. Despite the fact that the islands' air force of Army B-17s was wiped out on the ground on 7 December and that the small US Asiatic Fleet was ordered south to join Allied fleets in the Netherlands East

Above : Marine antiaircraft crew aboard the carrier *Wasp* during a lull in operations near Guadalcanal on 7 August 1942.

Indies to try to hold off the Japanese naval offensives in that area soon thereafter, the American defenders were determined to fight as long as possible to delay the Japanese juggernaut while hoping that reinforcements would arrive. The Marines of the 4th Division, recently arrived from Shanghai, were put under the command of Army General Douglas MacArthur for the defense of the archipelago and were assigned the job of defending the beaches of Corregidor Island—'the Rock' at the entrance to Manila Bay—against Japanese attacks. As the Japanese landed in various spots on Luzon on 20 December 1941 and fought their way toward the capital of Manila, Bataan Peninsula and Corregidor nearby became the last bastions of the islands' defenses. American troops of all three services were thrown together to prevent or at least delay the all-but-inevitable fall of the archipelago. Much to the dismay of the Japanese attackers, the combined American forces with their Filipino allies held off the invading troops through December, then January, February and March 1942.

But despite the desperate heroism of the troops, Bataan fell in early April, rendering Corregidor completely vulnerable to fresh Japanese artillery, air, and naval gunnery attacks despite the determination of the defenders to resist to the last man. Almost incessant battering of the Corregidor defenses were preliminary to an amphibious assault upon the besieged fortress. Despite the best efforts of two battalions of the 4th Marine Regiment—aided by Army, Navy and Philippine troops to a total number of 3891 officers and men—the full-scale invasion of 4–5 May could not be held off. When the Japanese managed to land tanks, and Lieutenant General Jonathan Wainwright (who had succeeded General MacArthur when the Army commander was ordered to leave the Philippines to make his way to Australia to lead the Allied offensive back against the Japanese aggressors) was informed that half of the defenders of Corregidor were either dead or wounded, he made the heartrending decision to surrender the Philippine defense forces. Knowing that almost 700 of his Marines were either dead or wounded, the commander of the Marine forces on Corregidor, Colonel Samuel L Howard, ordered the colors of the 4th Marine Regiment burned and led his men into captivity on 5 May. All of the prisoners were then forced to undergo the infamous 'Bataan Death March' into captivity. It had taken the Japanese five months to overwhelm the defenders of the Philippines, and the Marines had displayed the valor that was their proud tradition. America—and its military forces—had taken a beating at Pearl Harbor, on Guam and Wake, and now in the Philippines in the early months of the war, but it was clear that the nation and her allies suffered no lack of courage and determination to turn the tables as time and circumstances permitted. The Japanese had indeed won the initial rounds, but the Pacific war was far from over.

Below : A Marine unit ready to move up to the front line during the unavailing defense of Bataan in March 1942. Few were to survive the fighting and the subsequent imprisonment by the Japanese.

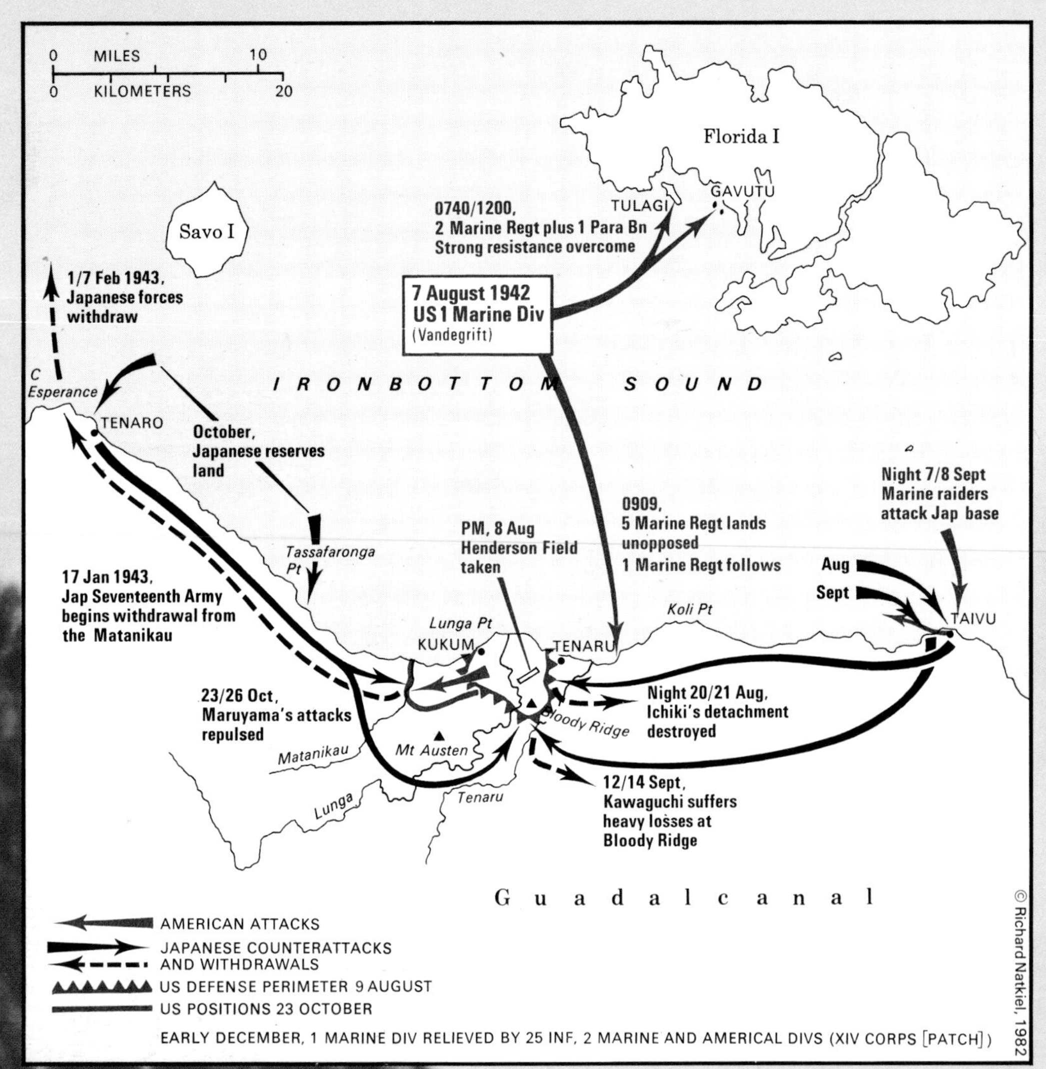

Start of the Long Road Back: Guadalcanal

During the first eight months of the war the Japanese had moved down through the Pacific islands on a path of conquest that seemed unstoppable. In spite of the monumental defeat the Japanese Imperial Navy had suffered at the hands of the US Navy off Midway early in June—aided by the gallant defenders of Midway Atoll which included Marine air units—the Japanese Army had not been stopped on its sweep south through the Pacific waters. The Americans had been driven from Guam, Wake and the Philippines. The British had suffered defeats in Burma, Malaya, Hong Kong and Singapore. The Dutch were driven out of the East Indies. And the Far East navies of all the Allied forces had been virtually destroyed in the process. Next in the path of Japanese conquest was New Guinea (the key to the conquest of Australia), the British islands of the Bismarck Archipelago, and then the 900-mile-long Solomon Island chain. If these could be taken, fortified, and turned into air and naval bases, the war in the South Pacific would be won for the Japanese. From these southerly locations supply lines from the United States mainland and Hawaii to Australia could be cut.

Determined to retain the initiative and consolidate their conquests, the Japanese landed and took New Britain Island and its important port of Rabaul in January 1942. Building it up as a naval and air base, they began the systematic bombing of Port Moresby on the coast of southeast New Guinea and landed troops on two locations on New Guinea itself. Australia was now in mortal peril. In March the Japanese began their invasion of the Solomons, meeting virtually no resistance from the hard-pressed British or Australians. In May they moved onto the island of Tulagi, off Florida Island in the southern Solomons, and made it their own. They now had possession of one of the best anchorages in the Solomons. Within a month they had crossed the bay to the south and had landed on the neighboring island of Guadalcanal, there to build an airfield on the north shore of the island just inland from Lunga Point. If this airfield was completed, Allied-held islands to the south would be in peril and the Japanese fleet anchored in Tulagi could move out at will to interdict the Allied fleets moving to Australia. If Australia, denied American men and supplies, fell to the Japanese, any American counter-offensives might have to come from Pearl Harbor thousands of miles away in the Central Pacific or even from the United States itself.

Out of these circumstances emerged one of the Marines' greatest battles of World War II. Denied support from its Australian and New Zealander allies who were busy fending off attacks on their own territories, the blunting of the Japanese moves in the Solomons by seizing Tulagi and Guadalcanal away from them would have to be an American affair. According to the plans drawn up by the American military commanders, the Navy would take in the invading American forces against Tulagi to the north and Guadalcanal to the south, the 1st Marine Division under Major General Alexander A Vandegrift would carry out the assault tactics, and the Army would come in to relieve the Marines as soon as a beachhead had been secured and reinforced. Vandegrift was forced to assemble his invading forces at Fiji from all over the Pacific and from bases at home. Many if not most were inadequately trained for the job they were to do (the Corps had been swollen to 143,000 men by June 1942 but few recruits were adequately trained for the tasks that lay ahead).

Unbelievable confusion reigned at Wellington, New Zealand, where the forces were assembled for the final push. Logistics broke down to the point that it was almost impossible to prepare for the amphibious operation. And because of too few supporting naval vessels, vital supplies of food, ammunition and fuel for the Guadalcanal and Tulagi landings were drastically cut back. If the landings in the southern Solomons were not too vigorously contested, if the Navy provided adequate protection against Japanese counterattacks, and if the Army and additional supplies followed soon after the initial attacks by the

Left : Map of the operations on Guadalcanal.
Right : General Vandegrift at work in his tent on Guadalcanal.
Below : A Marine Raider unit comes ashore on Guadalcanal in November 1942.

Leathernecks, Operation Watchtower stood some chance of success. Vandegrift had grave doubts, but given the consequences of further Japanese advances in the Solomons and their effects on the war in the Pacific, orders were tapped out and the Marines prepared to do their job. At last they were going on the offensive.

The Solomons assaults on 7 August 1942 came as a complete surprise to the Japanese. The defenders on Tulagi and on the nearby islands of Gavutu and Tanambogo had no forewarning before sighting the 76-ship invasion force but put up a furious defense from caves, natural redoubts and man-made dugouts until blasted out by grenades and dynamite. Before being quelled after three days of furious fighting, the defenders lost about 700 troops (almost 90 percent of their number), many by suicide charges. The Marines lost 144 dead or missing and almost 200 wounded. Valuable lessons were learned about the determination of Japanese forces to resist to the end from fortified emplacements and about the difficulty of assaulting heavily-defended islands. Across the bay, the landings on mountainous, jungled Guadalcanal to the south were virtually unopposed, and the Japanese airstrip (80 percent complete) was soon in American hands. It had been easy, almost too easy. The Japanese had lost not only their airfield but also precious supplies of trucks, repair facilities, gasoline and even food. But what the Marines did not realize—nor, almost fatally, did their naval counterparts—was that the Japanese, having lost Guadalcanal, had every intention of recovering it by all means possible. The battle for Guadalcanal was only beginning, not ending.

Bad news reached the Marines on Guadalcanal on 8 August. Because of his aircraft losses and the 'need to refuel' (although he had 17 days' fuel left), Vice-Admiral Frank Jack Fletcher was removing his carriers from the area (even before the landings he had promised only two days' support). This meant that Rear Admiral Richmond Kelly Turner, commander of the amphibious force, would have to remove his transports even though all the Marines had not debarked and more than half the vital supplies needed by the Marines on the beach were still in the ships' holds. Turner would leave the next day whether all the transports and supply ships were unloaded or not. But even an ordered hurry-up unloading operation was not destined to go smoothly because that night Japanese naval forces moved in through the Allied picket line undetected and the 40-minute Battle of Savo Island took place. Although the Japanese destroyed four Allied cruisers in the furious battle, their commander, believing the American carriers were still in the area and not wanting to be caught in daylight by their planes, pulled out of the fight and returned to Rabaul. The American transports were untouched, but weighed anchor the next morning nevertheless. The 10,000 Marines of the 1st Division were alone—for how long no one knew.

Above: A Vindicator dive bomber takes off from Midway to attack the Japanese fleet.

With Japanese bombers raiding every day at noon and with the Imperial Navy cruisers or destroyers showing up almost every night to shell the Lunga Point beachhead, the Marines wondered how long they could last, especially since their food supply could be counted only in terms of days and their heavy equipment and coastal defense guns had not been unloaded before the transports left for New Caledonia. Yet despite the constant enemy harassment, the Marines continued to hold out and complete the airstrip captured from the Japanese (which the Americans named Henderson Field after a Marine airman, Major Lofton R Henderson, killed at Midway). So successful were their efforts that on 20 August the first contingent of Marine aviators—in 12 SBD dive bombers—flew into Henderson Field. Other planes followed, and the 'Cactus Air Force' (the code-name for Guadalcanal was 'Cactus') was in business. It would have to be, for the 10,000 isolated Marines were about to taste the full fury of a Japanese counter-invasion.

On 18 August destroyers from Rabaul had landed 1000 Japanese soldiers 20 miles east of Lunga Point at a land projection called Taivu Point. Not waiting for reinforcements to arrive, the Japanese commander, Colonel Kiyono Ichiki, on the night of 21 August ordered an attack on the left flank of the American defense line fanning out from Lunga Point. The ensuing defense of the perimeter by the Marines came to be known as the Battle of the Tenaru River and was as bloody an assault as the Marines had ever tasted in their history. Wave after wave of Japanese troops swept on against the Marines' rifle, machine gun, antitank gun and artillery fire. Before the fight was over by early morning, 800 elite Japanese soldiers had died. Colonel Ichiki burned his regimental colors and committed suicide on Taivu Point. The reinforcements never arrived; their convoy subsequently was attacked and forced to abandon the landing in the Battle of the Eastern Solomons on 24 August.

The Japanese had been repulsed, the Cactus Air Force was proving its worth against enemy shipping, and supplies from naval transports began to move in once again. Still the issue was far from settled, and air raids on Henderson Field and the beachhead continued as daily occurrences while sickness began to decimate the Marines as they struggled to hold the island. Dysentery and malaria almost seemed a worse enemy than the Japanese. General Vandegrift wondered how long his men could hold out. One thing he knew: the Japanese would be back to attempt to retake the island and Henderson Field.

By mid-September 6000 more elite Japanese troops had been landed by destroyers near Taivu Point. Their commander, Major General Kiyotake Kawaguchi, decided that part of them would move west toward the American position at Lunga Point while another moved into the jungle to attack the Americans from the south. A third contingent would land west of Lunga Point near the village of Kokumbona and move on the Marines along the coast from that direction. Thus attacked from three sides, the Americans would be wiped out and Henderson Field would belong to the Japanese. Air units from Rabaul were scheduled to land on 13 September. (As in the previous attack on the American perimeter, the Japanese commander had been promised more men if needed, but he decided they were unnecessary.)

Everything went wrong with the three-prong attack. The Japanese moves were uncoordinated, troops got lost in the jungle and bogged down in the mud, and, most importantly, the Marines held off the main Japanese thrust from the south in the famous Battle of Bloody Ridge of 12–14 September 1942. The Japanese troops at one point got to within 1000 yards of the airfield, but furious Marine resistance pushed them back. The other two prongs of the attack—along the coast from the east and west—fared no better and never breached the Marine lines. What was left of the Japanese forces (about 1500 died in the attacks to only 143 Marine casualties) struggled off to the west through the mountains to areas held by their compatriots, fighting starvation and despair every step of the way.

Still the Japanese commanders refused to give up; they immediately began planning for a major invasion to take place the next month. Given their position on Rabaul and their supplies of manpower at this stage of the war, they might well have succeeded. But encouraged by developments on Guadalcanal, the American military commanders had beefed up Vandegrift's Marines with additional men (there were now 20,000 land and air Marines on Guadalcanal), supplies and airplanes. Furthermore, some Army troops had arrived to replace the Marines when conditions permitted, and a second airstrip had been added to Henderson Field. If the Battle of Guadalcanal, in the last analysis, was a battle of logistics as well as of courage and tenacity, the Americans were matching their enemy step by step. Still, control of the sea in the southern Solomons remained the crucial ingredient, and the Japanese Navy's sorties down 'the Slot' through the center of the Solomons every night—the Marines called these sorties the 'Tokyo Express'—hardly let up. Until the Japanese Navy had been driven off, the harassment of the Marines on Guadalcanal was ended, and the island was securely in American hands—or until the Americans had been driven out of the Solomons—the battle for Guadalcanal would continue. Too much was at stake for it to end without a clear victor.

Frustrated at the failure of the two previous invasions of Guadalcanal to drive the Americans into the sea, Admiral Isoruko Yamamoto, commander of the Pacific Theater, from his headquarters at Truk far north in the eastern Carolines, assigned a full division to take the island from the Marines. He placed the troops under Lieutenant General Haruyoski Hyakutake. They landed at Kokumbona west of Lunga Point in October and began their move toward Lunga and Henderson Field on 16 October. But like the ill-fated west prong of the attack of a month before, the 8000-man force, poorly coordinated, slogged through the heavy jungle to attack the Marines on 26 October to no avail. Giving up on the attack after having 3500 of his men killed, Kyakutake moved his battered survivors to the western end of the island to hold out until the Imperial Navy took control of the waters around Guadalcanal. This too proved to be illusory, for in a series of naval battles around the island during the months of October and November (known as the Battle of the Santa Cruz Islands and the three Battles of Guadalcanal off Cape Esperance and Tassafaronga Point on the western part of the island) the American Navy—now under the aggressive Admiral William F Halsey—although severely battered (including the loss of the carriers *Hornet* and *Enterprise*), finally prevailed to turn the whole campaign around. So many ships had been sunk in the Sealark Channel between Guadalcanal and Tulagi by this time that the Americans called this expanse of water 'Ironbottom Sound.'

In one of the November battles 6000 Japanese troops were killed when their transports were attacked by American naval units and destroyed by planes from Henderson Field. During the months of the Guadalcanal campaign as they fought off air attacks and attacked enemy transports, the Cactus Air Force shot down 400 Japanese planes and sank ten transports while losing only 100 of their number. Thereafter Japanese supplies and reinforcements slowed to a trickle, Hyakutake and his men were isolated, and supplies and reinforcements began to flow into Vandegrift and his Marines in a steady stream. On 9 November 1942 Vandegrift and the 1st Marine Division were finally relieved—after four months of bloody fighting—by the 2nd Marine Divi-

Above: Admiral Yamamoto, Commander of the Japanese Combined Fleet and mastermind of Japanese strategy until his death in April 1943.

Below: Lieutenant Mitchell Page receives the Medal of Honor from General Vandegrift for gallantry during the Guadalcanal fighting.

Left: Putting out a small fire on a Marine Wildcat fighter following a Japanese air attack on Henderson Field, Guadalcanal. The 'Cactus Air Force' played a vital part in the battle.

sion and the Americal and 25th Divisions from the Army. (By the next year Vandegrift would be commandant of the Marine Corps.)

The Battle of Guadalcanal was over for the gallant but battered 1st Marine Division, although the Army spent the next few months mopping up Japanese forces in the vicinity of Lunga Point and extending their perimeters. They also moved towards Hyakutake's survivors on the western tip of the island. Early in February 1943 units of the Japanese Navy moved down 'the Slot' for the final time to evacuate the 13,000 sick and wounded survivors of the third major attack on the Marines on Guadalcanal. In all, a total of 36,000 Japanese had been assigned the task of removing the Marines from Guadalcanal. These 13,000 starving and demoralized soldiers hurriedly evacuated in the dead of night were all that were left on the 'island of death,' as they called it. Guadalcanal was securely in American hands; a foothold had been gained in the Solomons; and the sea lanes to Australia, and to her troops bravely holding off the Japanese on New Guinea, New Britain, and the nearby islands, had been secured.

The Pacific war had been turned around on land at Guadalcanal as it had been turned around on sea by the epic Battle of Midway earlier during those same crucial months of 1942. The US Marines, having faced their first major engagement of the war, having been left to their own devices against fanatical Japanese attacks, and having been forced to defend their lives and their nation's honor in the sour, steamy jungles of an island most had never heard of a few months before, had proved their effectiveness in the bloody cauldron of island warfare that was to be their lot in World War II. The cost had been 1152 Marines dead and 2799 wounded.

Above : Marines come ashore on Rendova Island, New Georgia at the start of the landings on 30 June 1943.
Below : Marine wounded being ferried offshore by landing craft.

Climbing the Solomons Ladder

As the American military planners contemplated their war efforts of 1943, three fundamental decisions were made. First, the campaign against the Japanese in the Pacific Theater would take the form of a giant two-pronged movement. One arm would advance upward from New Guinea and the Solomons toward the Philippines; the other would move across the Central Pacific in a series of island-hopping invasions of the Japanese-held islands. This right-hand prong would also be heading for the Philippines, but it would also place American forces within long-distance bombing range of the Japanese inner defenses and even the home islands. These giant pincers would move simultaneously toward their objectives.

Second, Army units would carry the fighting and make up the bulk of the landing forces in MacArthur's Southwest Pacific Theater, while the Marines would carry the landings in the Central Pacific with a Marine general in charge. To carry out these tasks, the Corps would be expanded to over 300,000 officers and men by mid-1943. It was within the context of this rapid buildup and the necessity of providing all fighting men possible to the Pacific war that the Marine Corps was forced to break its former all-segregated stance and allow blacks into

Above left: Marines on the beach at Bougainville ready to advance inland, November 1943.
Left: Dead Japanese on Bougainville. The 60,000 strong Japanese garrison reacted slowly to the Marine landings on 1 November 1943.
Below: Marines man the firing line, ready to repel one of the series of battalion-size attacks mounted on the beachhead on Bougainville in November 1943.

its ranks. This it did with great reluctance, initially assigning the blacks only to all-black units under white officers and non-commissioned officers and to defense and labor units. Women enlistees added to the Corps were detailed only to administrative and clerical jobs. As the war progressed, black Marines made combat landings and fought well. 15,000 blacks eventually wore Marine green before the war ended.

Third, facing a wartime strategy of island assaults, the Marine Corps requested and received new specialized landing craft invaluable for their assigned missions. By 1943 LSTs (Landing Ship, Tank), LSDs (Landing Ship, Dock), LCIs (Landing Craft, Infantry), LCTs (Landing Craft, Tank), and LVTs (Landing Vehicle, Tracked) were being added to the Marine arsenal of war. All except the LSDs could unload men and equipment directly on the beach of enemy-held territory. Thus the problems faced at Guadalcanal in getting onto a beach safely and then being rapidly reinforced were eliminated somewhat, although amphibious landings against enemy-held islands would continue to be a perilous undertaking—as the history of the Corps throughout the remainder of the war was to demonstrate dramatically.

The movement up the Solomons ladder began in February 1943 when an Army division and a Marine raider battalion seized the Russell Islands northwest of Guadalcanal. The islands proved to be undefended. Their seizure meant that fighter bases soon to be built there would be available for movements up through the central Solomons (plus three more airstrips had been added at Guadalcanal). But the principal targets were two islands in the New Georgia group in the central Solomons: New Georgia Island, which had a Japanese airfield at Munda on its southern shore, and nearby Rendova, from which artillery support could be supplied for the taking of Munda. The Marines were to aid two Army divisions in taking Munda on New Georgia by supplying two defense and two raider battalions to land with them. They were also assigned the task of helping the Army take Rendova. Although the campaign did not go well, particularly for the inexperienced Army units, and lasted from June until August 1943, the Marines were able to aid the Army appreciably by beating off Japanese counter-offensives around the airfield at Munda, by effecting artillery support from Rendova with their new 155-mm 'Long Toms,' and by playing a part in the air cover for the operation by supplying six of the 32 fighter and bomber squadrons flying out of Guadalcanal and the Russells assigned to the task.

The next step up the Solomons ladder was the island of Bougainville to the northwest. If Bougainville were taken, the great Japanese base at Rabaul would be within range of American fighters and dive bombers. Bougainville was as tempting an assault target as it was dangerous. The entire 125-mile length of the island was made up of swamps and jungle reaching up and across its mountainous interior. On Bougainville's southern tip at Buin the Japanese had built four airfields. Two more airfields were located at Buka and Bonis on the northern tip. And the island was defended by 40,000 seasoned troops. But the American military commanders fooled the Japanese completely as to their intentions by creating two diversionary landings, one taking place on the Treasury Islands nearby carried out by New Zealand troops and another on 27 October 1943 on the island of Choiseul to the southeast by the 2nd Marine Parachute Battalion (minus parachutes, as usual). And the Navy shelled both the northern and southern ends of the island just before the troops landed, convincing the Japanese commander that those would be the areas in which the Americans would land. Instead, they hit the beaches at Cape Torokina on Empress Augusta Bay halfway up the west coast of the island. The 3rd Marine Division and the Army's 37th Division met little initial resistance when landing on 1 November and had 14,000 troops ashore by nightfall, but they found that developing a perimeter in the impenetrable jungles hugging the shoreline was next to impossible. Fortunately, the Japanese commander, Lieutenant General Haruyoski Hyakutake (who had incurred the defeat of the third invasion of Guadalcanal), was not convinced that the Torokina landing was anything more than a diversion and thus held his troops back while the Americans fortified themselves around the landing site and began to prepare an airfield. There at Torokina they were forced to drive the Japanese off the surrounding hills from which they had a clear field of fire on the invasion forces. One such enclave, dubbed 'Helzapoppin Ridge,' was not taken until Christmas Day.

Finally convinced that the main American effort was indeed at Torokina—and that air assaults from Rabaul would not dislodge the soldiers and Marines from their positions—Hyakutake began to move his thousands of troops from the northern and

Above: Men of the 2nd Marine Raider Battalion on Bougainville in November 1943.
Above right: Marines advance cautiously past a disabled American tank on the Numa Numa trail inland from the Bougainville beachhead.

southern ends of the island. But it took weeks for the soldiers to make their way through the swampy morass that was the Bougainville jungle, and when they arrived, the Americans were ready with mined trails and well-dug emplacements. By the time the first Japanese attacks began on the Americans' perimeter in March, the 3rd Marine Division had been replaced by the Army's Americal Division, but the attacks were strenuously—if not fanatically—carried out. After 17 days of savage fighting, the Japanese had sustained 7000 casualties—to the Americans' 1000—and Bougainville had been secured. By the end of April 1944, aircraft from three airstrips carved out of the Torokina jungle had joined with naval carrier-based planes and Army Air Force units from MacArthur's forces to the west to begin pounding the crucial Japanese base at Rabaul on almost a daily basis.

In the meantime MacArthur had sent the 1st Marine Division, the tested and now rested veterans from Guadalcanal, to take another key base in his drive toward the Philippines. This was Cape Gloucester on the far western end of New Britain Island. Cape Gloucester controlled the Vitiaz and Dampier Straits between New Guinea and New Britain. With the straits in American hands, the sea path northwest was safe for passage. It was assaulted on 26 December 1943. Although well covered by Allied air power, which consistently beat off Japanese air attacks from Rabaul on the other end of the island, it took the Marines three weeks to subdue the 10,000 stubborn enemy troops in and around Cape Gloucester. But the job was done. (Thereafter, but not as a consequence of this operation, the 1st Marine Division was lifted from MacArthur's command and shifted to the Central Pacific campaign.)

Rabaul with its 135,000 troops had been designated as the next target, but having faced the jungle warfare of New Georgia, Bougainville and Cape Gloucester, and not wanting to repeat those agonizing experiences if possible—and with MacArthur's attention being returned to completing the domination of New Guinea to the southwest, while the Central Pacific drive was about to begin in earnest as the right arm of the two-prong strategy—the American military commanders made the decision to bypass Rabaul and let its troops, cut off from resupply, die on the vine. No longer usable as a naval anchorage—as countless air attacks had proved—and rapidly having its air forces destroyed by the American flyers of all three services, including Marines, Major General George Kenney's Fifth Air Force from New Guinea, and naval units from American carriers, Rabaul now represented no danger to the Allies as the left prong of the grand strategy moved to the northwest towards its destination in the Philippines.

The Gilbert Islands: The Horror of Tarawa

In order to move west across the Pacific from Hawaii toward the Philippines and possibly Formosa, and then to proceed northward toward the Japanese home islands, it was necessary for the American

forces to assault and capture the Central Pacific island chains known as the Marshalls and the Marianas. But first the Japanese would have to be removed from the Gilbert Islands to the southwest of Hawaii and almost due south of the Marshalls in order to clear the left flank of the movement. Like all the other Central Pacific islands, the Gilberts were far different from those found in the South Pacific with their mountainous ranges and lush jungle vegetation. The mid-Pacific islands were made up of atolls formed by volcanic eruptions below the sea. The islands making up the often diamond-shaped atolls were formed from the tops of the volcanic craters and were uniformly ringed with coral reefs but a few feet below the water, reefs that would tear to shreads anything that came in contact with their hard, crusty surface. The islands themselves were more or less flat, not mountainous, offering no protection to invading troops. And properly fortified with pillboxes and other deep emplacements made up of volcanic rock, coconut logs, and even reinforced concrete sides, they were almost impervious to artillery and bomb blasts—as the American attackers found in late 1943.

Two atolls in the Gilberts, Makin to the north and Tarawa 100 miles to the south, were the targets for the invasion fleet of 200 ships that made its way to the Gilberts to begin *Operation Galvanic* in November 1943. On board the transports were the 2nd Marine Division and part of the 27th Infantry Division. The men—totaling 35,000 in all—had their assignments: the Army would take Makin (with some of the Marines in reserve) and the Marines would take 18-mile-long Tarawa Atoll with Betio Island on the bottom of its triangular shape as the primary target. The amphibious force commander, Major General Holland M ('Howlin' Mad') Smith, decided he would stay with the Army for the taking of Makin Atoll as it was assumed this would be the easier target to pursue. An abortive Marine raid back in August 1942 carried out under Lieutenant Colonel Evans Carlson had revealed that Makin Atoll was lightly defended. Things should not have changed much in a little over a year.

But although there were few Japanese on the principal island of Butaritari on Makin, the operation took four days of hard fighting after the landings of 21 November. The 165th Regimental Combat Team of the 27th Division moved very cautiously across the island, too cautiously for 'Howlin' Mad' Smith who, believing in the Marine Corps practice of moving with all dispatch whatever the obstacles, personally intervened to get the operation moving at a faster pace despite whatever the Army thought of his methods. To Smith, having a 20-to-1 advantage over the Japanese defenders precluded any reason for slow movement. The delays on Makin, however, paled into insignificance when compared to the problems the Marines were running into at Betio to the south.

Bettio's less than 300 acres nowhere rose above ten feet in elevation but were fortified with coastal defense guns, 40 artillery pieces in bunkers, a long sea wall four feet in height on the lagoon or inner side (where most of the Marines were scheduled to land), and at least 100 machine guns in pillboxes. The Japanese pillboxes, bunkers, and supporting ammunition dumps were all interconnected with trenches for effective use by the 4300 troops on the island. And ringing Betio and the atoll was a submerged coral reef thoroughly mined with entanglements between the breaks in the sharp coral ridges. Most of the Marines were to approach Betio in shallow-draft LCVPs (Landing Craft, Vehicle and Personnel), or more commonly called 'Higgins Boats.' These, it was hoped, would clear the forbidding coral reefs. The first three waves of Marines were to be taken ashore in LVTs, or Amtracs, which could both 'swim' in the lagoon and then move on their caterpillar treads across the reefs and then onto the

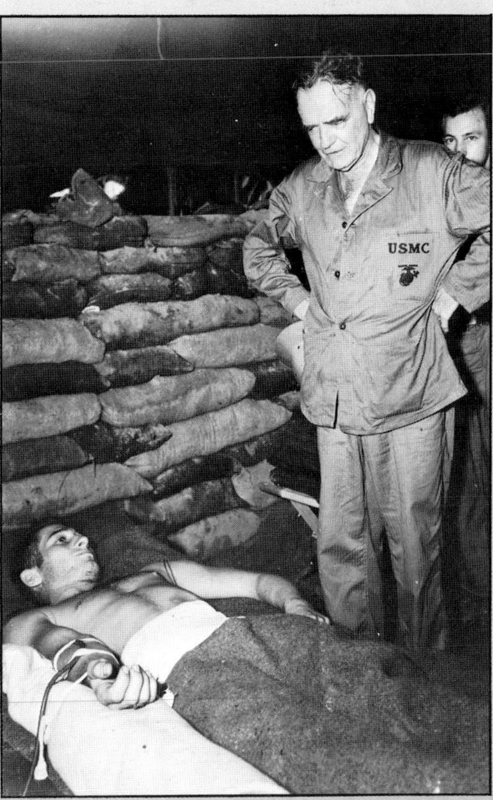

Above: Admiral Halsey talks with an injured Marine in a beachhead hospital on Bougainville. *Main picture, below:* Amtracs head for the shore, Tarawa, 20 November 1943.

beach, but only 125 of these were available. Most of the Marines and supplies would have to move into the beach in the Higgins boats. Four landing areas were designated on the northern shore of Betio: Green Beach on the outside of the atoll, and Red Beaches 1, 2, and 3 on the lagoon side. All would prove to be infernal stretches of real estate for the 76 hours following the landings on the morning of 20 November 1943.

As the amphibious landings proceeded, everything seemed to go wrong. The Navy lifted its gunfire too soon, allowing Japanese artillery to open up on the assembling landing craft. The planned half-hour air strikes were not only delayed but also lasted only seven minutes. And the leading boats of the invasion armada found themselves under murderous fire from shore as the naval bombardment and air strafing ended a full 18 minutes before the Marines hit the beach. Undaunted by the pre-invasion bombing, shelling and strafing—which had virtually no effect on them—the Japanese defenders rushed to their undamaged weapons and opened a withering fire upon the invaders. Not only were some of the LVTs destroyed in the water—over half never reached the beaches—but also the remainder either landed at the wrong beaches in the withering fire or found they could not traverse the four-foot sea wall. Their Marine occupants died in droves while trying to escape from them by jumping into the water and wading ashore. The Higgins boats following behind got hung up on the coral reefs, forcing their combat-laden occupants to endure fiery deaths from Japanese shore fire or from attempting to wade ashore in water often up to their armpits.

Those who made it to shore could only crouch down behind the sea wall unable to move because of murderous crossfire from the enemy guns. Some made it to the

Above: A wounded Marine is taken to a landing craft for evacuation to a hospital ship during the Tarawa operation.

Below: Men of the 2nd Marine Division being evacuated from Tarawa after the conclusion of the battle. The shattered trees attest to the violence of the fighting.

safety of a pier on Red Beach 3 where they hid under it and behind it trying to figure out their next move. The fears of the assault commander, Colonel David M Shoup, about the whole plan—including the coral reefs and the Higgins boats' ability to navigate over their jagged edges—now seemed to be coming to fruition. Control was rapidly vanishing on the beach—by now a confused expanse of dead and wounded men, wrecked equipment, and constant enemy fire—and communication with the areas on the beach and with the ships offshore broke down almost completely. The invasion was rapidly turning into a debacle of the first order. Standing in the command post he established at the end of the long pier, Shoup, although wounded, tried to make order out of the chaos as subsequent waves of Marines fell to the same grisly fate as their buddies had endured in the first waves.

The only way off the beach was for the Marines to fight their way forward inch by inch and yard by yard, taking whatever casualties as were necessary, until they could get close enough to the pillboxes to knock them out one by one. It was a grisly, bloody business, but the Marines did it. By noon General Smith, still back with the Army at Makin, had decided to send the 6th Marines to help out at Betio (the Army on Makin would have to get along without them). This allowed the reserves waiting off Tarawa to be committed to the fight ashore, but because of communications difficulties these reserves remained offshore during the first night because they had no orders as to where to land. When they began to come ashore the next morning they came under murderous fire as they slogged through the surf. Some 350 of the 800 men in the relief force were killed or wounded before touching the beach.

Above : Marines on the beach at Tarawa firing at Japanese positions around the island's airfield.

Fearful of complete annihilation of the relief Marines, Colonel Shoup ordered all the Marines on the beach to move forward against the Japanese emplacements despite the withering fire. Many Marine heroes died in those morning hours, but about noon of this second day the battle finally turned in favor of the Americans. The tide in the Tarawa lagoon shifted, allowing Higgins boats to clear the reefs with supplies. Two battalions on Red Beach 2 punched their way through to the south shore, and Green Beach on the outside of the lagoon was finally cleared. By evening the 6th Marines had arrived from Makin and were making their way across Green Beach.

By the morning of the third day on Tarawa the Marines had slugged their way out of Red Beach 3 and were approaching the bombproof blockhouse which served as the headquarters of Rear Admiral Meichi Shibasaki, the commander of the Japanese defense forces. This was soon reduced to ashes as Marine assault engineers dropped grenades down the air vents of the blockhouse, followed by gasoline poured down the vents to be detonated by TNT charges that followed in short order. By that evening hundreds of Japanese had fled to the eastern end of Betio, and as the night wore on they launched savage counterattacks against the Marine lines. More than 300

Below : On the beach at Tarawa. A heavily-laden squad of Marines moves off to attack Japanese positions around the airstrip.

died in savage hand-to-hand combat with the Marines.

By noon of the fourth day, 23 November 1943, it was all over. Betio was in American hands. The cost had been 1027 Marines dead or presumed dead and over 2200 wounded. On the other hand, only 17 Japanese were still alive on Betio, great numbers committing suicide by placing the muzzles of their rifles in their mouths and pulling the triggers with their toes rather than surrender. The remainder of Admiral Shibasaki's defenders and civilian construction workers on Tarawa—4700 in number—were dead. Makin and Tarawa Atolls were secure for the continuation of the trans-Pacific offensive.

Betio had been a hard lesson for the Marines and the American military commanders in the Pacific, and the military was flooded with condemnatory articles and letters when the pictures of the carnage and the casualty figures were released back home. But the military profited greatly by the bloody experience. More and better

Above: Crew of an LST opens the bow doors to allow the Marine LVTs to disembark for the assault landing on Roi, 1 February 1944.

LVTs would be produced for future operations and UDT (underwater demolition teams) would precede landings to clear obstacles for the landing craft from now on. The military also learned that massed artillery shelling and bombing would not destroy pillboxes and blockhouses. Tests conducted subsequent to the Tarawa experience proved that rockets and high-angle armor-piercing shells from naval guns alone would do the job. These and other lessons were not only learned but also applied as the Pacific war continued. In this sense, the Marine victims of Tarawa had indeed not died in vain.

Taking the Marshall Islands

The Tarawa and Makin campaigns caused no sidetracking of the drive to the west. On 1 February 1944, covered by a vast naval armada, American Forces stormed ashore in the Marshall Islands southwest of Hawaii and on the line to the Philippines. The newly-formed 4th Marine Division took the islands of Roi and Namur containing the main Japanese air base in the Marshalls at

Above : Seabees and Marines aboard an LVT wait for the order to land, 2 February 1944, Roi island.
Below, main picture : Marine reinforcements land on the Marshalls on the second day of the operation.

Above: Admiral Kelly Turner, naval commander of the Kwajalein landings and numerous other Marine operations of the Pacific War.

the northern tip of Kwajalein Atoll. At the same time the 7th Army Division attacked Kwajalein Island at the southern tip of the atoll. And simultaneously Majuro Atoll was taken without resistance by Army units, to be used as a base for the American Navy and its fast carrier task forces. By 4 February the central Marshalls had been taken with only slightly more than 300 lives lost. New, more heavily-armored LVTs (Amtracs) carried the troops to shore, better naval and air firepower made destruction of the enemy's fortifications more complete, and command ships stationed offshore with failsafe communications systems controlled the action without interruption. The Tarawa experience was not repeated.

Because the Kwajalein landings had gone so smoothly, Admiral Nimitz decided to send the assaulting troops directly 300 miles farther to the northwest. Marshalls and specifically to Eniwetok Atoll, site of an important Japanese base and an excellent lagoon for a naval anchorage, but not before the Navy's fast carriers had punished the Japanese naval bastion at Truk in the eastern Carolines 770 miles away with two days and one night of punishing bombing raids. Forty-one ships and 200 Japanese planes were destroyed in the raids, and the fear of Japanese interference from Truk vanished. On Eniwetok, however, the soldiers of the 106th Infantry and 27th Division and the Marines of the 22nd Regiment who landed on 17 February found that the Japanese defenders had to be 'dug out' yard by yard despite the 'softening up' by artillery and bombing that had preceded their landings. Still, two of the principal islands fell to the Marines in four days, while the Army's campaign against Eniwetok Island itself ended early in March. The remainder of the Marshalls fell or were bypassed with little difficulty. The Americans suffered less than 600 killed. The sacrifices of Tarawa had indeed begun to pay immediate dividends for the Marines and soldiers who continued the Pacific war.

Below: General Holland Smith, pointing, commander of the Marine landing force in the Kwajalein operation.

Fight for the Marianas

By June 1944 the American Military Forces were moving toward their next objective in the long road back across the Central Pacific; the Marianas Islands with their crucial island of Guam containing air bases and a superb harbor. Not only would the taking of the wooded and mountainous Marianas put them only 1500 miles east of the Philippines and only 1300 miles southeast of Japan itself, but also it would cut Japanese supply lines to the south (further isolating the great Japanese base at Truk in the eastern Carolines) and put their home islands within range of the Army Air Force's new long-range B-29 bombers. Reclaiming Guam would also represent a great moral victory as the island had fallen to the Japanese in the first days of the war. Retaking Guam from the occupying Japanese would be the first liberation of American territory in the Pacific.

Above: Marines of the 2nd Division dig in on the beach on Saipan on the first day of the landings.

Admiral Chester W Nimitz, commander of the Pacific Theater, decided that the islands of Saipan and Tinian to the north of Guam should be taken first. This would cut off Japanese air defense to Guam when that island was invaded three days later. Saipan was garrisoned by over 25,000 troops well dug in on the 15-by-5-mile island dominated by 1500-foot Mount Tapotchau at the center. Assigned to take it were three Marine divisions (the 2nd, 3rd and 4th), one Marine brigade, and the Army's 27th Division. The invasion plans called for the 2nd and 4th Marines to land on 15 June on the southwest coast, the 2nd turning left to assault Mount Tapotchau, the 4th racing across the island to Islito Airfield. The amphibious assault that bright and clear day did not go well as the Navy had not sufficiently softened up the landing area and the amtracs with the assault troops came under furious and deadly Japanese fire. More than 2000 casualties were suffered. Still, 20,000 Marines made it ashore and

Above : A wounded Marine is given treatment by a Navy corpsman on the beach at Namur, Kwajalein Atoll.
Left : Marines land on Aur Atoll in the Marshalls in April 1944. The atoll was in fact undefended by the Japanese.

that night held off the first of many suicide attacks launched by the Japanese. But if the initial landings were not reinforced, the soldiers and Marines would be in serious trouble on Saipan.

At this point the Navy came to the rescue by beating off a major Japanese attempt to disrupt the invasion of the Marianas. In what came to be known as the Battle of the Philippine Sea, Admiral Raymond Spruance and the Fifth Fleet intercepted the First Mobile Fleet under Vice Admiral Jisaburo Ozawa west of the Marianas and decimated it. Much of the glory rightly fell to the naval air crews who met the Japanese carrier plane onslaught west of Saipan on the first day in what soon came to be called 'the Great Marianas Turkey Shoot.' On the second day they pursued the Japanese fleet and inflicted even more damage. By the time it was over, the Americans had lost 130 planes and 76 of their crewmen, but the Japanese had lost almost 400 carrier planes, dozens of land-based airplanes from Guam, and three aircraft carriers. The Japanese carrier navy had been effectively destroyed in two days of furious combat. But this epic naval battle also meant that the Japanese defenders on Saipan would not be relieved. American efforts to dislodge them continued until all were wiped out. This proved to be a tremendous undertaking.

After eight days of fighting, the southern end of Saipan was in American hands, but the enemy forces on Mount Tapotchau and the northern end of the island remained to be subdued. As the 2nd Marines swung left to assault the mountain, the 4th Marines

Above : Marine Major General Harry Schmidt, left, Navy Under Secretary Forrestal and Admiral Spruance inspect the newly-captured base at Kwajalein.

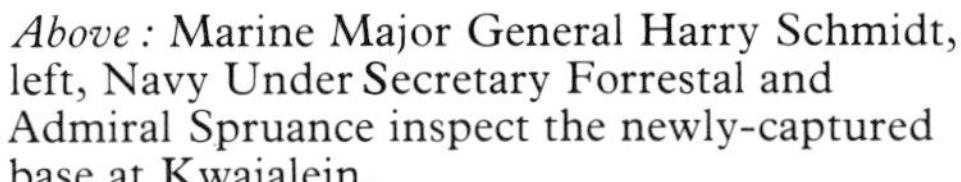

swung out and then left to move up the far side of the island. The 27th Division was in the middle. When the Army units in the center could not keep up and threatened the two flanking movements, General 'Howlin' Mad' Smith demanded and received the dismissal of the Army's Major General Ralph Smith—with whom he had clashed on Makin for his dilatory approach to war—and the Army began to move.

By 6 July the sweep to the north was succeeding with Mount Tapotchau taken and the Japanese holding only the northern third of the island. Facing defeat, Admiral Chuichi Nagumo, commander of the carrier forces at Pearl Harbor, loser at the Battle of Midway, and now naval commander on Saipan, shot himself with a pistol. Lieutenant General Yoshitsugu Saito, commanding the Japanese Army forces, sliced himself in the stomach with a samurai sword; then an aide shot him in the back of the head. But before his ritualistic suicide, Saito had issued a message to his troops to follow him to glory against the enemy. They did so the next morning more than 2500 Japanese staged a massive banzai attack against the Americans. Their fanatical attack rolled forward against the 27th Division in particular. The Americans used every weapon available to stop them, including 105mm howitzers. When it was over, mounds of Japanese bodies lay in front of the American lines.

Still the carnage was not ended. Even though the Americans declared the island secure on 9 July, in the days that followed hundreds of Japanese civilians committed suicide at Marpi Point at the northernmost point of the island by throwing first their children, then themselves, off the 800-foot ledge into the sea. Hundreds of Japanese soldiers joined them despite repeated Japanese-language loudspeaker messages that captives would be treated well and would not be tortured and killed, as the military commanders had told them. Some of the soldiers jumped into the sea; others pulled the pins from grenades and held them against their bellies. Over 29,000 Japanese died on Saipan as war casualties or suicides before it was over. The Americans had also paid the price in blood with over 16,000 casualties, of whom over 3400 were killed in action. But the significance of the American victory on this island of blood was not lost on the Japanese government and its military; many were now sure the war was lost.

Tinian, just three-and-a-half miles to the south of Saipan, was the next objective because it contained three Japanese airfields. But while Tinian was fairly flat (unlike Saipan), it had a high rocky coastline well fortified with coastal batteries. The only break in the forbidding coastal wall was in front of Tinian Town on the southwest corner, but this area had been heavily fortified by the Japanese. To land there would mean very heavy casualties. Accordingly, the military commanders decided to land between the jagged coral cliffs on the northwest corner of the island through two gaps in their rugged face. These were undefended, but if the Japanese discovered that this was the landing site, the whole invasion might well fail as the tiny gaps in the coral cliffs could be easily plugged by the Japanese. Therefore, to allow the invasion a chance of success, on 24 July the invasion fleet containing the 2nd Marine

Above : Marines employ a captured Japanese mountain gun during the battle for Saipan.
Above right : A Navy corpsman gives aid to wounded Marines on 7 July 1944 during the last stages of the fighting on Saipan.
Right : A Marine flamethrowing tank attacks a Japanese pill box on Saipan. The vehicle is a modified version of the Stuart light tank.

Division appeared off Tinian Town, bombardment began, and the amtracs began moving toward shore. But instead of landing, they only milled about, convincing the Japanese that their shore batteries had discouraged any landing. Meanwhile, 15,000 Marines of the 4th Marine Division landed and made their way through the openings on the northwest corner and established a firm perimeter. When the Japanese reacted that evening, it was too late. With the 2nd Marines following them ashore, the Leathernecks of the 4th Marines were able to fend off their counterattacks, inflicting over 1400 deaths on the attacking Japanese. Within a week the Marines of these two divisions, aided by tanks, swept the island, and Tinian was in American hands.

Guam, 100 miles to the south, was meanwhile being assaulted by Marines and soldiers. On 21 July the 3rd Marine Division landed at Asan on the west coast of the island just below the capital of Agana to swing south and take Apra Harbor, while the 77th Army Division and the 1st Provisional Marine Brigade landed at Agat to the south to swing north to entrap the Japanese defenders on the Orote Peninsula where the main Japanese airfield was located. Progress away from the landing sites was agonizingly slow, but by 25 July Orote Peninsula had been cut off. That night, after apparently becoming thoroughly drunk to carry out their suicide mission of breaking out, the Japanese made a savage attack on the

Americans hemming them in. Carrying conventional weapons, bottles and even baseball bats, they assaulted the American lines. Artillery was ordered to fire directly into the charging lines of Japanese; they died in mounding clusters until the survivors fled back onto the peninsula. That same night a more carefully planned Japanese attack confronted the 3rd Marines to the north. Slipping through gaps in the American lines, the Japanese soldiers made a strenuous attempt to reach the beachhead. After desperate hand-to-hand fighting, the Marines repulsed the attack, but not until 3500 Japanese had paid with their lives. These were the last major actions on the valuable island.

Fighting went on for two more weeks, but the American hold on Guam was never seriously threatened. Many Japanese fled into the hills and hid out for months—and even years—thereafter, but by now Guam was securely in American hands, Saipan was being prepared as a major base for long-range bombers, and Truk to the southeast was cut off from support. The Americans could now look to the reconquest of the Philippines.

Above : Marines on the beach at Saipan. In the background a Buffalo amtrac modified to give fire support to the landing force.

Bloody Peleliu

Yet one obstacle remained. The Palau Islands, part of the western Carolines and 500 miles east of Mindanao in the southern Philippines, would stand astride the American left flank as it moved toward the Philippines. They would also threaten MacArthur's right flank as he moved northward toward the same goal. Some military planners, notably Admiral William F Halsey, argued that the islands should be bypassed as they represented no great danger to either movement. But Admiral Chester W Nimitz insisted that the Palaus be taken, and plans were made accordingly. Little did anyone know that the taking of Peleliu Island in the chain would rank in blood with Tarawa. Over 1200 Marines and 277 soldiers would die and another 6200 would be wounded before the island was taken after six weeks of fighting. Over 10,000 Japanese soldiers and civilians would also taste death in the carnage on Peleliu.

Peleliu is the major island in the Palau group. The whole is enclosed by a giant coral reef. Peleliu itself is an elongated island six miles by two. At its southern end was located the Japanese airfield. North of the airfield lay Umurbrogol Ridge, its mountainous spine making its way to the northern extremity of the island. The formidable ridge was honeycombed with coral caves. These old mining caves had been enlarged and perfected to aid and protect the defenders. Some of them had sliding steel doors behind which artillery pieces were hidden; after the guns fired their rounds, the doors could be slid closed so that they could neither be seen nor destroyed. All of the caves were well stocked with food and ammunition. The 10,000 Japanese troops on the island knew they could give the American invaders more than their money's worth. They were also under orders not to engage in pointless suicide attacks, but, rather, they were to try to contain the Americans on the beaches. If this was not possible, they were to pull back to defense lines from which mortar and artillery fire could enfilade the invaders. Furthermore,

Below : Fighting in Garapan village, Saipan, on 23 June 1944. The village was not completely captured until 2 July.

Above: During the fighting on Peleliu in September 1944, a Marine is picked off by a Japanese sniper.

troops about to be overrun were not to kill themselves, but were to remain hidden to strike the enemy from the rear after they passed. Lieutenant General Sadae Inoue, the overall commander in the Palaus, and Colonel Kunio Nakagawa, commanding on Peleliu, would not repeat the useless bloodletting of Saipan. They were determined to attain victory by stealth and effective military tactics.

The three-day preliminary air and naval bombardment of Peleliu was considered thorough and protracted. Little remained above ground near the landing area on the southwest coast of the island. The Navy was more than satisfied, yet the underground fortifications so carefully constructed by the Japanese had hardly been touched. The initial landings by the 1st Marine Division on the beaches west of the airfield on 15 September 1944 seemed easy, but as the Japanese emerged from their caves and began to pour mortar, artillery and machine gun fire on the waves of Marines, amtracs were hit and Leathernecks began to die by the score. Nor could the Navy support vessels help as their artillery could not penetrate the steel doors behind which the Japanese artillery was prepared to fire before emerging to rain its hellish fire on the Marines below on the beach. The Marines were able to hold the beach, but that was all.

Company K of the 1st Marine Regiment commanded by Colonel Lewis B 'Chesty' Puller was having a particularly difficult time at the north end of the beachhead because of furious fire coming from a Japanese emplacement on a rocky point of land that became famous that day, as afterwards, simply as 'the Point.' Dozens of men were dying and hundreds were taking wounds from five concrete pillboxes and a maze of trenches on that small stretch of land. Within two hours less than 30 men were still alive and unwounded from two entire platoons, but 'the Point' was being taken by the gutsy Marines. They gradually put the pillboxes out of action in the only way possible: crawling up to them through withering machine gun fire and throwing grenades through their firing slits. Still the left flank was in danger, so Puller threw up a defense line in case the Japanese counter attacked, for if this line was gapped the whole beachhead would be in danger.

The next crucial sector for the Marines, however, emerged at the airfield. At five o'clock in the afternoon hundreds of Japanese infantrymen emerged from beyond the airfield and began to move toward the Marine positions carefully and deliberately, taking cover where they could. This was no banzai attack but a well thought-out movement, for behind the infantry came tanks, over a dozen of them. Moving quickly through their infantry, they made straight for the lines of the 5th Marine Regiment. The charging Japanese tanks were stopped only by the appearance of a dozen more-heavily armed and armored Marine Sherman tanks that rumbled onto the airstrip to open fire on their Imperial counterparts. The Shermans and a Navy dive bomber stopped the Japanese charge, but it had been too close for comfort, and many Marines had died in desperate efforts to hold the center of the line. The airfield was still in American hands and the Japanese soldiers to the south of the airstrip had

Below: Marine landing craft drive ashore during the assault on Peleliu covered by the prelanding bombardment.

meanwhile been cut off by the 7th Marine Regiment. Yet the Japanese were far from finished on Peleliu.

Colonel Nakagawa decided at this point to withdraw his troops to the protecting caves and pillboxes on Umurbrogol Ridge. Since the 5th Marines had moved across the airfield toward the eastern side of the island and the 7th Marines were still cleaning out the Japanese from the southern tip of the island, it was up to Puller's 1st Marine Regiment to take on Nakagawa and his troops in their impregnable bastion, by now all but denuded of vegetation by gunfire and bombing but presenting a bloody challenge to his decimated forces as they faced artillery and mortar fire seemingly without end. On 17 September Puller's Marines began making their way up the coral ridges—'Horseshoe,' 'Death Valley,' and other deathtraps—that formed the mountainous stronghold. They were aided by naval gunfire, tanks, and bazookas. Cave after cave on the rocky mountainside was cleaned out the first day, only to be lost the next by a furious counterattack. Three days later, after more furious fighting on what the Corps came to call 'Bloody Nose Ridge,' Puller's 1st Marine Regiment had sustained 1700 casualties in the six days of fighting since the landings. Nor could the 7th Marine Regiment make any progress against the Japanese defenders when it relieved the battered 1st Marines on 20 September.

At this point units of the Army's 81st Division were moved onto the island. Then the 5th Marines swung back to the left of Umurbrogol and, covered by accurate naval gunfire, moved along the narrow west coast of the island. Utilizing their tanks and amtrac-mounted flamethrowers, they forced their way through and took the northern section of the island, then turned to assault Umurbrogol from the rear. Gradually the 321st Army Combat Team, the 5th Marines, and the 7th Marines moved in to surround, then work their way up, the formidable slopes of the forbidding ridge spining its way along Peleliu. Yard by yard the soldiers and Marines crawled their way up Umurbrogol, neutralizing pillboxes by flamethrowers, grenades and TNT as they went. By late October more Army troops had replaced the 5th and 7th Marines, but still the battle continued. Only after another full month of fighting was the cave-ridden citadel that was Umurbrogol finally taken by the Army. Only 700 of Colonel Nakagawa's 6500 men were still alive by that time. It had taken almost 1600 rounds of light and heavy ordnance to kill each of Nakagawa's 5800 men who died on Peleliu in 1944. The 1st Marines had sustained over 6000 casualties. Whatever glory the Marines—and their

Above: Explosions aboard the escort carrier *St Lo* after a kamikaze hit.
Below: The Battle of Leyte Gulf. The American escort carriers come under surface attack from Kurita's battleships.

Army compatriots—had gained on Peleliu they wanted to forget. Peleliu, along with Tarawa, stands even today as a gory lesson in the wretched warfare as it was fought in the Pacific coral islands on the way to eventual victory over the determined Japanese. After the savagery of Peleliu, it was imperative that the assaulting Marines be allowed to rest and refit before continuing the job they had been trained to do.

Marine Air in the Philippines

The reconquest of the Philippines was basically carried out by the Army. However, General MacArthur, the Southwest Pacific Theater commander, making his way up the northern shore of New Guinea in preparation for this return to his beloved Philippine Islands, requested and received the aid of the 1st Marine Aircraft Wing (1st MAW) for his landings in the archipelago. The 1st MAW, in turn, received from MacArthur's air commander, Lieutenant General George C Kenney, permission to assist the land forces by close air support and began training in the Solomons for this mission.

The 1st Marine Air Wing was not called into action initially as the American forces

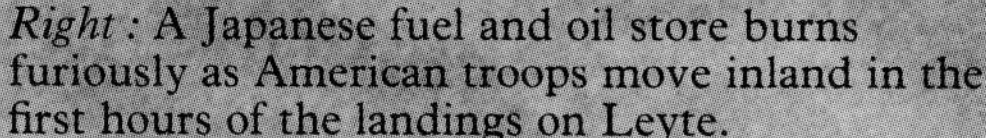

Right: A Japanese fuel and oil store burns furiously as American troops move inland in the first hours of the landings on Leyte.

Right: Brewster Buffalo fighter aircraft in flight. The Buffalo served with Marine units in the early part of the war.

bypassed the landings on the island of Mindanao in the south and struck instead at Leyte in the center of the archipelago on 20 October 1944 as a preliminary to the main attack on Luzon to the north. However, the massive Japanese naval surface raid on the American invasion fleet known as the Battle of Leyte Gulf from 23–26 October and the *kamikaze* suicide raids on the fleet convinced MacArthur that more land-based air cover was absolutely necessary, and early in December the 1st MAW got the call to hurry to the Philippines from the Solomons.

The Marine dive bomber and fighter crews who reported to Leyte had their skills tested in the weeks that followed. They flew against Japanese reinforcements on the sea, flew night fighter cover for the Navy, and supported ground operations with verve. In ground support operations they demonstrated their skill at extremely low level bombing runs, a skill the Army Air Force was forced to emulate. When the Army moved on to attack the main Philippine island of Luzon in early January 1945 the Marine flyers were there, providing air cover for the Navy and striking Japanese bases both on Luzon and on Formosa to the north. In carrying out their close air support missions here, the Marines also taught their Army and Navy brethren a new technique in air support tactics. They utilized air liaison parties (ALPs) in radio-equipped jeeps with the ground units to direct air strikes with great precision, thereby assuring greater striking power with less chance of hitting friendly troops. The Army was quick to pick up the Marine innovation, and the use of ALPs became standard practice in the conquest of the remainder of the Philippines. The seven Marine squadrons on Luzon flew almost half of all sorties against the enemy between late January and April 1945 although they represented less than 15 percent of American aircraft available in the area.

Below: A Marine lieutenant briefs his platoon before the landings on Iwo Jima. The unit is from the 4th Marine Division.

Above : Men of the 5th Division in a forward position facing the Japanese defenses on Mount Suribachi.
Below right : The battle for Iwo Jima.

By March 1945, with Luzon gradually being cleared of Japanese, most of the Marine air units were shifted to the southern Philippines where they assisted the 8th Army and the Filipino guerrillas on Mindiano in clearing out the Japanese from that island. In this operation the Marines flew an excess of 10,000 sorties between March and July and again demonstrated their proficiency in close air support. Eventually all of the Philippines were brought back under American and Filipino control, and ALP-directed close air support had come to stay in the Pacific war. The Marines had made a valuable contribution to the liberation of the Philippines and to saving the lives of thousands of assault troops as the fighting wore on in the summer of 1945 with the Americans moving ever closer to the Japanese home islands.

Eight Square Miles of Hell: Iwo Jima

As the conquest of the Philippines was being carried out, military planners turned away from Formosa as the next possible target and decided, instead, to move north to Iwo Jima in the Bonin Islands and to Okinawa in the Ryukyus. From there the Japanese home islands would be within flying range of medium bombers, and Okinawa would be used as the staging area for the invasion of Japan. Furthermore, Iwo Jima was the site of two Japanese airfields with another being built which had to be taken, and the island would also be valuable as a base for fighter planes to escort the long-range B-29 'superfortresses' on their attacks on Japan from the Marianas. Iwo Jima was almost half way between the Marianas and Japan, being 650 miles from each. The invasion of Iwo Jima was set for 19 February 1945.

It would be hard to imagine a worse death-trap for an invading force than 'Iwo.' The small volcanic island of less than eight square miles was shaped like a porkchop with its tip to the south. At that tip Mount Suribachi rose 600 feet into the air, dominating the sandy beaches below. North of the southern coastal plain crowned by Suribachi rose the Motoyama Plateau, anchored at each end by cliffs dropping to the sea. Given the layout of the forbidding island, the landing would have to come at the south, Suribachi would have to be taken, and then the Marines of the assaulting V Amphibious Corps would have to work their way up Motoyama Plateau, blasting out the Japanese defenders as they went. And 21,000 Japanese troops, well dug in in over a thousand caves and well supplied with tanks, artillery and ammunition, were waiting. On Suribachi and the Motoyama Plateau the Japanese also had hundreds of concrete blockhouses. The Japanese commander, Lieutenant General Tadamichi Kuribayashi, had been fortifying his island for eight months and now ordered his troops to fight in place until death, killing as many Marines as they could. They succeeded. Before the fighting was over, more than 26,000 Marines had been killed or wounded —along with almost 3000 naval personnel—

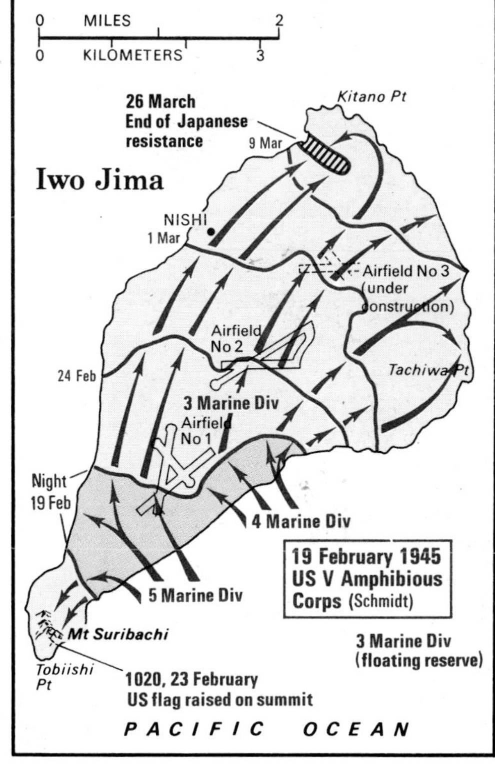

Above : General Holland Smith (nearer) and Admiral Kelly Turner during the Iwo Jima campaign.
Right : Marine wiremen at work on telephone lines leading up to the front.

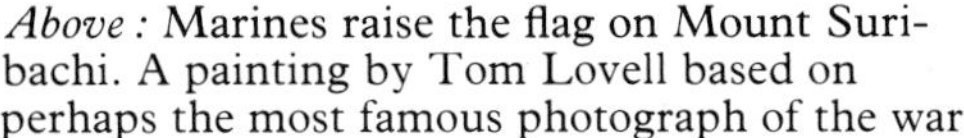

Above : Marines raise the flag on Mount Suribachi. A painting by Tom Lovell based on perhaps the most famous photograph of the war.

on the volcanic scrub wastes of the tiny island.

The Marines' 70,000-man assault force under General Holland M Smith, the V Amphibious Force, was made up of units of the veteran 3rd and 4th Marine Divisions and the newly-formed but veteran-packed 5th Marine Division. Learning their lessons from the cave warfare of Peleliu, the Marines had with them a large stock of bazookas, flamethrowers and flamethrower tanks, plus demolition teams. But first the landings had to take place on the south-eastern shore of the island. The 4th and 5th Marine Divisions were assigned to make the landings with the 3rd Marines in reserve. Both would wheel to the north to assault Motoyama Plateau while the 28th Marine Regiment would take Mount Suribachi. This would mean that initially almost 50,000 Marines would be packed onto the small beachhead under the noses of Japanese gunners on Suribachi and the Plateau, but geography determined there was no other choice. The Marines would have to land and fight their way to their objectives as best they could since naval gunfire could do little against the blockhouse and cave defenses fashioned by the Japanese.

On the morning of 19 February the Marines in amtracs and landing boats moved toward the forbidding shore not knowing that preliminary bombing and shelling had knocked out only 17 of the more than 730 major defense installations on the island. The Japanese held their fire until the Marines began to crowd onto the beaches. Then all hell broke loose. Artillery and mortar fire began to decimate the Marine ranks almost at will. By nightfall over 2000 casualties had been sustained, and the beachhead was an incredible scene of crowding and confusion. There was no place to go on the beaches tangled with men, equipment, tanks and the mangled bodies of Marines blown into fragments by the withering Japanese fire. The surviving Marines dug in where they were, and the next morning began moving yard by yard into the interior, taking casualties in horrifying numbers as they ran and crawled forward against the enemy. Four days of slogging death were required before Mount Suribachi had been assaulted and the defenders wiped out. On 23 February patrols of the 28th Marine Regiment made it to the top of Mount Suribachi and raised a small American flag in

Below : Marines use explosives against Japanese positions near the foot of Mount Suribachi. Explosive charges were often the only way to attack the Japanese dugouts.

victory. Soon thereafter another patrol reached the summit of Suribachi; its Marines had with them a larger flag taken from an LST. This second flag-raising, dramatically captured for all time by an Associated Press photographer, became an overnight inspiration to the Corps and to the American nation and lives today as the most famous symbol of the Marines and their victories in the Pacific.

But at the moment the hard-pressed Marines on Iwo Jima had more important things to do than consider the symbolism of a flag-raising. The heights of the Motoyama Plateau had to be taken. On the Leathernecks went, moving up the face of the rise, sustaining appalling casualties with Marine blood flowing into the black volcanic dirt as they made their way forward. Of one 900-man battalion making the assault up the face of the plateau of death, only 150 were neither killed nor wounded in the hard fighting. For two more agonizing weeks the Marines clawed their way up the face of the plateau. Flamethrowers, grenades, TNT and air strikes were their constant companions as they blasted the Japanese defenders from their caves and blockhouses one by one. Marine artillery battalions pounded the Japanese positions around the clock. Before the main enemy lines had been penetrated and the high ground had been seized on 10 March, almost 13,000 Marines had been killed or wounded. Yet the fighting and dying continued as the Marines worked their way north to clear the tiny island of its stubborn defenders. Almost all of the island's 21,000 Japanese troops died in place as ordered. By the time the island was declared secure and the mangled remains of the 3rd, 4th and 5th Marine Divisions were pulled out on 16 March, 6000 Marines and Navy doctors and corpsmen had paid with their lives and another 20,000 had been wounded in taking the tiny chunk of volcanic Pacific real estate.

The ration between casualties taken to casualties inflicted on the enemy on Iwo had been the highest ratio ever recorded in the history of the Marine Corps. As Admiral Nimitz later remarked regarding the Marines on Iwo Jima, 'uncommon valor was a common virtue,' and 22 Marines received Congressional Medals of Honor for heroism—12 of the awards were presented posthumously—during the month-long campaign. This was more than a quarter of the total awarded to Marines during the course of World War II. The Marine Corps, in the face of determined resistance, had written one of the most glorious chapters in its proud history on tiny but crucial Iwo Jima in February and March 1945.

Okinawa: The Last Battle

Okinawa, the 60-mile-long major island in the Ryukyus chain and only 360 miles from Japan, was the next obvious target. While air units pounded the airfields and harbors of Japan, Formosa and the Ryukyus from the fast carrier task forces and land bases in the western Pacific in preparation for the invasion, a vast naval armada of more than 1200 vessels assembled for the landings. More than 183,000 men organized into the US Tenth Army (made up of the XXIV Army Corps and the III Marine Amphibious Corps) were gathered and prepared for the massive operation against the island and its 100,000 defenders. The Marine segment included the 1st, 2nd and 6th Marine Divisions. Several Marine air groups and squadrons were included in the covering Tactical Air Force. After the Okinawa beaches and airfields had been pounded for a full week, on 1 April 1945 the landing force of soldiers and Marines left their ships and headed for the Hagushi beaches on the southwest coast of the island north of the city of Naha. Almost 90,000 Marines were in a second landing force that made a feint at the southeastern beaches on the opposite side of the island and then landed at Hagushi.

Initially all went very well as Japanese resistance over the beach and island was light. Within four days the island had been split, and the 6th Marines moved northward while the Army moved south. On the basis of the light resistance encountered thus far, all dared to hope for an easy campaign, but the Japanese were prepared to defend Okinawa to the last man in a protracted war of attrition, particularly on the southern third of the island. Forcing the Tenth Army to bleed for Okinawa while their *kamikaze* attacks decimated the Fifth Fleet might well convince the Americans not to invade the home islands. At the least, the Japanese defenders would delay the invasion for a considerable length of time. They were prepared to concede the beachhead and to fight a delaying action in the north, but from that point on the Americans on Okinawa and with the fleet offshore would pay dearly for their efforts to dislodge them from their last bastion of resistance.

As the 6th Marine Division moved north it ran into the Japanese positions on the hilly Motobu Peninsula. Particularly difficult to assault was a hill complex known as Yae Take. The 4th and 29th Marine Regiments were finally able to take the hilly region by 20 April, but only at the cost of almost 1000 casualties. For the next week the Marines moved across the northern end of the island until all effective Japanese resistance had been ended.

The Japanese commander was determined that the southern third of Okinawa would be defended to the death. He had established an entire series of defensive positions across the island from west to east. The main defensive line began at Naha on the west, stretched across the heights of Shuri town and castle towards the center, and anchored itself around Yonabaru on the eastern shore. Fortified caves and emplacements on both the forward and reverse slopes of the ridges of the defensive line, complemented by limestone cliffs and ridges, constituted the Japanese defenses. During the first two weeks of April the American soldiers and Marines flung themselves against the Japanese line. Their three-division strength failed to crack it, and the Japanese even counterattacked on 12–14 April. So badly was the fighting going and so high were the casualty counts that the military commanders considered bypassing the Naha-Shuri-Yonabaru line by carrying out another amphibious assault. And in the meantime the Fifth Fleet was undergoing no less than ten large-scale *kamikaze* attacks of almost 1500 planes against their ships and men. These attacks, along with conventional air strikes, eventually sank 30 naval ships, damaged over 300 others, and killed or wounded almost 10,000 American naval personnel. On both land and sea the invasion of Okinawa was going very badly for the American forces. Something had to be done.

The amphibious end run was finally rejected by the military planners, and, instead, the 6th Marine Division from the north and the 1st Marine Division in reserve were thrown into the Naha-Shuri-Yonabaru line. Along with the Army units, they began the slow and bloody advance against the stubborn Japanese defenders in their emplacements. In fighting every bit as ferocious as that of Iwo Jima, the Americans threw massive artillery barrages, naval gunfire bombardments and tons of bombs against the Japanese positions (during the campaign American field artillery fired 1.7 million rounds against the enemy). Usually only flamethrowers and dynamite blasted the defenders from their caves and fortified positions as the Marines and soldiers climbed their way up the hills under machine gun fire and grenade poundings, hugging the ground as they went. The Marines of the 6th Division took tremendous casualties fighting for Sugar Loaf Hill, while the 1st Division did the same in taking Dakeshi Ridge and Wana Ridge. Only during the third week of May did the tide of battle begin to turn. One week later, having lost 50,000 men, the Japanese commander ordered a retreat from the remainder of the fortified positions along the Naha-Shuri-Yonabaru Line. By the end of the month Naha had fallen to the 6th Marine Division, and the 1st Marine Division had broken through near Shuri, although they had to beat off a fierce Japanese counterattack be-

Below: Major General Lemuel Shepherd, commanding the 6th Marine Division, studies a map shortly after the first landings on Okinawa.

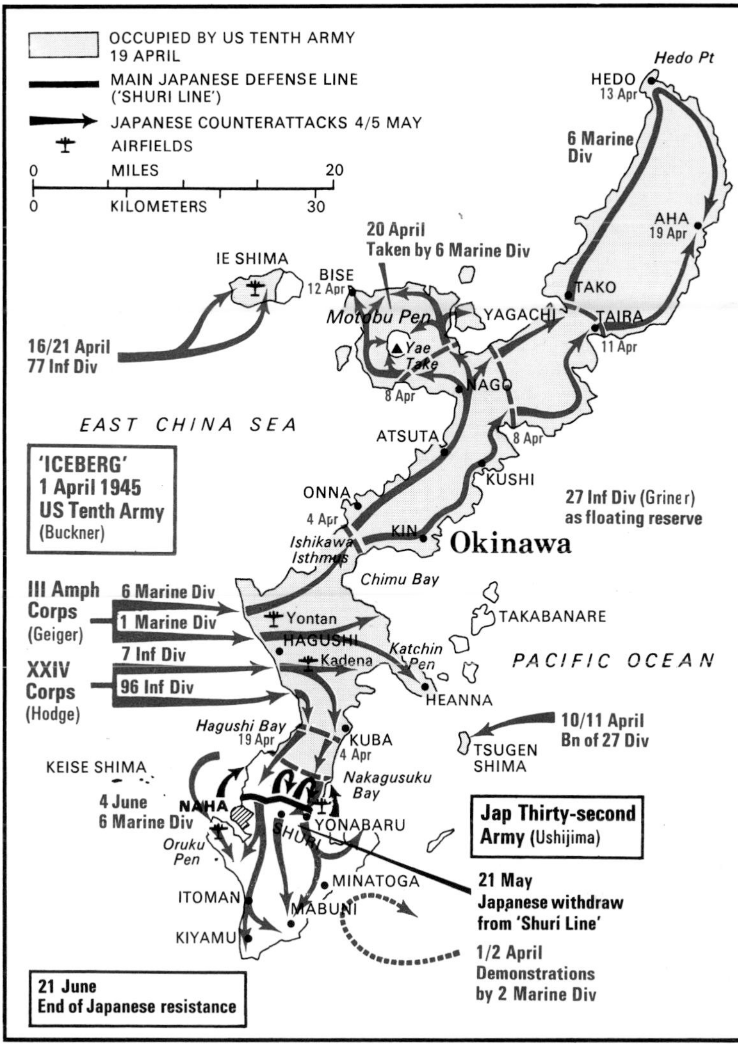

Above : A TEM Avenger bomber on a close support mission over Okinawa in June 1945. *Above right :* Map of the Okinawa campaign. *Right :* Marines close in on a Christian church near the Shuri castle on Okinawa which had been used by Japanese snipers.

fore planting the American flag on Shuri castle. The whole Naha-Shuri-Yonabaru line was in American hands by 31 May, but the Japanese, regrouping to the south, were far from finished as a fighting force even after two months of fighting.

The battles raged on in the south of Okinawa. The 6th Marine Division was given the task of clearing the Oroku Peninsula and its 2000 defenders. It took an amphibious assault and a solid week of bloody fighting before the peninsula fell. Meanwhile the 1st Marine Division was losing over 1000 men in taking Kunishi Ridge to the west. The southern shore of Okinawa was finally reached on 19 June, but mopping up of the remnants of the Japanese defenders continued for a few more days.

The battle for Okinawa was the last for the Marines in World War II. It had extended over 82 agonizing days. More than 100,000 Japanese defenders had died, inflicting over 19,000 casualties on the Marine Corps (including over 3000 dead). The entire US Tenth Army casualty list showed 65,000 killed and wounded, and the Navy had suffered 10,000 casualties. Okinawa, the last campaign, was also by far the bloodiest campaign in the whole Pacific war. And if Japanese defensive efforts on Okinawa were any measure of that nation's willingness to defend itself against an American invasion of the home islands, the American military from the highest general or admiral down to the lowest private on the line knew what to expect when the next assault began, for it would be against Japan itself. Plans were being prepared. The Marines—along with their Army and Navy compatriots—could now look forward to the greatest task of the war, invading Japan and finally ending the long, bloody Pacific conflict with the complete subjugation of the enemy.

But this was not fated to be, for after the dropping of atomic bombs on Hiroshima and Nagasaki the Japanese finally surrendered in August 1945. Unspeakable relief spread over the six divisions of the Fleet Marine Force Pacific when news of the surrender arrived, for three divisions had already begun training for the invasion of Kyushu and the remaining three were scheduled to invade Honshu early in 1946. Now only occupation tasks remained. The Marines' greatest period of testing and valor had come to an end. *Semper Fidelis* had indeed been proved a worthy motto of the Corps, as it had so often before in its proud history.

The Tally

At the end of the war the Marine Corps had in uniform 458,000 officers, men, and women. During the course of World War II more than 669,000 wore the Marine green. These had represented some 5 percent of the total of over 16.3 million Americans who served in the armed forces during the war. From December 1941 until August 1945 some 19,733 Marines had given their lives for the cause of freedom. Another 67,207 had been wounded in action. Theirs had been a Pacific war. Approximately 98 percent of all Marine Corps officers served in the Pacific Theater during the course of the war; 89 percent of the enlisted ranks also served there.

Since the beginning of the conflict the Marines had made 15 landings utilizing six divisions across the broad expanse of the Pacific. The Army had made 26 landings with 18 divisions. Both had fought extremely well in the amphibious landing tactics new to warfare, but the Marines were widely recognized as the amphibious landing specialists. In developing in their mission during the Pacific campaigns, the Marines had developed and utilized new weapons and combat specialties to aid in their tasks. In fighting jungle wars in the South Pacific, atoll warfare in the Central Pacific, and cave warfare on Peleliu, Iwo Jima and Okinawa they had added greater firepower to aid their infantry in the form of bigger and better tanks, armored amphibians and massed artillery. Their air wings had over 2300 confirmed 'kills' to their credit and had created the whole field of modern, accurate close air support for ground troops. Above all, on V-J Day the Marines believed in themselves and their amphibious assault mission. And they believed in themselves as the elite of America's—if not the world's—fighting forces. Yet the postwar world, military planners and politicians were soon to challenge not only the Marine Corps' mission, but even its very existence as a fighting force.

Right: Men of the 15th Regiment (6th Marine Division) are brought up to the front line near Naha on 6 June 1945, Okinawa campaign. *Below:* A Marine photographer explains the workings of one of his cameras to an elderly Okinawan. Many Okinawan civilians believed that they would be mistreated by the Americans.

KOREA AND OTHER CONFLICTS

'Never Shone More Brightly'—1950-1955

During World War II, while the bulk of the Corps was distinguishing itself in the Pacific, Marines in other areas of the world were carrying out duties as couriers, intelligence operatives, support factions in the French and Belgian Resistance, and ships' detachments. Marine officers and advisers served with the British in Europe and the Middle East; other detachments raided the Japanese on the China coast and manned outposts in Cuba, the Virgin Islands, and Ireland. Finally, a group of 256 men and officers were designated combat correspondents, taking typewriters and cameras—along with their rifles—into combat in the Pacific.

Wrapping up

In the months following the end of World War II, Marines of the 4th, 2nd and 5th Marine Divisions debarked in Japan as part of the American occupation forces. Others went to China to repatriate Japanese troops and to try to keep the peace between the forces of the Nationalists and the Communists, warily eyeing one another and waiting for a chance to renew their civil war. Other Marine units were sent to garrison various Pacific islands. But despite these essentially constabulary duties, demobilization was proceeding apace as the American public demanded that the cry of 'bring the boys home' be answered immediately, even though the world situation called for caution in the face of forces released by the changed political situation, especially in Europe where dislocations among nations and peoples scarred the Continent and the power of the Soviet Union hung over Europe's horizon.

By January 1946 the 3rd, 4th and 5th Marine Divisions had been disbanded. By July of that year the Marine Corps had been cut from its wartime strength of 485,000 to only 156,000 officers and men, and more cuts were on the way. In another year the number would only total 92,000. Marine occupation troops were pulled out of Japan in 1946, and the units in China were being drastically cut back.

The Marine Corps survives

The greatest danger to the Corps came not from its cuts in personnel, which, after all, were expected and accepted in the aftermath of the war. The Corps could well live with its reduced numbers. The greatest threats came from the Corps' sister services. The Army wanted to take over all land-based military forces, thus wiping out the Marines' amphibious specialty. The Army leaders argued that amphibious warfare was now obsolete in the wake of the atomic bomb. Who would the Marines land against anyway, when threat of atomic destruction would force any aggressors back to the path of peace? And any land actions could well be handled by the Army. On the other hand, the Army Air Force, believing in the absolute supremacy of air power in the modern age, not only wanted to be an independent service but also was determined to take over all military air functions. This would wipe out the Navy's carrier-based air arm as well as the Marine Corps' carrier- and land-based units.

In order to protect itself and also to illustrate that fast assault tactics were not only practical but necessary, the Marine Corps began to develop the idea of using helicopters for swift envelopment tactics. They could come in from the sea by air rather than over the water. What would later be called 'vertical assault' tactics were thus born in the cauldron of necessity as the Marines faced the possibility of extinction from the Army and the Air Force and wondered at times whether or not it would be sacrificed to the Navy's determination to keep its air power even if something else—like its Marines—had to go.

Defense of the Marine Corps and its missions lay more in the political realm than in redefining and refining its missions in a highly complex world of unrest among the great superpowers and the restive lesser powers. Utilizing its best manpower available to make a case for itself; superb public relations abilities in the person of its Commandant, General Alexander A Vandegrift; and its political friends on Capitol Hill—and after two years of serious political infighting by the various services through their friends in Congress—the Marine Corps and the Navy won their battles. The National Defense Act of 1947 specifically stated that the Navy would retain its air wings and the Marine Corps would remain as a separate and distinct service as a branch of the Navy.

The Corps had won its right to exist with its prescribed missions recognized in law. Its greatest postwar challenge had been met. Its number continued to decline as a result of Congressional budget-cutting (by June

Previous page: Marine 105mm howitzer in action near Chinchon-ni, Korea, on 15 April 1951.
Right: Mao Tse-tung (second from left) and other Chinese Communist leaders in discussion with American officials during the US Government's unsuccessful attempts to mediate.
Below: General Marshall with Communist and Nationalist leaders at Yenan in April 1946.

1950 only 75,000 men and women wore the green and only 28,000 were with the Fleet Marine Force on station and combat ready), but the US Marine Corps was capable of expansion on land, at sea, and in the air.

Portents in North China

After the armistice, the civil war in China heated up, Communist forces beginning to gain the upper hand over the Nationalists. In 1945 Marines occupied four key cities in North China, including Peking. They were there not to fight the Communists but rather to maintain order and commerce, and to help in repatriating the Japanese. Nationalist forces began deploying in the area as General George C Marshall, President Truman's ambassador-at-large, tried unsuccessfully to bring the factions to the bargaining table.

Then in 1946 the Communists commenced a program of sabotage and harrassment which clearly endangered the widely-separated US Marine units. As was expected, it was not long before the Marines found bullets flying in their direction. It happened first on 29 July of that year, when a convoy heading for Peking was ambushed. A brisk firefight ensued in which the 40-man Marine escort suffered 16

Below: Men of the Chinese Communist 8th Route Army ready to welcome General Marshall shortly before his arrival in Yenan in April 1946.

casualties, including four killed, before getting away.

There followed a series of incidents in which Marines were attacked by Chinese Communists. The last major incident came near Tangku; an American supply depot was raided by 350 Communists, who were after ammunition. The small detachment drove them away, but not before five Marines had been killed and 16 wounded.

When the capital of Manchuria fell to the Communists in November 1948, the Nationalist cause was clearly in serious trouble. The Marines were withdrawn in May of 1949; but it was not to be long before they and the Communist Chinese were meeting again over the barrels of guns.

The price of unpreparedness

The United States had no combat forces in Korea when units of the North Korean Peoples Army (NKPA) struck across the 38th Parallel at 0400 hours on 25 June 1950, a rainy Sunday morning in Korea. It was the first Saturday afternoon of summer in Washington, where time is 14 hours earlier than in Korea and Japan. President Harry Truman had gone to his home in Independence, Missouri, for a brief vacation. After dismantling the greatest war machine in history, Americans felt smugly secure in the knowledge that any future war involving the US would be quickly terminated by the newly organized USAF's B-29s carrying atomic bombs.

The reality was that the condition of the US military, as described by General Matthew Ridgway, was one of 'shameful unpreparedness.' The United States had only 12 combat divisions, including two Marine Corps divisions, and only the US 1st Army Division in Europe was at full strength. Four US Army divisions were on duty in Japan as occupation forces, manned mainly by young recruits short on training, experience and physical condition.

US Marine Corps strength, which was at 485,113 at the end of World War II, had been whittled to 74,279 on the eve of hostilities in Korea. After World War II popular sentiment was against a large standing military establishment. And there was an eagerness, as after World War I, to trim the federal budget by skeletonizing the military. In his *A Brief History of the 10th Marines*, Major David N Bruckner notes that in the autumn of 1946 the unit had been reduced to 17 officers and 115 enlisted men. The total complement of a 4.5-inch Rocket Battery consisted of a captain, a sergeant major and a corporal. By the end of the year the manpower of the battery had been cut to one master sergeant.

The US had provided the Republic of Korea (ROK) army with several hundred members of a Korean Military Advisory Group (KMAG), scattered about South Korea for training a defensive force of about 70,000 men, including a Coast Guard. The ROK forces were equipped with about 90 105-mm howitzers plus some halftracks and scout cars. Many of the ROK officers had been given commissions for political reasons. Most could not speak English and few of the KMAG personnel could speak Korean. When communication between ROK and KMAG officers was possible, the Korean officers often refused to accept advice from the Americans for fear of 'losing face' with their own men. Except for a few ROK soldiers who had encountered North Korean infiltrators, the ROK army had never experienced hostile fire and was therefore unpredictable.

Top right: Troops of the 3rd ROK Division in the Diamond Mountains area during the advance to Wonsan in October 1950.
Below: United Nations' equipment is burned during the evacuation of Wonsan in December 1956.

The NKPA, in contrast to the ROK army, had a strength of 135,000, including eight full strength infantry divisions and two at half strength, five constabulary brigades, and an armored brigade with Soviet T-34 tanks. The NKPA also was supplied with 180 Soviet bombers, Yak fighters, and other aircraft and 122-mm guns with a range of 17 miles. The North Korean army was staffed by combat-tested cadres who had served with the USSR Red Army against the Japanese in Manchuria or with the Peoples Republic of China forces in the Chinese Civil War. Others had undergone three years of training under the direction of Soviet officers who served directly with NKPA troops at the division level.

North Korean Premier makes it official

More than seven hours elapsed between the start of the invasion of South Korea and receipt of official notice from the US Embassy in Seoul by the State Department in Washington. One reason for the delay was that the opening bombardment and border crossings by the NKPA were not unlike harassment and maneuvers that had been going on intermittently for months along the 38th Parallel. But any doubt was erased when North Korean Premier Kim Il Sung, a Soviet-trained general, announced in a radio broadcast at 0930 hours (1930 on 24 June in Washington) that his forces had begun an invasion.

As Soviet-built aircraft began strafing South Korea's capital city of Seoul, KMAG and the US Embassy activated a prepared emergency plan for evacuating American civilians. Orders began trickling through the chains of command within a few hours after official notice was received in Washington at 2126 hours. The US 7th Fleet began a blockade of the Korean coastline and USAF planes provided cover as approximately 600 US citizens and selected personnel from other countries were evacuated without incident aboard the SS *Reinholt*. President Truman authorized the contribution of whatever forces and equipment might be available for 'cover and support' of the ROK forces. Direct aid began 26 June 1950 when the US transferred 10 P-51 Mustang fighter planes to the South Koreans and convoys of military trucks started moving equipment and ammunition to USAF transport planes waiting at bases in Japan.

On 27 June 1950 North Korean tanks reached the outskirts of Seoul and the ROK government evacuated the capital. At the same time, KMAG personnel caught in Seoul hiked 16 miles through the mud to Kimpo Airport to catch the last flights to safety. By June 28 the Communist North Korean flag was flying over Seoul.

ROK troops delayed Communist advance

Two or three precious days were gained in delaying the advance of the North Korean Communist forces because of the canny intuition of one KMAG officer, Army Lieutenant Colonel Thomas McPhail, who convinced the commander of the ROK 6th Division to cancel all week-end passes beginning 23 June. Intelligence reports told of new NKPA units near the border with well-camouflaged tanks and artillery. When the attack came, only the ROK 6th Division was ready to respond. The division held its position until 28 June when faced with envelopment; as friendly flank units fled southward it withdrew. Some units of the ROK 1st Division also made a tough stand outside Seoul with one company fighting relentlessly until the last man was killed.

Above: A Marine sniper uses the telescopic sight on his M1 rifle to pick his targets carefully during street fighting in Seoul.

General Douglas MacArthur of the US Far East forces in Tokyo flew to Suwon, about 20 miles south of Seoul, on 29 June 1950 for a personal inspection of the area and briefings by KMAG officers. MacArthur radioed the Joint Chief of Staff that ROK forces were 'incapable of gaining the initiative' and recommended immediate commitment of US ground forces to prevent the complete loss of South Korea. President Truman at first authorized the use of one Regimental Combat Team (RCT) but later changed the authorization to the use of ground forces under MacArthur's command when it was learned that the nearest RCT was in Hawaii, more than 4000 miles away.

Thus was created a makeshift infantry battalion known as 'Task Force Smith,' named for its commanding officer, Lieutenant Colonel C B Smith. The Task Force was composed of 21st Regiment units of the 24th Infantry Division based in Japan and included a 105-mm howitzer battery, two rifle companies, two 4.2 mortar platoons, a 75-mm recoilless rifle unit, and six 2.36-inch bazooka teams. The Task Force was flown immediately to Pusan, the railhead for a train and truck ride to the front at Osan. From 1 July 1950 until other 24th Division units arrived by sea, Task Force Smith was the only US combat unit fighting the North Korean army.

Below: British Royal Marines land during a joint US/British raid behind enemy lines on Chinnapo on 14 June 1951. Such raiding missions were not uncommon after the first winter of the war.

Task Force Smith under Communist fire

The American unit, fresh from the soft life of occupation duty in Tokyo, made its first stand in a roadway between Seoul and Chonan on 5 July 1950 when a NKPA infantry division behind 30 T-34 tanks attacked. Despite their lack of training and experience, the makeshift army unit held off the entire North Korean division for seven hours, knocking out five of the T-34 tanks with howitzer shells. But they were greatly outnumbered, outgunned, outmaneuvered and finally out of ammunition.

As Task Force Smith withdrew to escape encirclement, units of the 24th Infantry Division's 34th Regiment were moving northward and provided rearguard action. But the NKPA troops continued their advance, catching the 34th Regiment in a bloody trap with fighting at such close quarters that the commanding officer, Colonel Robert R Martin was killed while dueling a T-34 tank with bazooka rockets from a distance of 15 yards. Survivors tried to withdraw to allied lines under cover of darkness, sometimes abandoning their boots which became stuck in the thick rice-paddy muck.

For more than two weeks during July 1950, the 24th Infantry Division units battled North Korean Communist forces almost continuously, going without sleep or food while fighting five separate delaying actions without reserves over a distance of 70 miles. Besides the enemy, the infantrymen had to fight mildew, rot and rust, flies, fleas and lice; often they went shoeless, hungry and bleeding in a country where any Korean in civilian clothing could be either a friend or a Communist infiltrator armed with hand grenades.

General Dean betrayed for five dollars

For several days after 20 July the fighting raged through the streets of Taejon where Communist snipers appeared suddenly on nearly every rooftop. The 24th Division commander, Major General William Dean, became separated from his men while assisting a wounded soldier. He was injured in a fall and blacked out. When General Dean recovered he found himself deep in Communist-held territory and tried to make his way back to American lines, dodging NKPA patrols and going without food for 20 days. Finally, he approached a Korean civilian to ask for food. The Korean turned General Dean into the Communists for the equivalent of $5.00 and the NKPA held him as a prisoner of war until September 1953. General Dean later said he 'kept his sanity' by counting the number of flies he killed during his imprisonment.

As the 24th Division units withdrew from Taejon, reinforcements from the 7th and 25th Infantry and 1st Cavalry Divisions began arriving in South Korea from Japan as General MacArthur rounded up most of the remaining army units on Japanese occupation duty for the fighting in Korea. The 5th RCT from Hawaii, authorized for the fighting in Korea on 30 June 1950, finally arrived on 1 August, along with the 2nd Infantry Division. Lieutenant General Walton Walker was named to replace General Dean as the entire ROK army and US ground forces in Korea were pushed back into the 'Pusan Perimeter,' a triangular-shaped corner of South Korea facing the Sea of Japan. From an apex at Taegu the friendly forces held a 75-mile defense line running to the east coast and another extending to the south coast of Korea. Although the US Navy and Air Force planes, accompanied by aircraft from other United Nations members, had cleared the skies over South Korea of Communist planes, the NKPA continued to advance toward Pusan by moving at night and hiding during daylight hours when they could be spotted by the planes.

First Marine units arrive

The NKPA advance finally was stopped by the arrival 2 August 1950 of the 1st Provisional Marine Brigade led by Brigadier General Edward A Craig. Army General Ridgway later credited Craig's crew with halting the enemy 'in its tracks.' The brigade included the 5th Marines and the Marine Aircraft Group 33, and although below strength like the army units—with two rifle companies per infantry battalion instead of three and four artillery batteries rather than six—it 'saved the day,' according to Ridgway, and 'provided real muscle.' TheMarine force was equipped with M-26 Pershing tanks with 90-mm guns, making them a fair match for the Soviet T-34s, which had hides generally too tough for the World War II bazooka shells issued the first army troops sent to Korea. Like the US 2nd Infantry Division, the Marine brigade had been dispatched by sea from the West Coast of the United States.

On 7 July 1950 the United Nations Security Council had authorized a UN military command with General MacArthur as Commander in Chief. Under a unified command, units from various countries were integrated into US Army company size and larger units. Each US Army company was authorized to utilize up to 100

Below : Scene during the epic retreat to Hungnam. Men of the 5th and 7th Marines are shown regrouping near Yudam-ni in a picture taken on 29 November 1950.

South Korean recruits. Larger non-US units, such as the 27th British Brigade, served as units of the US 8th Army. However, the US Marine Corps units were exempt from the order integrating South Korean recruits into company-size commands.

Marines join Task Force Kean

The 1st Marine Brigade went into action within five days after completing the sea voyage from Camp Pendleton, California. It was assigned with a ROK battalion and the 5th and 35th Army RCTs to a Task Force, named for 25th Infantry Division commander Major General William Kean, with a mission to block a drive by the veteran NKPA 6th Division to take Pusan from the southwest. On 7 August 1950 Task Force Kean launched a counteroffensive against the NKPA troops who held a mountain ridge near Chinju. In temperatures near 100 degrees Fahrenheit the Task Force battled the North Koreans for four days, at times firing 105-mm howitzers at point blank range at the Communist troops. The NKPA troops, sometimes dressed in civilian clothing, infiltrated the UN positions to locate the Marine command post and spot targets for the well-camouflaged North Korean guns. The NKPA units also used a favorite tactic of infiltrating to attack the Marine units from the rear. In addition to the killed and wounded, many casualties were caused by heat prostration.

After the initial engagement, the Marines captured Kosong on the southern coast of Korea, thereby securing the left flank of the US 8th Army position and forcing the North Koreans to retreat. General Walker then assigned the 1st Marine Brigade to duty along the southern portion of the Naktong River to fight alongside the battle-

Above: Men of the 1st Marine Division in Korea. In the background DUKWs and amtracs.
Above right: A Korean and an American Military Policeman question a Korean refugee, to check for possible smuggled weapons.
Below: Marine artillerymen of the 1st Marine Division in action in October 1952.

weary 24th Infantry Division. The safety of Pusan, which was rapidly growing into a large UN supply base, was virtually guaranteed by the Task Force victory.

More action to the north

While the UN forces had the advantage of shortened supply and communication lines within the Pusan Perimeter, the North Koreans were overextended. The NKPA had planned to forage and confiscate food from the South Korean areas they overran, but now found they had to resupply themselves from the north. When US B-26s destroyed their vehicles and supplies, the NKPA resorted to the use of ox carts and human porters to transport food and ammunition. Women were pressed into service as porters. Makeshift bridges were built from logs tied together and held beneath the water surface by large rocks; from the air they could not be detected because of the murky water covering the logs. The innocent looking oxcarts and A-frame backpacks of the Korean 'refugees' also concealed mortars and machine guns as well as rice for troops in the south.

In mid-August, as pressure built around the provincial capital of Taegu, near the apex of the Pusan Perimeter, the 1st Marine Brigade was shifted northward to the right flank of the US 24th Infantry Division, taking positions around Changnyong. This time the US Marines faced the

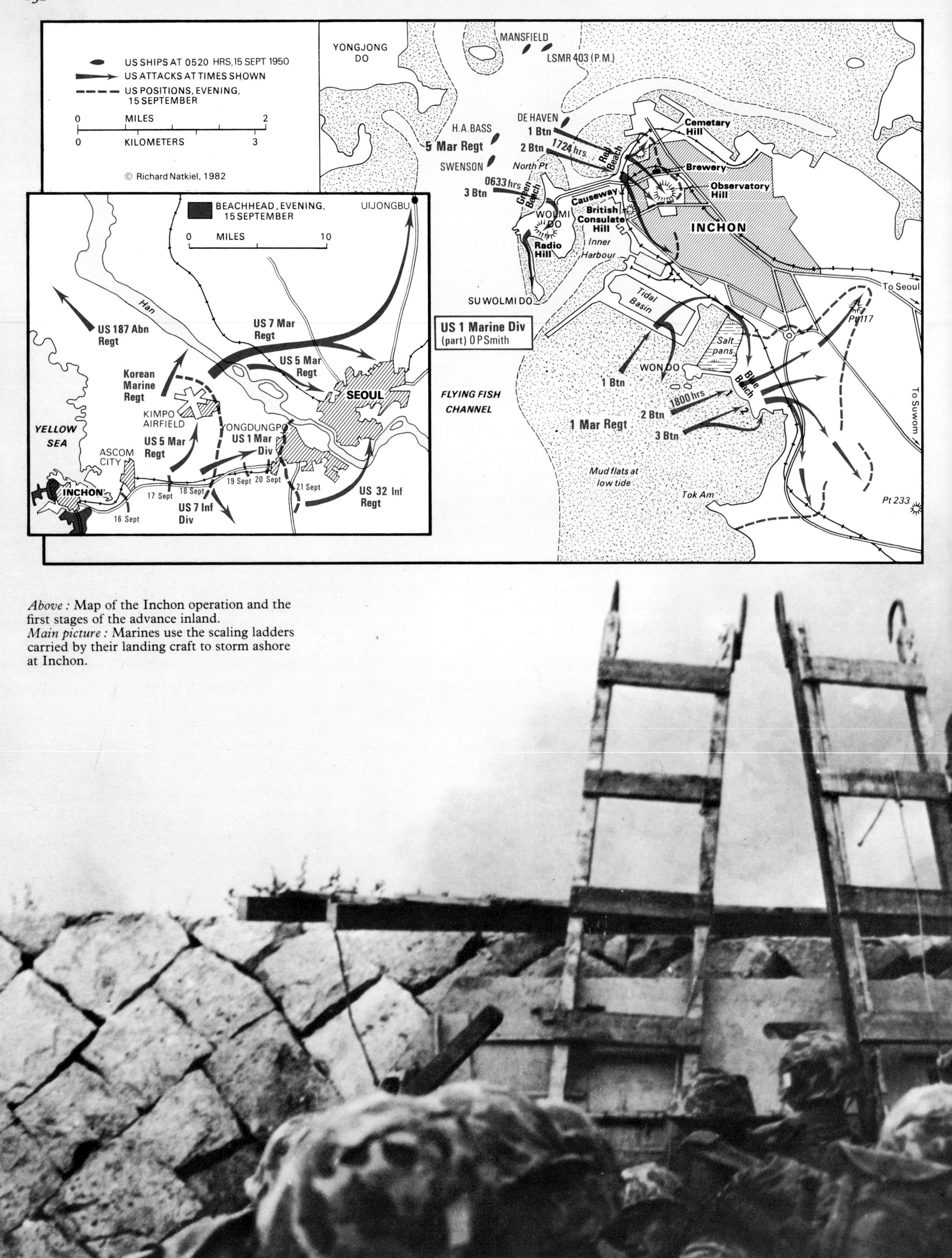

Above : Map of the Inchon operation and the first stages of the advance inland.
Main picture : Marines use the scaling ladders carried by their landing craft to storm ashore at Inchon.

NKPA 4th Division and after a number of determined counterattacks drove the North Koreans to the west bank of the Naktong River while ROK and US infantry troops prevented the fall of Taegu to three North Korean divisions. The 24th Division, which had fought alongside the Marines in two battles within two weeks was replaced by the US 2nd Infantry Division after the fight at Changnyong; the 24th had suffered 30 percent casualties in the first six weeks of the Korean War.

The last great battle along the Naktong River began 31 August 1950 as the Communist forces mounted their heaviest assault against the Pusan Perimeter. Fighting flared along most of the perimeter and breached the lines in many places, requiring the 24th Division to return to combat as the NKPA threatened to cut rail and highway lines. Fighting side-by-side with the 2nd Infantry, the men of the 1st Marine Brigade used rifles, grenades and bayonets to hold the Yongsan-Changnyong sector. They were helped by a rainstorm that flooded the Naktong River and disrupted North Korean efforts to ferry in reinforcements.

Marines lead Inchon Invasion

While UN army units fought along the Naktong River on the western edge of the Pusan Perimeter and the Taegu-Pohang line on the north, the 1st Marine Division was being formed in Japan by Major General Oliver P Smith. The 1st Provisional Marine Brigade was withdrawn from the Pusan Perimeter for the division, which also would include six battalions of Marines transferred from the Mediterranean, the United States and shipboard units. The 1st Marine Division would become a part of the newly activated X Corps which also would include the US 7th Infantry Division being fleshed out with 8000 South Korean soldiers.

X Corps would play the leading role in one of the most daring military ventures in history—the invasion of Inchon from the Yellow Sea. The Inchon landing was such a bold and seemingly impossible undertaking that many top officers in the Pentagon, experienced in World War II amphibious landings, doubted that it could be done. Because of Inchon's location on the Yellow Sea it was subjected to tides that varied by 30 feet during the day in a narrow circuitous channel through mile-wide mud flats. The harbor was guarded by shore batteries on the island of Wolmi-do, situated in the channel. And the date selected for the landing, 15 September, would fall during the typhoon season. There would only be two hours on 15 September when the tides would be high enough to effect an amphibious assault. And when General MacArthur presented the plan in early August, he only had six weeks to organize the men and equipment needed for the invasion.

Above: The landing force heads for the shore, Inchon, 15 September 1950.

Organization of X Corps

Creating a military corps with two freshly rebuilt wartime strength divisions on less than two months notice was something of a miracle in itself. On 19 July 1950 President Truman called up the Organized Marine Corps Reserve. Six days later, units from Camp Lejeune, North Carolina, began boarding trains for the West Coast of the US. On 30 July, the regimental Headquarters Battery, Service Battery, 4.5-inch Rocket Battery and the 1st and 2nd Battalions of the 10th Marine Regiment left for Camp Pendleton, followed by the regiment's 3rd Battalion. After arriving in California, the 10th Marines were redesignated the 11th Marines.

The US Army's 7th Infantry Division,

led by Major General David G Barr, had been on occupation duty in Japan since 1949. The original 7th Division had been cannibalized to provide troops for the 25th Infantry and 1st Cavalry Divisions after the loss of Taejon in late July. What was left of the 7th Division in Japan before South Korean soldiers were added was for a while the entire garrison remaining in Japan.

The situation back in the States was not much better until the call-up of reserves by the president. In July 1950 the entire General Military Reserve in the United States consisted of the 82nd Airborne Division and a poorly trained under-strength 3rd Infantry Division. The Joint Chiefs of Staff had rejected MacArthur's request for either one or both of those divisions, which would have left the nation without a combat division. And there was Genuine fear at the time that the Korean War itself was merely a Communist diversion to conceal a Soviet invasion elsewhere.

Far left: A Marine symbolically destroys a photograph of Stalin, found during the recapture of Seoul.
Left: General MacArthur and General Almond, commander of X Corps, on a visit to a 1st Marine Division command post, 20 September 1950. The Marine officer nearest the camera is Colonel L B Puller.
Below: Men of the 1st Marine Division move past a burning North Korean T34 tank as their own armor moves up the road in support, 17 September 1950.

Proving the impossible possible

It was because the Communists considered the capture of Inchon by an amphibious landing impossible that it succeeded. Once the plan was approved, Major General Edward Almond, a member of MacArthur's staff in Tokyo, was named commander of X Corps. A young navy lieutenant, Eugene Clark, was put ashore near Inchon two weeks before the planned invasion to gather information about gun emplacements, the sea wall and other details. Clark was so successful in his espionage effort that when the first UN landing craft approached the Inchon harbor, he was able to turn on the lighthouse lamp to help guide the ships.

As a diversion while planes and naval guns bombarded the Inchon area in advance of the landing, a fleet led by the battleship *Missouri* bombarded Communist installations on the east coast of Korea. Because the mission, given the code name 'Operation Chromite,' required 260 assorted vessels and high tide at Inchon could only be used for two hours to avoid stranding landing craft on the mud flats, men had to be put ashore in stages. The 3rd Battalion of the 5th Marine Regiment went ashore as the first wave at 0630 hours as bombarding naval guns ceased firing. Their objective was Wolmi Island, where shore batteries guarding the harbor were located.

The island was not as well fortified as had been anticipated and the Wolmi was secured within the first hour. When the afternoon tide came in, another wave of Marines attacked the sea wall which rose four feet above the prows of the landing craft. Some of the men scaled the wall with ladders, others rammed holes through the wall and still other units blasted openings with dynamite. By the end of the day the Marines had secured their Inchon beachhead.

The battle to retake Seoul

With each high tide for the next several days, units of the 1st Marine or 7th Infantry Division came ashore until the port area was in control of United Nations forces. Inchon fell with little resistance and the Marines advanced toward Kimpo Airport, Korea's largest airfield, located west of Seoul. The 7th Infantry advanced south-eastward toward Suwon, Meanwhile, at Kimpo the Marines needed tanks to defeat NKPA troops who mounted an attack described in the official records as 'fanatical.' Once Kimpo was secured, however, US C-54 and C-119 transports began landing at intervals of a few minutes apart with ammunition, fuel and other supplies. If the scene was reminiscent of the 1948 Berlin Airlift it was because the same commander, Major General William H Tunner, had been sent to Tokyo to manage the Korean Airlift.

Marine and Navy aircraft had supported the Inchon landing and continued support

as X Corps Marines advanced toward Seoul. It was hoped the capital city, built around the base of a mountain, could be captured with the same light resistance encountered at Inchon and Kimpo. But the North Korean Communists had converted the tree-shrouded slopes of the mountain into a fortress. The NKPA intended to make the battle a street-by-street fight and had concentrated their best firepower in the area. Casualties among the X Corps troops became heavy before they even reached the city limits.

The North Korean defenders of Seoul included the NKPA 9th Division, which had been moved northward from the Pusan Perimeter to meet the UN forces on a new front. Marines fought yard by yard, and sometimes foot by foot, through sandbagged buildings and barbed-wired streets against small arms, machinegun and mortar fire. In the suburb of Yondungpo, advancing UN troops were subjected to heavy artillery fire. Although General MacArthur announced on 26 September 1950 that Seoul had been retaken, fighting was still going on and the capital could not be returned to the ROK government until 29 September.

The gap is narrowed

According to the original plan, the US 8th Army, composed of the ROK I and II Corps and the US I and IX Corps, was supposed to break out of the Pusan Perimeter with the start of the Inchon landing. Radio broadcasts and airdropped leaflets were used to urge the NKPA troops south of Seoul to surrender. The Communist radio, however, refrained from mentioning the UN success at Inchon so the psychological warfare effort had little success at first. On 20 September 1950 the US I Corps—composed of the US 1st Cavalry and 24th Infantry Divisions, the 27th British Commonwealth Brigade and ROK 1st Division—broke through the NKPA defenses along the Naktong River. The US IX Corps—consisting of the US 2nd and 25th Infantry Divisions and ROK units—forced the enemy back in the Masan-Chinju area. At about the same time, the ROK I and II Corps forced four NKPA divisions to withdraw 70 miles along the northern side of the Pusan Perimeter.

Caught between the 8th Army and X Corps, the NKPA troops abandoned weapons and tons of rice as they tried to escape to the north. Many simply changed to civilian clothing and mingled with the

general population. But the United Nations forces soon controlled all highway and rail routes to North Korea. As the gap between the 8th Army and X Corps narrowed, the 70th Tank Battalion of the US 1st Cavalry Division found forward elements of the US 7th Division south of Suwon and forged the link on 26 September. By the end of September the UN forces controlled an area of Korea four times that held before the Inchon landing.

The chase into North Korean turf

On 7 October 1950 the 8th Army relieved X Corps Marines in the Inchon area as the Marines were readied for a second amphibious assault elsewhere in Korea. On the previous day, the United Nations General Assembly had given approval to a request by General MacArthur for authority to pursue the NKPA in North Korea and destroy the remnants of the army. ROK President Syngman Rhee had already announced that his armies would continue to attack North Korean units, with or without United Nations permission, and the ROK 3rd Division began a push up the east coast of North Korea on 1 October. By mid-October the UN forces had captured 135,000 North Koreans—equal to the total NKPA army before the invasion—and had reached the North Korean capital of Pyongyang.

The 1st Marine Division had been scheduled to make an amphibious landing at the North Korean port of Wonsan, on the east coast, on 20 October 1950 after being withdrawn from the Inchon-Seoul area. Meanwhile, the ROK 3rd Division, which had jumped the gun by invading North Korea before the advance was authorized by the UN, had already taken Wonsan on 11 October 1950. When the 1st Marines arrived at Wonsan, the port was in UN hands but the Marines could not land until the Wonsan harbor had been cleared of some 2000 mines. The 1st Marine Division finally made an 'administrative' landing on 26 October 1950.

Above: M26 Pershing tanks and infantry of the 1st Marine Division pass by as a group of North Korean prisoners is led to the rear by South Korean troops, 26 September 1950.

The Drive to the Yalu River

Retrospective critiques suggest that later misfortunes could be traced to the master plan for invading North Korea by moving X Corps to the east side of the Korean

Above: Left to right, Admiral Radford, Commander in Chief Pacific Fleet, General MacArthur, Secretary of the Army Pace and Army Chief of Staff General Bradley during MacArthur's Wake Island conference with President Truman.

peninsula and the 8th Army to the Inchon-Seoul sector. The 8th Army had been assigned the responsibility for providing logistical support for X Corps as well as the 8th Army, but without giving the 8th Army tactical control over X Corps. The 8th Army experienced difficulty in obtaining supplies and transportation facilities. And the general north-south lines of mountain ridges in North Korea made communication between X Corps in the east and the 8th Army in the west virtually impossible. But the plan called for a second linkup of the 8th Army and X Corps south of the Yalu, with North Korean forces destroyed, before the onset of winter weather.

Actually, the 7th Regiment of the ROK 6th Division, attached to the 8th Army reached the Yalu River on 26 October 1950, the same day the 1st Marines finally were able to enter Wonsan. But the ROK troops encountered stubborn resistance from what appeared to be North Korean units making a last stand. Heavy fighting also developed at Unsan and Tokchon along the Chongchon River, south of the Yalu River, around 31 October 1950. Some of the captured enemy were found to be Chinese wearing North Korean uniforms but they were believed to be 'volunteers' from the Peoples Republic of China. During the first ten days of November, however, elements of 12 different Chinese Communist divisions had been identified in the area of the Changjin (Chosin) Reservoir. Then Chinese and NKPA units cut in behind X Corps' forward elements, including the 1st Marine Division.

Over the wild terrain yonder

The 1st Marine Division had been ordered to the Yalu over terrain as formidable as any likely to be encountered by a military unit. The only road leading to the objectives of Kanggye and Manpojin was a narrow winding path that in one sector rose 2500 feet above a canyon, a sheer granite cliff on the 'safe side' of the road. At another point, the road wound over a 4000-foot high pass where winter wind-chill factors usually were well below zero degrees Fahrenheit. The terrain was generally wild, rugged and trackless.

As General Smith proceeded northward along the mountain pathway, he had the foresight to have his men prepare an emergency airstrip at the southern end of the Changjin Reservoir. If necessary, it could be used to resupply the Marines and to evacuate casualties. Smith also stockpiled ammunition, fuel, and other supplies in case they were needed. His experience and intuition led him to believe his troops were extremely vulnerable to attack in the isolated granite gullies and gorges of northeastern Korea. His planning to insure a defensible route for withdrawal would pay dividends when and if the Chinese Communist armies struck, as they had been promising in radio propaganda broadcasts.

General MacArthur had expressed his confidence that the Chinese would not enter the Korean War and that the remnants of the NKPA could be eliminated 'in two weeks.' MacArthur even suggested that American troops could be 'home by Christmas,' a month away when the November offensive was scheduled to begin.

Right: Typically fierce Korean winter weather lashes Marines of the 1st Division as the retreat from Koto-ri begins in early December 1950.

The tide turns

Only one American unit ever reached the Yalu River. The 17th Regiment of the 7th Infantry Division captured the North Korean town of Hyesanjin during the last week of November 1950, about a month after ROK troops reached the Manchurian border town of Chosan. A ROK Capital Division unit attached to X Corps had progressed as far as Sodong along the northeast coast, the farthest point reached by any of the UN troops at that time.

The appearance of Chinese forces was at first something of an enigma. They would appear, then disappear, just as the first Soviet MiG-15s appeared briefly to oppose United Nations pilots near the Yalu, but just as suddenly jetted back to some airfield in Manchuria. X Corps, reinforced by the addition of the US 3rd Division, a group of British Royal Marines and two ROK Divisions, the 3rd and Capital, resumed its northward probe toward the Yalu, but this time with caution. As November temperatures dropped below freezing, a lull developed in the fighting and there was relatively little action for X Corps from about 10

November 1950 to 24 November. Radio Moscow had announced on 19 November 1950 that North Korean and Chinese forces had withdrawn to prepare a counteroffensive leading to a Communist victory—but the message was considered a bluff.

On 24 November 1950 General MacArthur announced the start of a major offensive to destroy the remnants of the NKPA. The 8th Army would advance northward through western and central Korea to the Manchurian border while X Corps would carry out an enveloping drive to the northwest. One day later Communist troops began a counteroffensive that broke the ranks of the ROK II Corps at Tokchon, exposing the right flank of the 8th Army. The 8th Army had engaged the 4th Field Army of the Peoples Republic of China. On 27 November X Corps was attacked along both sides of the Changjin Reservoir by the Chinese 3rd Field Army. The objective of the PRC armies was to pin the 8th Army against the west coast and X Corps against the east coast and open a route to the south for North Korean and Chinese division advancing through central Korea.

'An entirely new war'

General MacArthur summoned Generals Walker and Almond to Tokyo for a four-hour discussion of the situation. He explained that it was 'an entirely new war,' with Chinese armies that had entered the fighting without a declaration of war and without the official sanction of the Peoples Republic of China, which could not be held responsible for the actions of military 'volunteers.' Because of the conditions under which MacArthur had been allowed to pursue the NKPA into North Korea, United Nations planes could not conduct reconnaissance missions or attacks beyond the Yalu River frontier with China. Plans were made to withdraw the 8th Army by land and X Corps by sea through the port of Hungnam-Hamhung, below the Changjin Reservoir.

The US 2nd Division took the brunt of the fighting with the Chinese Communist forces for six days, providing a delaying action while the rest of General Walker's 8th Army withdrew below the North Korean capital of Pyongyang. The 2nd Division suffered so many casualties that it was declared combat ineffective and was withdrawn into South Korea. By the middle of December the 8th Army had withdrawn below the 38th Parallel and formed a defensive perimeter around Seoul.

The evacuation of X Corps

On the day following the crushing attack by the Chinese Communists on the ROK II Corps assigned to protect the right flank of the 8th Army, General Almond ordered the 1st Marine Division to attack northwest and cut the enemy lines of communication at Mupyong-ni. But before the Marines could execute the mission, the Chinese Communists began the second phase of their counteroffensive with the objective of destroying X Corps. From the snow-covered mountains around the Changjin Reservoir, six Chinese Communist Divisions attacked the Marines and neighboring battalions of the 7th Infantry Division. The 5th Marines under Lieutenant Colonel Raymond Murray and the 7th Marines commanded by Colonel Homer Litzenberg had started to relieve General Walker's troops when they were hit by hostile fire from assault batta-

Above: Marine infantry begin a counterattack near Hagaru-ri, 26 December 1950, after an air strike by Marine Corsair fighter-bombers.

lions of the Chinese 79th and 89th Divisions near the village of Yudam-ni. The two Chinese divisions then were given support by the Chinese 59th Division attacking from the south.

Fighting continued into the night with hand grenades and mortar fire in temperatures that dropped to 18 degrees below zero and froze BARs and carbines. The Marines fought on with M-1s and Browning machine guns, at one point setting fire to a building to provide enough light to see the waves of attacking Chinese. It was now that General Smith's advance planning helped prevent a withdrawal from turning into a disaster.

Battles of the Changjin Resezvoir

General Almond authorized General Smith to abandon his heavy equipment if such a move would speed his withdrawal. But General Smith announced he would not abandon any equipment he could use and he would withdraw only as rapidly as he was able to evacuate his wounded men.

It was a distance of nearly 60 miles from Yudam-ni at the north end of the Changjin Reservoir to the evacuation port of Hungnam, over the same treacherous mountain trails the Marines had traveled on their way toward the Manchurian border. Smith intended to fight all the way to Hungnam and to bring out all the equipment and personnel that could be moved. Only those killed in action would be left behind. He even conducted a burial service for the Marines killed in the first round of fighting at Yudam-ni.

The 5th and 7th Regiments joined forces in their withdrawal and acquired reinforcements along the way, including survivors of two battalions of the 7th Infantry Division who had fought the same Chinese Communist divisions near the Changjin Reservoir and a group of British Commandos.

Communist rifle and machinegun fire plagued the X Corps troops from every side and the enemy tried to trap the men numerous times with road blocks and

Above : 5th and 7th Regiment Marines near Yudam-ni at the start of the retreat to Hungnam. *Left :* MacArthur and, left, General Oliver Smith who led the 1st Marine Division.

blown bridges. Because the supply route had been cut in several places by Chinese Communists, the US Combat Cargo Command made daily airdrops of ammunition, food and medicines during the running battle along the western edge of the reservoir. Air Force and Marine transports and even Navy torpedo bombers were used to drop tons of supplies to the X Corps troops.

The greatest courage was required

In an official US Government report on the Korean War, the War Office said that for General Smith's Marines 'the greatest courage was required to effect the retreat to the coast,' where an evacuating fleet was gathering. As the Chinese battled to maintain their envelopment of the Marines, Task Force Dog commanded by Brigadier General Armistead Mead of the US 3rd Infantry Division fought inland from the coast to Chinhung-ni, on the road between Hungnam and the Changjin Reservoir, to clear a path for the 1st Marine Division.

General Smith's men were always under fire from Chinese Communists on the mountain slopes. Although the Marines tried to keep to high ground whenever possible, the men often had to move through open gorges and down steep mountain sides. For anyone who could walk, movement was by foot; only the dead and badly wounded were allowed to travel by vehicle. Meanwhile, Marine, Navy and Air Force fighters and bombers blasted away at Chinese troop concentrations which continued to shower death on the Marines 24 hours a day as they worked their way through the corkscrew corridor to safety.

In addition to the emergency airstrip built by the Marines at Koto-ri, the 1st Engineer Battalion worked through the night to build an additional emergency airstrip on the frozen ground at Hagaru, at the south end of the Changjin Reservoir. The airstrip was completed in 12 hours, including the occasional 'work breaks' required when the engineers had to put aside their construction equipment and take up rifles to fight Chinese Communist patrols that threatened to halt the project. The airstrips at Koto-ri and Hagaru served to evacuate more than 5000 casualties during the withdrawal, in addition to their use in supplementing air drops of supplies.

A bridge blown, a bridge built

After fighting their way through three Chinese Communist divisions between Yudam-ni and the 4000-foot Toktong Pass through the mountains west of the Changjin Reservoir, the 1st Marines encountered a fourth Chinese division, the PRC 58th, a part of General Chen Yi's 3rd Chinese Field Army, as they approached Hagaru on 6 December 1950. In five days of fighting the troops had moved about 12 miles closer to Hungnam and some of the more perilous miles were still ahead of the units. At one point the Marines had to fight on the frozen surface of the reservoir in order to rescue a 7th Infantry Division unit being decimated by Chinese Communist troops.

Near Koto-ri the Communists attempted to trap the Marines by blowing up a bridge that spanned a chasm. The bridge actually was a hydroelectric spillway apron but the only means of getting the division's mechanized equipment out of the North Korean mountains. Without the bridge the Marine transportation and wounded would have to be abandoned while the troops, carrying whatever light weapons they could pack, would have to cut back across the mountain ridges held by the Chinese Communists.

General Smith then ordered a military miracle. Although the task had never been performed before in the history of warfare, the Marine general requisitioned a 16-ton steel bridge to be air-dropped. The Combat Cargo Command responded by dispatching eight C-119 transports, each carrying a two-ton bridge section to Koto-ri. The flying boxcars dropped the spans, which were assembled by Marine engineers and moved into place across the narrow ravine. The bridge was built under heavy enemy fire as two Marine companies held the high ground commanding the crossing and prevented the Chinese troops from closing the trap. The span enabled the 1st Marines to continue their trek to Hungnam without leaving behind the heaviest of equipment.

Breakout at Chinhung-ni

After surviving attacks by the Chinese Communist 58th Division from the west and the Chinese 76th Division from the east on the road between Hagaru and Koto-ri, the 1st Marines had to face the Chinese 60th Division on the west and the Chinese 77th Division on the east to get beyond Koto-ri. The distance from Koto-ri to Chinhung-ni was ten miles and the 1st Marine Division with their entourage of 7th Division and British Commando remnants at one time were fighting along the entire length of the road, the advance elements striking the outskirts of Chinhung-ni while the rear guard was still battling Chinese Communists at Koto-ri. Each Marine unit had to fight its way back to join other Marine units to its rear.

Task Force Dog, meanwhile, had driven to Chinhung-ni and was able to meet up with a battalion of the 1st Marine Regiment working southward to open the last obstacle in the road to the plains below Chinhung-ni. It had taken 13 days of constant exposure to enemy fire in bitterly cold mountain terrain for the bearded survivors to reach the final leg of the road to Hungnam. The 3rd Infantry Division's 65th Regiment provided rear guard action for the Marines after they got beyond the range of Chinese Communist artillery near Chinhung-ni. Other 3rd Division units held defensive positions around the Hungnam Perimeter. Additional cover was provided by elements of the 7th Infantry Division that had not been involved in the Changjin Reservoir debacle.

Right : A Marine patrol ready to set out, Wonju sector, 22 February 1951.

Above : 5th Regiment Marines during the bitter retreat to Hungnam.
Below, main picture : Equipment and landing craft on the shore at Inchon, ready for the move of the 1st Marine Division to Wonsan in October 1950.

'In a superior manner'

General Smith and his half-frozen, exhausted Marines reached the Hungnam perimeter on 11 December 1950 as the nearly 200 vessels organized for evacuation of the beachhead got underway. General MacArthur flew to the beachhead on the same day and praised the men for their 'high morale and conspicuous self-confidence' throughout the heavy fighting. MacArthur added that 'Although highly outnumbered, you have come through in a superior manner.' The Marines not only brought out their wounded and all movable equipment but prisoners and captured enemy equipment.

But the fighting in North Korea was not ended for the X Corps troops. The scene at Hungnam was like a rerun of the British evacuation at Dunkirk in 1940. From Hungnam harbor General Almond established a perimeter extending in an arc with a 22-mile radius. The Chinese 3rd Field Army battered at the perimeter and was joined after the start of the evacuation by two North Korean divisions. Army, Navy and Marine Corps personnel, meanwhile, worked around the clock in subfreezing weather to load the Marines, 350,000 tons of cargo, 17,500 vehicles, ROK, US and British troops, 98,000 Korean refugees and even Soviet self-propelled 76-mm guns and other captured equipment onto the waiting vessels.

Final rounds of the year

The Hungnam evacuation required two weeks to complete. Each day the perimeter was allowed to shrink a bit as fully loaded ships departed. A 7th Fleet flotilla poured 34,000 rounds from 5-, 8- and 16-inch guns into the attacking Chinese and North Korean Communist troops. The guns were augmented by 5-inch rocket launchers. During the nights thousands of star shells and illuminating projectiles were fired to prevent a surprise night attack. The entire 1st Marine Air Wing, one fourth of the total USAF 5th Air Force and Navy and Marine planes from Rear Admiral E C Ewen's Fast Carrier Task Force 77 and Rear Admiral Richard Ruble's escort carrier group provided air cover.

As the perimeter became smaller each day, engineers destroyed anything in the port area that could have been used by the attacking Communist forces. Bridges, buildings, railroad equipment and rail lines were blown up. As Christmas Eve approached, only a small beachhead remained under a cloud of smoke and debris from demolition blasts. On 24 December 1950 rear guard elements of Major General Robert Soule's 3rd Infantry Division fired their final rounds of the year at the Communist enemy and while carrier-based planes and warships of the 7th Fleet pounded the approaching Chinese and NKPA troops, the 3rd Division men climbed into their landing craft and amphibious tractors and left the beachhead.

At 1436 hours on 24 December 1950, reported a message from the carrier *Philippine Sea,* all troops had been safely removed in the greatest sea evacuation in American history.

Below: North Korean prisoners, captured by men of the 1st Marine Division.

General Ridgway takes command

By 31 December 1950 all United Nations troops were back below the 38th Parallel and all of North Korea was once again in the hands of Communist military forces. The badly mauled 1st Marine Division had been evacuated to Pusan but would be back in action again within a month following the reorganization of X Corps and the 8th Army to form a single command. The reorganization was determined as a means of correcting the difficulties of operating X Corps and the 8th Army as separate but interdependent commands during the drive to the Yalu River. Meanwhile, General Walker, Commander of the United Nations ground forces, had been killed 23 December 1950 when his jeep collided with a ROK truck as he was traveling north of Seoul. Lieutenant General Matthew Ridgway, World War II commander of the 82nd Airborne Division, was named as Walker's replacement. General Ridgway arrived in Korea on 26 December to take command of the UN ground forces.

On 30 December 1950 General MacArthur advised the Joint Chiefs of Staff in Washington that the Communist forces could—if they wanted to make the effort—drive the United Nations troops out of Korea. It was estimated that the Chinese Communists had sent 21 divisions into Korea to aid 12 North Korean divisions and their total manpower was about 500,000. In addition, the Communists had massed a reserve force of about 1,000,000 troops along the Yalu, according to intelligence reports. The UN forces totaled 365,000, of which the largest single contingent was composed of ROK troops. The US 8th Army was the second largest UN force. And there were now token or larger contingents from Great Britain, Australia, Canada, New Zealand, India, South Africa, France, Greece, the Netherlands, the Philippines, Thailand, Turkey, Belgium and Sweden.

'Maximum punishment, maximum delay'

It was decided by the UN military commanders to establish a series of prepared defense perimeters extending as far back as the 1950 Pusan Perimeter. The strategy was to inflict as much damage on the attacking Communist forces as possible with a minimum of UN casualties, then withdraw in an orderly manner to the next prepared defense line to the rear. There was even a contingency plan to withdraw the UN troops to Japan if necessary. Some of the defense lines were prepared with trenches, barbed wire and sandbags. Fortunately, the deep defense lines were not needed because a later inspection revealed that Korean civilians had pilfered barbed wire and sandbags from the defenses for personal use. Nevertheless, the 'fight and roll' technique planned by Ridgway, based on a study of Chinese Communist tactics in the Chinese Civil War and again in the fighting north of the 38th Parallel, indicated it would achieve 'maximum punishment and maximum delay.'

The fight-and-roll tactic got its first test almost immediately as the Communist Armies began the New Year with a 1 January 1951 offensive in great force. Because the Chinese Communist troops moved as self-sufficient fighters, carrying enough food and ammunition to last several

Above: General Eisenhower, in his uniform as Supreme Allied Commander Europe, confers with President Truman in November 1951.

days and advancing by foot, they had to stop periodically to resupply themselves as their lines gradually became overextended. By inflicting maximum punishment, then falling back to a prepared defense line, Ridgway's troops were able to decimate the ranks of the Chinese Communist and NKPA forces.

The second drive to the north

Although the 1st Marine Division did not participate in the first week of the Communist January offensive, which forced the UN troops below the 37th Parallel, carrier-based US Marine aircraft covered the withdrawal of UN personnel through the Inchon area. By the end of the first week, contact with the enemy in the Suwon-Seoul area virtually disappeared, but pressure by the NKPA II Corps on the central and eastern defense lines increased considerably. On 10 January 1951 Communist troops had broken through the lines to the right of the US 2nd Division and infiltrated the ROK III Corps. To prevent further enemy penetration, General Smith's Marines were summoned to move northward from Masan to the Andong-Yongdok road where the Communist forces threatened to cut the supply routes of the ROK troops in the eastern sector.

With the mission to rescue the ROK III Corps executed and completed, the next major action involving the Marines in Korea was a contact with strong guerrilla forces south of the UN defense line on 23 January 1951 two days before Ridgway's Operation Thunderbolt was launched to take the United Nations forces back to the 38th Parallel. The Marines were busy with guerrilla groups in the south for nearly a month.

Large concentrations of guerrillas and remnants of the NKPA II Corps ranged between Andong and Usong, posing a serious constant threat to Ridgway's supply routes. The Communist forces would appear suddenly from the countryside, attack a truck convoy, then fade back into the countryside. All efforts to destroy the guerrilla groups had failed until units of the 1st Marine Division developed a technique of surrounding the guerrillas and preventing their escape. Once the hostile bands of guerrillas were encircled, the Marines would attack them with mortars and artillery. Observers estimated that such tactics reduced the strength of the Communist guerrillas in the south by 15 percent between January and February. The effectiveness of the Marine technique also was noticeable in a reduced level of activity. The guerrilla bands appeared less anxious to engage UN troops in large numbers, preferring to appear in brief skirmishes after which they would quickly disperse.

Operation Killer

On 21 February 1951 General Ridgway began a general assault on the Communist positions, an operation that required relieving the 1st Marine Division of its anti-guerrilla mission in the south. The new mission, dubbed Operation Killer, was frankly intended to produce a maximum number of enemy casualties with a minimum loss of UN troops. For this operation the Marines were committed near Wonju as part of IX Corps and during the first week of the advance General Smith, the commander of the 1st Marine Division, was named US IX Corps commander as a temporary replacement after army Major General Bryant Moore died of a heart attack following a helicopter crash into the Han River.

The Marines, meanwhile, had seized the high ground overlooking Hoengsong. Opposition was heavy but the enemy action was plainly an effort to delay the advance. As the UN troops moved northward through the Wonju area, the early Marine objective, they found the hills littered with dead Communist soldiers. It was estimated that 5000 Chinese troops were killed in the Wonju-Hoengsong offensive in seven days of fighting.

Below: Generals Ridgway (left) and MacArthur during a visit to the front in 1951.

Above: On the march in Korea. The harsh terrain and the poor roads in Korea meant that it was difficult for the United Nations' troops to make full use of their superior firepower. Greater emphasis was, therefore, placed on the training and determination of the individual foot soldier.

Above: 1st Marine Division in action near Hongchon.
Below: MacArthur at Wonju in February 1951.

Operation Ripper

Operation Killer had advanced the United Nations line to about halfway between the 37th and 38th Parallels by 1 March 1983 and was one of the more effective battle plans of the UN commanders. However, according to General Ridgway's retrospective of the event, he was advised by the Pentagon that there were objections in Washington to the use of the word 'killer' in the name of the operation because it had an adverse 'public relations' effect. Thus, beginning in early March 1951 the name was changed to 'Operation Ripper' but Ridgway's offensive continued.

By 15 March Operation Ripper had taken the UN forces back to the 38th Parallel and across the Han River in the west, and the capital city of Seoul changed hands a fourth time in less than nine months. Much of the city was rubble, including the US Embassy, there were no utilities and only 200,000 ragged civilians remained of the once bustling city's normal population of 1,500,000.

In the central zone Marines secured Hongchon and advanced toward Chunchon where fierce fighting erupted. NKPA troops had ensconced themselves in bunkers that were little affected by artillery and attacks by aircraft. Because Chunchon was a Communist supply and communications center it had to be destroyed. The 187th Airborne RCT was alerted to make a drop and assist the Marines but the project was cancelled when Marines went into the bunkers to dislodge the enemy with bayonets on 18 March 1951.

By the end of March, Operation Ripper was declared a qualified success. The geographical objectives had been achieved but the enemy had not been destroyed.

MacArthur is fired by President Truman

By early April 1951 some units of the US IX Corps had advanced beyond the 38th Parallel toward the so-called Iron Triangle bounded by Pyongyang, the North Korean capital, Chorwon and Kumhwa. The Communist forces, meanwhile, had massed 63 divisions with 500,000 men facing the United Nations troops. The Chinese Communists also were reported to have added at least a half-dozen new airbases in North Korea, including an airstrip built in Pyongyang by converting one of the main streets into a runway and tearing down the buildings on either side.

On 11 April 1951 General MacArthur was dismissed by President Truman from his four UN, Allied and US commands in the Far East. The five-star general was fired because of his public demands for a tougher stand against Communist China, contrary to policies of the United States and the

Above: Marine recoilless rifle team attacking a strongpoint near Chinchon-ni, April 1951.

United Nations. Beginning in March, MacArthur had predicted a 'theoretical military stalemate' if his forces had to continue what he called a 'halfway war' against the Chinese Communists in Korea. MacArthur explained that under the conditions imposed by the US and the UN, his troops could not expel the Communists from Korea and the Communists could not run the UN forces from the peninsula. Every time the UN troops drove the Communist forces northward, their supply and communications improved because their lines between North Korea and China was shortened.

When it was suggested that the 38th Parallel be established as a truce line, MacArthur objected that there were 'no natural defense features anywhere near' the 38th Parallel, adding that to set up an impregnable defense 'on any line across the peninsula' would require so many men that, if he had that many, he could push the Communists back to the Manchurian frontier. As the US Senate approved sending four more divisions to General Eisenhower's NATO command in Europe, MacArthur recommended in a letter to House Minority Leader Joseph Martin the arming of Chiang Kai-shek's troops on Taiwan for an invasion of the Chinese mainland.

James Van Fleet replaces General Ridgway

When the Pentagon recommended arming South Koreans for guerrilla activity, MacArthur rejected the proposal, saying ROK guerrillas were ineffective and US interests would be better served if the weapons were used instead to arm the Japanese National Police Reserve. MacArthur further issued a public statement urging a direct attack on Communist China, a naval blockade of the Chinese coast and a face-to-face meeting in the field with the commander of the Chinese Communists to discuss peace. President Truman, in dismissing MacArthur, explained that MacArthur had violated rules governing the issuing of public statements that had not been cleared by the US Administration and for 'acts that could touch off World War III.' General Ridgway was sent to Tokyo to replace General MacArthur. Lieutenant General James A Van Fleet was dispatched to Korea to take command of the UN ground forces there; Van Fleet was commanding general of the US 90th Division in World War II and was credited with masterminding the Greek government's triumph over Communist forces between 1948 and 1950.

General Van Fleet arrived on the scene

Below: Interdiction of communications was a vital part of the Allied war effort.

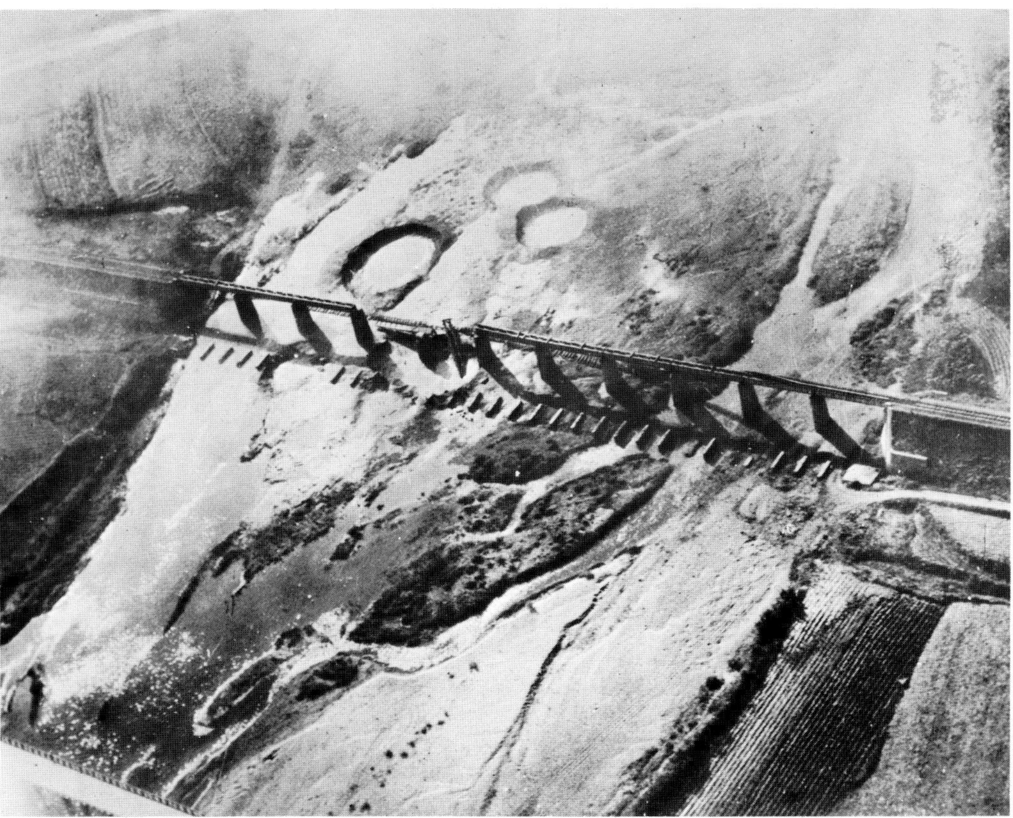

Above: Men of a 4.5-inch rocket battery attached to the 1st Marine Division wait to unload ammunition supplies, near Panjong-ni in August 1952.

14 April 1951 as the UN forces continued to edge northward while the enemy withdrew behind dense smokescreens created by burning off large areas of their front. The new commander continued the strategy of General Ridgway—'maximum punishment, maximum delay'—as the Communists broadcast radio messages promising a spring offensive either to drive the UN from the Korean peninsula or to destroy Van Fleet's troops in the field.

The enemy strikes back

The promised spring offensive began on the evening of 22 April 1951 with a four-hour artillery bombardment of the UN lines. It was a clear night with a full moon and by daybreak three Chinese Communist armies were moving across the entire peninsula. The Communist attacks followed the same pattern as in previous offensives, with 'human sea' assaults of massed infantry, blowing bugles and whistles, infiltrating to get behind the defense lines, and moving in so close that UN artillery and air support could not be used without endangering the UN's own frontline troops.

The Communists probed for a weak link, then struck at the ROK 6th Division which was between the US 24th Division on the left and the US 1st Marine Division on the right. As the ROK troops withdrew in confusion, the Communists attempted to move into the gap between the 1st Marine and 24th Infantry Divisions, which refused their exposed flanks and held their positions. The 27th Commonwealth Brigade rushed into the gap and stopped the Chinese advance south of the 38th Parallel. The 1st Marine Division retired southward and took up a new position near Chunchon.

When the Chinese cut the Seoul-Chunchon-Kansong highway near Kapyong on 26 April, Van Fleet ordered the entire IX Corps back to the Hongchon River, 20 miles south of the 38th Parallel. During the offensive, UN pilots flew 7420 missions in eight days and in one mission alone strafed 6000 Communist soldiers attempting to attack Seoul with an amphibious landing across the Han River. ROK marines on an embankment above the river finished off most of the Chinese troops that survived the air attacks.

Fighting on the No-Name-Line

Each of the defense lines originally established by General Ridgway had been given a code name identified with one of the states of the US—Wyoming, Utah, Kansas, Idaho. On 29 April 1951 General Van Fleet established a new line that was not given a state name and thereby became known as the No-Name-Line. It extended from north of Seoul in the generally northeastward direction across the 38th Parallel to Taepo-ri, on the east coast of North Korea. Van Fleet also shuffled the various units around to put more American troops on the west side of Korea, where the Chinese Communists had put the major weight of their offensive. The 1st Marine Division, however, was located near the center with the US 2nd Infantry and ROK 5th and 7th Divisions.

On 7 May 1951 the US Marines recaptured Chunchon after digging NKPA soldiers out of camouflaged bunkers along the highway to Wonju. Intelligence reports, meanwhile, indicated the Communists were planning a new drive. Fifty new airbases were being built and 1000 planes were sighted by reconnaissance cameras. The 1st Marine Aircraft Wing then stepped up its efforts in a coordinated attack with the 5th USAF. On 9 May 1951 a fleet of 312 F-80 Shooting Stars, F-84 Thunderjets, F-86 Sabrejets, F9F Panthers, F4U Corsairs and F51 Mustangs struck at airfields along the south bank of the Yaly River, destroying 15 Communist jet aircraft and more than 100 buildings. At about the same time, the No-Name-Line was turned into a No Man's Land with mine fields, artillery registered, bands of interlocking machine guns, 500 miles of barbed wire and 55-gallon drums of gasoline and napalm wired electronically for remote-control detonation. 'If the enemy comes,' said Van Fleet, 'I want to see so many artillery holes that a man can step from one to another.'

The second spring offensive

The enemy came on the night of 15 May 1951. Twenty-one Chinese divisions flanked by three North Korean divisions on the west and six on the east went for a sector in the center of the peninsula held by the US X Corps and ROK III Corps. The US 1st Marine Division held the left part of the line on terrain overlooking Chunchon plain. The US 2nd Infantry Division was to the right with the ROK 5th and 7th Divisions farther to the right. On 16 May, after holding their ground for a time, the ROK divisions fell back, broken and disorganized. The US 2nd Division, with French and Dutch battalions withstood enemy attacks until 18 May 1951. They, together with the US Marines, moved to fill the gap left by the two ROK divisions.

As the Chinese and North Koreans tried to encircle the 2nd Division, neighboring units rushed to help regain control. The 2nd Division held fast while the 38th Field Artillery Battalion fired 12,000 rounds of 105-mm shells at the Communist troops. Van Fleet's artillery use, which was five times the allowance of the previous ground forces commanders, led to later reports of an ammunition shortage and a Congressional inquiry. The 2nd Division suffered a total of 900 casualties but the Communist

Below: An HTL-4 training helicopter of the 1st Marine Air Wing in Korea in March 1951. Note the casualty evacuation litters fitted to the helicopter

Above: A Marine corpsman receives the Bronze Star for gallantry while serving with the 1st Marine Division.

attackers lost 35,000 dead, wounded or missing. By 20 May 1951 the US 1st Marine Division still held its position on the No-Name-Line and the US 2nd Division, with the 15th Infantry attached, began to retake its position on the line. The Communist spring offensive had been halted and the UN forces were preparing to take the offensive again.

'In hot pursuit of the enemy'

To help relieve enemy pressure on the US X Corps, General Van Fleet ordered several units—including the US 1st Marine Division—to send out patrols to a new phase line called the Topeka Line, just below the 38th Parallel. The following day, units of the UN forces began moving across the 38th Parallel toward the Hwachon Reservoir and the Iron Triangle. Van Fleet said the 38th Parallel 'has no significance in the present tactical situation' and his troops would 'go wherever the situation dictates in hot pursuit of the enemy.' Thus, the UN's own 1951 spring offensive rolled forward in May.

On 24 May 1951 General Almond ordered the 1st Marine Division to Yanggu and the 187th Airborne RCT to Inje to push the Communists farther away from the 38th Parallel and against the Hawachon Reservoir. Although rain, mud and the enemy slowed the offensive, the Marines made their final push toward their objective on 27 May. By June South Korea was virtually clear of Communist troops.

By June, General Van Fleet had lowered his sights a bit and it was explained that 'hot pursuit of the enemy' did not mean he intended another march to the Yalu River. In order to expend 'steel and fire, rather than human lives,' Van Fleet decided to find the most effective line across the Korean peninsula that offered optimum supply and communication lines and defensible terrain while making local advances in search of more favorable ground.

Operational Piledriver

On 1 June 1951 Van Fleet ordered reserve forces to begin building a virtually impregnable defense line at the position of the old Kansas phase line, running generally along the 38th Parallel for about the western half of Korea and swinging northward through Yanggu to a point above Kansong, approximately 30 miles above the parallel on the east coast of North Korea. All civilians were cleared out of the area, which was strung with barbed wire, laced with land mines and equipped with such amenities as covered shelters, road and trail blocks.

From this line, troops could work to the base of the Iron Triangle, which was a key supply and communications center for Communist troops, with terminals for rail and highway traffic coming from Manchuria. Operation Piledriver was the code name for the UN advances to Chorwon and Kumhwa, the base points of the triangle. Two tank-infantry task forces pushed all the way to Pyongyang on 13 June, but found it deserted and difficult to defend against Communist troops holding the high ground above the city. Chinese troops reoccupied Pyongyang four days later.

Probably the hardest fighting of Operation Piledriver involved the advance of the US Marines and the ROK 5th and 7th Divisions toward the 'punchbowl,' a volcano crater situated about 25 miles north of Inje and along the edge of the Kansas Line objective of Van Fleet. The route to the Punchbowl was blocked by a succession of well-entrenched NKPA II and V Corps troops who were adequately supplied with machine guns, mortars and artillery. After blasting the North Koreans out of one ridgeline of bunkers, the task had to be repeated at the next ridge. By 16 June 1958 the 1st Marine Division finally reached the Kansas Line. And for the rest of the month, the Marines fought a series of violent, bloody skirmishes about the Punchbowl, battles that were costly but did not result in a significant change in the positions of either side.

Call for a ceasefire

As the first anniversary of the Korean War approached, USSR Deputy Foreign Commissar and Soviet Delegate to the United Nations Jacob Malik proposed that the opposing sides in the war arrange for a

Below: Marines in training in a rear area try out a new pattern of winter clothing, Korea, December 1951.

ceasefire. The proposal was made on 23 June 1951, with indications that the ceasefire was actually requested on behalf of the Peoples' Republic of China. President Truman responded by authorizing General Ridgway to conduct negotiations with commanders of the Chinese and North Korean forces. A meeting was arranged at Kaesong, a town near Korea's west coast and between the front lines of the opposing armies, for 10 July 1951. Vice Admiral C Turner Joy, Far East Naval Commander for the US, was named delegate for the United Nations and Lieutenant General Nam Il, NKPA Chief of Staff, represented the Communist armies.

One of the conditions for the ceasefire negotiations agreed to by both sides was that hostilities would be continued until a truce was signed. However, neither side appeared willing to start any large-scale offensive while peace talks were underway. The front at that time extended from the Imjin River to Chorwon, parallel to the base of the Iron Triangle, swinging southeast along the southern edge of the Punchbowl, then north again to the Sea of Japan above Kansong. Van Fleet's troops improved their positions and consolidated the land they had just won. The US 1st Marine Division faced two strong NKPA Corps around the Punchbowl.

The Battle of Bloody Ridge

Much of the fighting in July 1951 centered about a 3980-foot peak west of the Punchbowl known as Hill 1179. It was defended by a regiment of NKPA troops and was being used to observe the UN lines during the ceasefire negotiations. ROK marines attacked Hill 1179 without success, after which Van Fleet ordered the US 2nd Division into the fight. The wooded slopes of Hill 1179 were so steep the American infantrymen had to climb hand over hand up the rocky cliffs while carrying full loads. Korean natives went with the troops, toting ammunition, armament and food on A-frame backpacks. After four days of struggle and supported by aircraft and artillery, the 2nd Division troops finally secured the crest of Hill 1179.

The next important round of fighting fell again to the US 1st Marine Division after the ROK 5th Division was driven off a mountain range, also west of the Punchbowl, called Bloody Ridge on the night of 27 August 1951. The 9th Regiment of the US 2nd Division was committed to retake the ridge in a seesaw battle that ran for five days, the infantrymen advancing only to be forced back. The Communist forces were well dug in and supported by artillery. The enemy did not yield its position until units of the 1st Marine Division joined in the battle, which became one of the bloodiest and most exhausting of the war. The fighting at times resembled scenes from a Hollywood movie, with Marines inching their way along rocky mountain slopes, carrying mortars as well as rifles and ammunition, to reach enemy foxholes. Much of the firing was at pointblank range after the Communist positions were reached.

Marines introduce helicopter troop lifts

Fighting for the many ridges along the UN line continued through September and into October 1951. After a seven-day mission by the 1st Marine Division to advance to the Soyang River above the Punchbowl, the Marines tried the first troop lift by helicopter in a combat zone. It was a military innovation that gave the troops a major tactical advantage in fighting that required hand over hand assaults over the knife-crested ridges of Korean terrain while carrying 60-mm mortars or 75-mm recoilless rifle rounds as well as their own rifles, ammunition and other supplies.

Below: Marine patrol returns to friendly lines, 1st Marine Division, 28 December 1951.

The helicopter was developed too late for effective use in World War II, but the Marines discovered the versatility of the rotary wing machines as early as August 1950 when they began to use helicopters for reconnaissance, rescue, casualty evacuation, liaison between units and laying communication wires.

The first Marine helicopters used in Korea were Sikorsky HO3S-1s, with room for three men. They were used during the Inchon invasion by unit commanders who could personally supervise fighting over a front of several hundred yards. Although there had been initial concern about the vulnerability of helicopters to enemy ground fire, losses turned out to be much less than expected. In fact, only two helicopter pilots were lost to enemy fire during the first six months of the Korean War.

During the fighting in the Bloody Ridge-Heartbreak Ridge-Punchbowl area above the 38th Parallel in late September 1951, the 1st Marine Division began transporting company-size units to the combat zones with the larger Sikorsky HRS-1 helicopters, each capable of carrying 1400 pounds of cargo or six fully-equipped combat troops. Using a squadron of the Sikorsky HRS-1s, the Marines could move a company 10 to 15 miles within a few hours over terrain that would have required a day or more by ground transportation. In October, the Marines began using helicopters to move whole battalions. After observing the success of the Marine experiments, the Army later began using helicopters for rapid troop transport to a battle zone.

Below: A Marine with Browning Automatic Rifle advances as his buddy prepares to give covering fire, Sintan-ni, December 1951.

Fighting and peace talks stalemated

The Communist delegation to the ceasefire negotiations broke off talks in August 1951 but called for a return to the peace table in mid-October after the UN firepower demonstrations in the Punchbowl area. Van Fleet had submitted plans for major offensive operations including an amphibious landing that would have taken the Marines to a point on the east coast of North Korea near Wonsan, the major port south of Hungnam. But General Ridgway in Tokyo vetoed the plans because of the optimistic outlook at that time for a truce and political discontent in the US about the price in American casualties for the amount of real estate gained. Van Fleet was instead ordered on 12 November 1951 to cease offensive operations and begin an active defense of the UN's main line of resistance.

As the year 1951 ended, fighting had tapered off into a routine of patrol clashes and skirmishes with the enemy over outpost positions along the 155-mile front. The US 45th Army Division arrived to replace the US 1st Cavalry Division and intelligence reports revealed that Chinese Communist troops had taken over the defense of the North Korean lines in the western and central sectors of the front. Communist attacks occurred sporadically at night. Conflict in the air also slowed as Communist pilots seemed reluctant to engage US Sabrejets. Navy planes from the carriers *Antietam* and *Valley Forge* bombed bridges and railyards. But the war generally ground into a stalemate that lasted into early 1952.

Marines reassigned to US I Corps

Because General Van Fleet believed the western sector had become more vulnerable during the spring of 1952, he shifted units along the front to concentrate greater US firepower in the area defended by the Chinese Communist troops. The changes required that the 1st Marine Division, which had been defending the Punchbowl area in the US X Corps zone, would be attached to the I Corps commanded by Lieutenant General John W O'Daniel. Small raids across the Imjin River were planned and the Marines were needed for the missions to utilize their amphibious experience and equipment. The ROK 1st Division, which was replaced by the US Marines, was moved to the right center sector and given greater responsibility for defending the battle line there.

As expected, the Chinese intensified their thrusts against the UN lines during May 1952. As measured in mortar and artillery rounds, the Chinese had increased their firepower from a total of 8000 rounds in July 1951 to 102,000 rounds in May 1952. They also moved their artillery closer to the UN lines and would mass eight to 10 guns on a single target. But the Marines encountered mainly patrol clashes and light probing attacks. The most ambitious Chinese attacks were directed against the US 45th Division, protecting O'Daniel's I Corps on the right wing. During June 1952 the 45th Division sustained 1004 casualties but cost the Chinese 5000 in a series of attacks and counterattacks.

Battles of the outposts

The 1st Marines saw action again after Major General Paul W Kendall became commander of the US I Corps in July 1952. Supported by mortar and artillery fire, two companies from the 7th Marine Regiment swept into Chinese Communist positions and inflicted 200 casualties on the surprised enemy before retiring. The battlefront had been relatively stable since the previous November but as summer followed spring, UN raids and Communist counterattacks increased. On 29 August 1952 the US 5th Air Force, accompanied by planes of the US Navy and Marine Corps, Australia and the United Kingdom, carried out the biggest air raid of the Korean War. Hundreds of planes flew over North Korea in a massive strike at the North Korean capital of Pyongyang, Communist supply installations, repair shops, troop concentrations, military headquarters and other targets. But Communist artillery bombardments also increased and in a single day in September 1952, 45,000 mortar and artillery rounds fell on UN defense positions. But even that record fell on 7 October 1952 when the US 8th Army received 93,000 mortar and artillery rounds from Chinese and North Korean guns.

In October 1952 Chinese troops that had concentrated their attacks during the late summer against US and ROK Army positions turned their attention to the sector of the front held by the US 1st Marine Division. In a series of harassing attacks, the Chinese Communists tried without success to overrun several of the Marine outposts.

The last offensive

At the end of 1952 General Van Fleet had 16 divisions manning the 8th Army's battle line. Included was the 1st Marine Division, which had acquired a ROK Marine regiment as an important adjunct. The UN also had four divisions available as reserve forces. During the stalemate that began in 1951, both sides had constructed such powerful defense lines that it would have been costly to either side to attempt to reduce the defenses of the opposing force. The Communists had suffered thousands of casualties attempting to breach the UN lines and Van Fleet advised that an occasional outpost could lose its usefulness if it became clear that the enemy was willing to capture it at any cost.

But through the spring and early summer of 1953, the Communist forces began signaling the start of a new offensive by attempting to seize outposts that overlooked the main defense line of the UN troops. By July 1953 the intensity of the enemy attacks had returned to the level of May 1951, before the start of ceasefire negotiations. The UN armies had a total strength of about 768,000, as opposed to nine Chinese and North Korean armies and corps on the enemy front line and an additional 11 armies and corps in reserve for a total of more than 1,000,000 men. About three-fourths of the frontline troops were Chinese.

General Van Fleet, meanwhile, retired after nearly two years as 8th Army commander and was replaced by Lieutenant General Maxwell Taylor.

The frequency and intensity of the Communist attacks began in March 1953, probing at sectors of the US I Corps line. On the evening of 26 March they assaulted several outposts of the 1st Marine Regiment. Two of three positions were overrun by enemy forces in regimental strength, and the Chinese advanced toward the main line of resistance until they were intercepted by a blocking force. The following morning, a Marine battalion counterattacked and recaptured one of the lost outposts. In fighting that continued through the day and into 28 March, the Marines drove the Chinese back and recaptured their other lost outpost.

However, the Chinese returned with a counterattack that drove the Americans back 400 yards. In the afternoon the US Marines once again drove back the Chinese and regained their outpost. Then the Marines dug in, reinforced their position and waited for the next Chinese attack. It came during the night of 28 March, spearheaded by a battalion of Chinese. More Marine reinforcements were poured into the battle while artillery fire was used to isolate the battlefield and prevent the Chinese from increasing the size of their force. By the next morning, the Chinese Communists withdrew after failing to make headway in their assault on the Marines.

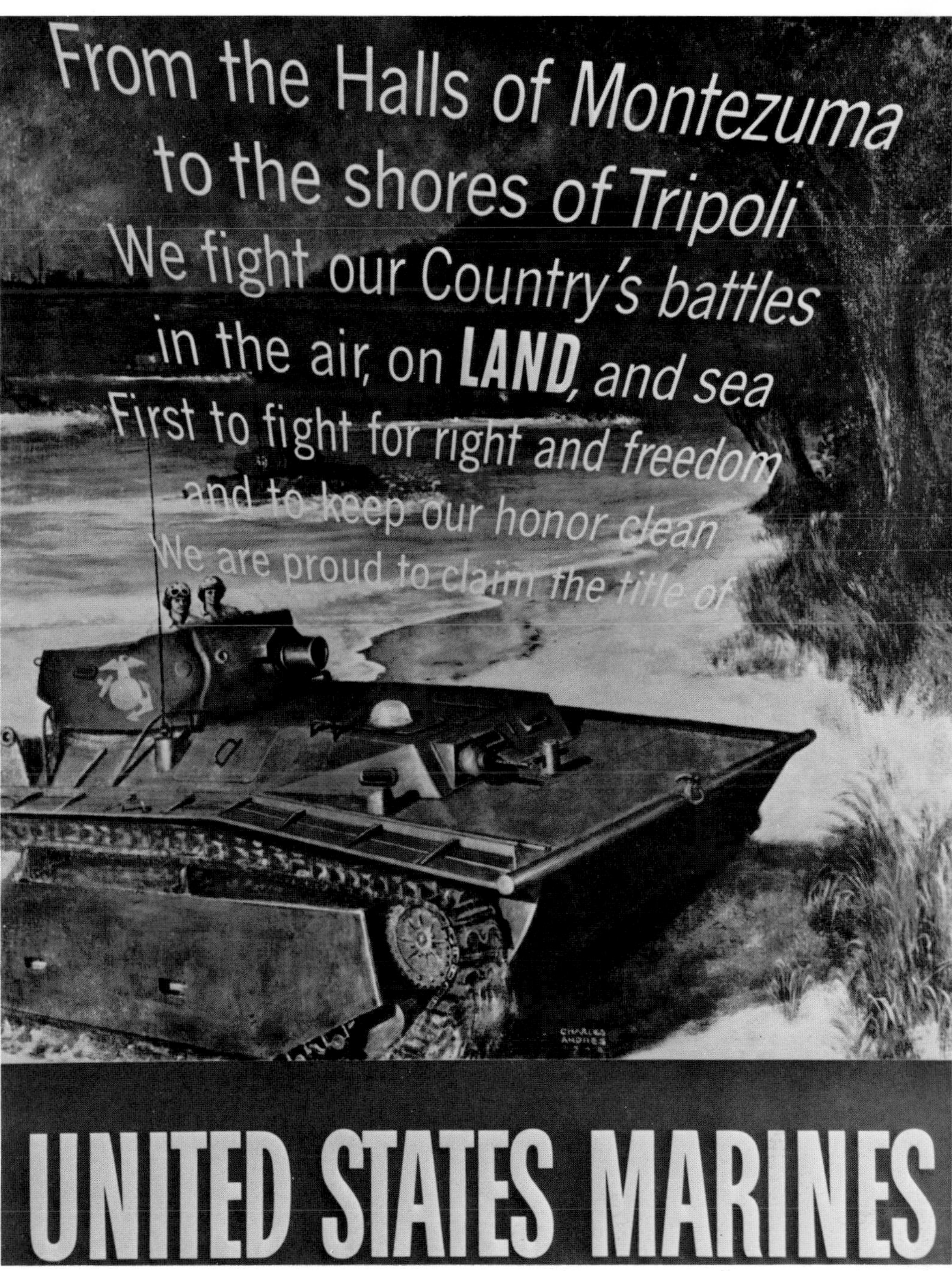

Above: A Marine recruiting poster of the Korean War period. Many of the recruits were veterans of World War II.

An armistice is signed

The Communists continued their attacks into June and July 1953. On the night of 10 June 1953, the Chinese struck down both sides of the Pukhan River to drive the ROK II Corps back 4000 yards in six days of the heaviest fighting in more than two years. By mid-June, the Chinese had lost 6628 men and II Corps 7377 casualties in the fighting. General Taylor brought in the 187th Airborne Regimental Combat Team and the 34th Regimental Combat Team to reinforce the UN positions. In the following month, July 1953, the Communists experienced tremendous losses in an attempt to end the war with a victory. The estimated losses for the Chinese totaled 72,000, including 25,000 killed. The Chinese had sacrificed the equivalent of seven of their divisions in attacking the ROK II and US IX Corps.

Meanwhile, the negotiators at the peace table at Panmunjom finally reached an agreement on an armistice and a team began drawing up the boundaries of what was to become the DMZ, or Korean demilitarized zone. The armistice was signed by North Korean General Nam Il and US Lieutenant General William K Harrison, Jr, the senior United Nations delegate to the armistice negotiations, at 1000 hours on 27 July 1953.

Above: Drill Instructor Sergeant Warren Plavets marches his platoon off after their graduation from basic training at Parris Island, a picture taken in May 1952.

The armistice took effect at 2200 hours on the same day, as a requirement of the agreement. The war had lasted three years, one month and two days. It had consumed the lives of hundreds of thousands of soldiers and civilians from two dozen nations around the world. Homes, fields and factories were destroyed, the nation's economy ruined and the populace threatened with famine and disease. General Dwight D Eisenhower, who had succeeded Harry Truman as President of the United States during the war, said: 'We have won an armistice on a single battleground—not peace in the world. We may not now relax our guard nor cease our quest.'

One of the greatest tributes paid to the members of the 1st Marine Division who served in the Korean War came later from a military chaplain who was with members of the Marine and Army troops who fought their way out of the Changjin Reservoir trap in North Korea in December 1950. The chaplain said he witnessed Army infantrymen who 'faked' injuries in order to be evacuated as casualties. But he also observed Marines who were wounded but who concealed their injuries so they would be allowed to continue fighting the Chinese Communist troops.

A different kind of peace

Another major war was over, but the next years of the Corps were not to be a replay of those after World War I and World War II, when its strength had been drastically cut. Even before the armistice was signed in 1953, the US Congress had passed in 1952 Public Law 416, which provided for three active Marine divisions and three air wings. Perhaps just as crucial for assuring the survival and integrity of the Corps, its Commandant was given a position on the Joint Chiefs of Staff, with co-equal status in decisions affecting the Marines. And in 1954 the Secretary of the Navy would further strength the Commandant's position by making him directly responsible to the Secretary, not to the Chief of Naval Operations. It was a recognition, if not a reward, of the fact that when the hostilities began in Korea, General MacArthur had called on the Marines, and they had done the job.

The Marines themselves had learned many lessons from the fighting in Korea, of which the versatility of the helicopter, already described, was only the most obvious. The Marines had also been confirmed in their high regard for amphibious landing forces and for the coordinated air support for Marine land operations. In the years that followed, the Corps would continue to develop its helicopter vertical-assault tactics, just as it had done with amphibious tactics in the 1930s (and with equal import for future operations). Training would also include both cold weather and jungle sessions. The Marines had developed a special thermal boot to protect feet from frostbite as a result of their early experiences in Korea; they had also learned the value of the 'flak jacket', or armored vest, developed by Marines to protect men in the front lines from abdominal and chest wounds. New weapons would also be adopted as a result of lessons learned in Korea: the M-14 would replace the old, familiar M-1, and the M-60 machine gun would replace the Browning automatic rifle.

Reflecting their firm respect and responsibilities, the Marines remained deployed around the world, with sizable units on Okinawa, Japan, and Hawaii, as well as at the home bases in the States. At Marine Headquarters in Washington, General Lemuel Shepherd Jr was replaced in 1956 as Commandant by General Randolph McCall Pate, who had been in office barely three months when, on 8 April 1956, an incident at the Parris Island training camp became one of the worst scandals in the Corps's history. An overzealous, if not downright irresponsible, Drill Instructor ordered an unauthorized night march, which led to six recruits drowning in Ribbon Creek. There was an immediate public outcry and protest over the Marines' traditional training methods—although most Marines were quick to defend them—and after Congressional hearings, numerous changes were made in these methods. Although individual cases of excessively rough, even brutal, training incidents would surface over the years, the Marines were at least credited with admitting to these failures. And the image of the Marines was enhanced, too, when in February 1962 Marine Lieutenant Colonel John H Glenn Jr became the first American to orbit the earth; Glenn went on to become a genuine

American hero, a Senator from his state of Ohio, and a candidate for nomination for the presidency, while many other Marines followed him into space.

But between the extremes, most Marines went about a more normal range of duties in the years following the Korean War. Some, for instance, found themselves performing essentially humanitarian tasks such as rescuing victims of natural disasters: in 1953, Greeks on the Ionian Islands, after an earthquake; in 1955, Mexicans, after a flood; in 1957, Ceylonese and Spanish, after floods; in 1960, Moroccans and foreigners, after an earthquake at the resort town of Agadir; in 1961, Turkish, after an earthquake; and British Hondurans, after a hurricane.

Marines also found themselves being assigned to another type of rescue mission in these years—helping individual Americans or friendly nationals when threatened by violence. Thus, in 1956, when war engulfed the Middle East briefly as a result of the Suez Crisis, Marines evacuated Americans from Alexandria, Egypt, and a UN truce team from Haifa, Israel, while two Marines held off a mob attacking the American consulate in Jerusalem. In 1958 a mob in Caracas, Venezuela, attacked the limousine carrying then-Vice President Richard Nixon, whose Latin American goodwill tour had run afoul of anti-*Yanqui* feelings (undoubtedly encouraged by leftist agitators); a battalion of Marines was put on standby on a cruiser off Caracas, but they did not have to go ashore. A somewhat similar incident occurred in Tokyo, Japan, in 1960, when Ambassador Douglas MacArthur II and the visiting White House Press Secretary James Hagerty were surrounded in their car by a mob; this time a US Marine helicopter actually rescued them.

Another type of rescue operation mounted by the Marines during these years came about when they were called in to display the full support or commitment of the USA when some friendly government seemed threatened by domestic or foreign violence. The most dramatic instance of this role for the Marines occurred in Lebanon in 1958. That summer, the pro-Western government headed by President Camille Chamoun felt threatened by a possible *coup d'etat* after a successful Communist coup in neighboring Iraq. On 14 July President Chamoun appealed to the USA and Britain for direct help; President Eisenhower consulted with his Joint Chiefs of Staff that day and then authorized a landing by Marines then in the Mediterranean. On the 15th the 2nd Battalion, 2nd Marines, part of the Sixth Fleet's landing force, went ashore some four miles south of Beirut; no shots were fired—indeed, the only obstacles were bathers at the beach. During the following two days, more Marines came ashore at other points around Beirut; although by no means welcomed by all Lebanese, the Marines ended up establishing an armed perimeter around Beirut by the end of July. The Marines did engage in some exchanges of fire with rebels (although the two Marine deaths came from accidental shootings by other Marines) but in general the American forces were praised for the restraint they showed. By the time the last Marines left at the end of September, a semblance of order had been restored to Lebanon, but events would conspire to bring the Marines back to Beirut many years later—and to a less peaceful rendezvous.

Marines in Central America and the Caribbean

One region of the world where the US Marines had a history of intervention was Central America and the Caribbean, where the United States had long taken it for granted that it would not stand by during certain manifestations of instability. Thus, in 1954, during a coup that overthrew the government of Colonel Jacobo Arbenz Guzman—a coup, not so incidentally, supported by the US government—a battalion of Marines was assigned to protect American nationals and American-owned property. That did not seem unreasonable, nor did it seem unreasonable in July 1958, when Fidel Castro was fighting his revolution against the Cuban government and the water supply of the US naval base at Guantanamo was threatened, that US Marines

Below: The intensification of the Cold War in the early 1950s led to renewed calls for Marine recruitment.

went into Cuban territory to protect that water supply.

A more controversial instance, however, came in April 1961, with the invasion of Cuba at the Bay of Pigs; although no Marines actively participated in the invasion, at least one high-ranking Marine officer played a significant part in the planning stage. Then, during the Cuban Missile Crisis of October 1962, when President Kennedy demanded that the USSR remove its missiles from Cuba and enforced a blockade, or quarantine, to effect this, the entire Marine Corps was placed on alert along with the entire US military throughout the world. More specifically, the 5th Marine Expeditionary Brigade, some 11,000 strong, actually sailed from Camp Pendleton, California, for the Caribbean, while the 2nd Marine Division was moved down to Key West, Florida, and various Caribbean stations.

Undoubtedly the most controversial intervention of the USA in Caribbean affairs in these years would come in 1965, when President Johnson ordered the US military into the Dominican Republic. The US Marines, of course, had occupied this nation between 1916–24, and ever since the assassination of Trujillo in May 1961, visits by US Navy ships and amphibious 'demonstrations' by US Marines had served to remind anyone who doubted it of the US commitment to maintaining order in this island state. Then, in late April 1965, a faction in the Dominican Army that was generally considered 'leftist' attempted a coup, and the US-backed president Donald J Reid Cabral asked for US aid. On 25 April a six-ship squadron of the US Navy's Caribbean Ready Group set out from Puerto Rico with some 1700 Marines aboard. The original, or at least announced, mission was simply to protect US nationals and aid in their evacuation should they become endangered. By 27 April there was such bloody fighting between the pro- and anti-government forces that the US ambassador asked that the Marines be assigned to assist in the evacuation. (There were already eight Marines comprising the security guard of the US Embassy, but they were powerless in the face of the violence in Santo Domingo.) Before that day was over, Marines, using helicopters and amphibious transports, managed to get some 1200 US nationals aboard US Navy ships.

But the fighting continued, and by 28 April it appeared that the leftist, anti-government forces were coming out on top. The military junta that now opposed these forces asked the US to provide military aid. At first, only platoons of Marines were brought to the US Embassy and to the evacuation site, where they could be regarded as still protecting US nationals. But soon they were engaged in firing back at the anti-government snipers. As reports of these developments were made to President Lyndon B Johnson, he and the Joint Chiefs of Staff decided to commit more Marines; by now it was clearly a decision to stop what was perceived as a pro-Communist coup.

Starting on the 29th, some 1500 Marines went ashore; the next day, elements of the US Airborne Infantry Division began to join them. As the American troops tried to make their way into the center of Santo Domingo, they engaged in some fairly intense fighting. In the days that followed, some 22,000 US Marines and Army personnel came ashore, and the anti-government forces were kept from taking over. A ceasefire was arranged through the agency of the Organization of American States (OAS); troops from five Latin-American nations began to arrive to take over from the US units, and by 6 June all the US Marines had left. But of the 6000 Marines who had gone ashore, nine were dead and 30 wounded.

Below: Apprehensive recruits arrive at Parris Island to begin training in 1951. As the picture shows the US armed forces were racially integrated by this time.

Above: Sporting their new Marine Corps haircuts recruits are issued with their uniforms, Parris Island 1955

President Johnson and his advisers were criticized by many for committing US forces to fight on behalf of a particular government—especially since it had itself seized power by a coup. But Johnson and his supporters had the example of Cuba in mind, and were determined not to let another pro-Communist government become established on a Caribbean island. And although even some high-ranking Marines insisted that 'only a fraction of the force deployed was needed or justified,' no one denied that the Marines had once again done their duty like the professionals they were.

The Far East: dominoes or quagmire?
But of all the regions where the US Marines had so often found themselves assigned to defend America's interests, perhaps it was the Far East that would prove to be the most troublesome—and costly. After mainland China was taken over by the Communist Chinese, the USA decided to continue supporting the Nationalists on Taiwan, and this support sometimes meant calling in the Marines. Early in 1955, for instance, the Communist Chinese took over an offshore island of Ichiang; this move appeared to threaten Nationalist Chinese on the nearby Tachen Islands, so a battalion of Marines was assigned to help some 24,000 of them evacuate to Taiwan. In 1958, when the Communist Chinese began to bombard the offshore islands of Quemoy and Little Quemoy, a Marine Air Group was assigned to Taiwan to help bolster the Nationalist Chinese air defenses.

But it was in Southeast Asia that the United States found itself increasingly involved in commitments that had increasing implications. Behind all these commitments, in fact, was the determination not to let these lands fall under Communist domination. Thus, even in 1955, when some 300,000 North Vietnamese—mostly Catholics, but in any case opposed to the Communist government of Ho Chi Minh—chose to flee to the south, US Marines assisted in this mammoth refugee operation.

Then a civil war broke out in Laos in 1959, and when it appeared that it might threaten the stability of neighboring Thailand, in 1961 the USA dispatched a Marine Expeditionary Brigade; eventually Marine helicopter units were also sent to Thailand, and before the Marines all left in August 1962, some 5000 had been assigned for duty there.

The justification, again, was that if one of these countries fell to the Communists, the others would begin to topple like a row of dominoes. Those opposed to American involvement, however, would employ another simile—that of a quagmire, into which America was sinking deeper and deeper. Whichever was the case, it was in another Southeast Asian land that the USA—and the Marines—were becoming increasingly involved. It was the troublespot to end all troublespots: Vietnam.

THE LONG STRUGGLE IN VIETNAM

'Our Tradition and Our Burden'—1955-1973

In early 1954 the Corps' total involvement in Vietnam was represented by the arrival there of one lone Marine advisor; by 1968 the number of Marines in Vietnam had grown to a peak strength of 85,755 men and women, more than a quarter of the total strength of the Corps. The circumstances that brought about the growth of Corps involvement in America's longest military action was a classic example of how deadly a brew the mixture of politics and warfare can create.

In the beginning

In a sense, the Vietnam War was an 'adopted war' for the United States. What was then known as the Indochina War belonged to the French who, by the time the first American arrived, had been in combat with the North Vietnam-based Communist army of Ho Chi Minh for nearly a decade. During that period the French formed a union with the South Vietnamese that placed the conduct of the war against the Communists under the aegis of a group titled the Franco-Vietnamese High Committee, made up of military men of each nation. One of the plans generated by the committee called for the creation of a strong South Vietnamese Navy and Marine Corps, but political squabbling in Saigon, along with opposition by the country's large army, brought these plans to all but a halt, so that at the end of 1955 the South Vietnamese Marine Corps consisted of only 90 officers and 3730 men.

The American Marines in Vietnam at this time were served with an organization called MAAG—the US Military Assistance & Advisory Group, Indochina—which was set up by presidential order to support the efforts of the French and South Vietnamese military. At French insistance MAAG's role was strictly that of a supply depot; its advisory functions were limited to the demonstration of US equipment and not related to operations or combat training.

Major growth of the American presence did not come until after the signing of a peace agreement in 1954 ended the Indochina War and led to the subsequent gradual withdrawal of the French military. This reduction in French forces created great difficulty for the embryonic South Vietnamese military, since they had been receiving military supplies directly from the French, who in turn got the materials from the United States. With the French leaving, title to the military equipment reverted to the United States, and the American administration felt obliged to move in and see to its distribution.

Soon, however, the pressure of circumstances made it necessary for the United States to take on a major role previously filled by the French in regard to the South Vietnamese military forces, that of providing for their training, organization and administration. Toward the end of 1954 the United States told the Vietnamese government it was willing to provide equipment and training support for 90,000 Vietnamese troops. When Saigon strongly rejected this number, the US raised the figure in increments during the following year to 150,000.

Also, in 1955, Marines with the Seventh Fleet aided in the evacuation of 300,000 refugees from North Vietnam to the south. That same year, working in conjunction with the French, the United States provided personnel for two training missions with the acronym titles of ATOM and, its replacement later in 1955, TRIM. A plan for the organization of the South Vietnamese Navy and Marine Corps was developed by a committee of TRIM, with the naval portion of the plan coming from a French study group and the Marine proposals coming from US Marines assigned to TRIM. In December 1955, after a detailed presentation of the plans of Lieutenant General Lee Van Ty, Chief of Staff of the Vietnamese Armed Forces, Ty accepted the organizational plan. As part of the implementation of the plan, US Marine Corps drill instructors provided Basic School instruction for Vietnamese Marine Corps recruits; the best of the graduates from these classes became DIs themselves and soon took over much of the work of training recuirts.

Involvement by attrition: advisory campaign

The next decade of war in Vietnam at first saw American military forces play a 'bridesmaid' role to the combat, close to the center of action but never committed to aggressive combat by direct orders. However, this situation gradually changed in an evolutionary way as American military personnel —working with base-keeping forces, medical field units and helicopter elements in ever-closer support of Vietnamese combat

Previous page: Marine CH-53 helicopter in flight over Phnom Penh in April 1975.
Below: Viet Minh troops during the victory over the French at Dien Bien Phu in 1954, which signaled the end of French rule.

Right: A Sea Stallion helicopter carrying a water trailer to Hill 119, six miles from the Danang base, 1st Marine Division, during the Vietnam campaign in May 1970.

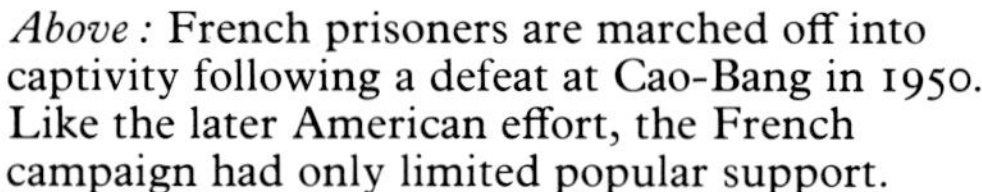

Above: French prisoners are marched off into captivity following a defeat at Cao-Bang in 1950. Like the later American effort, the French campaign had only limited popular support.

Above: Men of the 4th Marines during an amphibious landing at Danang.
Right: Marines move away from their transport helicopter during a search and destroy operation.

troops—began experiencing casualties from enemy action in steadily increasing numbers. Early in 1962 Marine Medium Helicopter Squadron 362 of the 1st Marine Aircraft Wing was ordered to Vietnam, in what was dubbed Operation Shu-Fly, to provide support for Vietnamese combat troops; Marine Corps commitment in the country at that time was approximately 600 personnel.

By far the largest number of American casualties were suffered in Viet Cong attacks on air bases from which planes of the US Air Force, beginning in February 1965, made strikes at North Vietnam; many of them operated out of the congested, ever-busy air base at Da Nang. Public indignation over these casualties grew steadily in the United States, and on 6 March 1965, it was announced in Washington that two battalions of Marines, about 3500 men, were being sent to South Vietnam to serve as security troops for the Da Nang air base, thereby freeing Vietnamese troops for combat duty. Secretary of State Dean Rusk, when questioned, said that the Marines would shoot back if fired upon; this was the first time an American administration had openly authorized ground forces in Vietnam to engage in fire fights with the enemy. It was a policy change of historic dimensions.

It was in the 'plan ahead' nature of the Marine Corps that it had well-formulated plans for exactly this mission—in fact, Da Nang was the objective area in the Corps Schools' well-practiced Amphibious Warfare Study No. XVI. The Bay of Da Nang above the air base was an excellent harbor—except during northeast monsoons—formed by the Hai Van Peninsula on the north and a sprawling promontory known as Mon Ky (or Monkey) Mountain to the south. The city of Da Nang, formerly the old French colonial city of Tourane, looked tattered and weary from years of warfare, yet its streets bustled with the noise and life of a population estimated at 200,000, more than half of them refugees and other displaced persons.

Involvement by attrition: defensive campaign

The seas were running rough before a northeast wind when the USS *Henrico*, *Union* and *Vancouver*, the ships carrying the 9th Marine Expeditionary Brigade, under Brigadier General Frederick J Karch, took up station 4000 yards off of Red Beach Two on the morning of 8 March 1965. The Marines had been warned that the refugees in Da Nang had been heavily infiltrated with Viet Cong, and that they therefore might receive fire from any quarter. But when the men in the first group ashore, Battalion Landing Team 3/9 came up the beach at 09:18, they were greeted instead by a crowd that included local dignitaries and slim Vietnamese girls who encircled the American's necks with strings of flowers. This friendly greeting was totally unexpected.

The arrival of BLT 3/9 by sea was coordinated with the arrival at Da Nang by air of BLT 1/3; this operation went off with such success that by the afternoon a halt was called to the airlift until the mountain of equipment on the ground could be cleared away; the inflights recommenced on 10 March and were completed by 12 March. Viet Cong interference with the operation was minimal, consisting only of some VC small-arms fire at incoming C-130 transport aircraft.

In addition to the 9th MEB's responsibility of sharing in the defense of Da Nang, it had the further mission of protecting the high ground directly to the west of the air base. When Company I, 3rd Battalion, 9th Marines, took over the hill, they nicknamed it '*the hungry i*' after their Company and a then-popular nightclub in San Francisco. After Company K dug in on Hill 268 to the north and engineers put in a road, a Hawk missile battery of the 1st Light Anti-Aircraft Missile Battalion under Lieutenant Colonel Bertram E Cook Jr took up firing positions. The defensive positions were text-book perfect; unfortunately for the Marines, the VC did not fight by text-book rules.

The problems of securing Da Nang were part of a larger problem, that of defending the military region known as I Corps Tactical Zone within which the air base was located. I Corps consisted of 10,000 square miles of variegated territory, about one-sixth of the total land area of South Vietnam. It was the farthest north of the four corps areas, with its upper boundary touching the border of North Vietnam, its eastern edge running along the China Sea, peaks of the Annamite mountains along the southern boundary, which continued upward at the Corps' western edge on a common border with Laos. The long, high stretch of the Annamites historically had separated the region designated as I Corps from the rest of Vietnam not only geographically but culturally as well; for example, one group of mountain people, the Montagnards, differed in a number of culturally significant

Above: Marines and an interpreter interview a Vietcong suspect. Distinguishing innocent civilians from Vietcong sympathizers was an endless problem in Vietnam.

ways from other Vietnamese. I Corps was a rural area; the basic social unit was the hamlet, of which there were literally hundreds. These, in turn, were combined in political units designated as villages, districts and provinces.

While command of military operations in I Corps was nominally under General Nguyen Chanh Thi, Vietnamese troops in fact controlled only the cities of Da Nang and Hoi An, and very little else other than outpost district headquarters which floated like warships in a sullen sea of Viet Cong. These outposts, fortified by surrounding breastworks of bamboo and mud, were scattered here and there throughout I Corps, most of them garrisoned with little more than a company-sized unit of Vietnamese troops who usually stayed within their protective mud walls.

By 12 April the Marine strength in the Da Nang area had reached about 5000. That day a reinforced company from 2nd Battalion, 3rd Marines, was lifted 42 miles north by helicopters to Phu Bai, seven miles from Hue, to secure an air base and communications facility; two days later other Marine units joined them in strength. Hué, South Vietnam's third largest city, once was the country's royal capital, and its people had never forgotten Hué's one-time splendor. Hué's students showed their proud, independent spirit by being a continuing source of political disquietude, as were the city's militant Buddhists.

On 7 May the designation of the Marine units in I Corps was changed from the 9th MEB into III MAF—Third Marine Amphibious Force. The organization was to have been called an 'Expeditionary' force, but it was decided all the way up at the level of the Joint Chiefs of Staff in Washington to change it to 'Amphibious' following the appearance of comments in Saigon newspapers that the term 'Expeditionary' evoked memories of the colonial days of the French Expeditionary Corps. General William C Westmoreland, Commander, United States Military Assistance Command, Vietnam (ComUSMACV), made it clear at this time that the mission of the Marines in Vietnam still was a defensive one, but he added that this included the task of undertaking, when authorized, limited offensive operations directly related to the security of their bases.

Also on 7 May, I Corps' string of coastal defensive positions was added to when the 3rd Marine Amphibious Brigade under Brigadier General Marion E Carl, the Corps' first air ace, came ashore on a barren beach at Chu Lai, 55 miles southeast of Da Nang, meeting no opposition. The specific purpose of this landing was to secure an area for the construction of a new air base that would relieve some of the growing congestion at busy Da Nang. Two days after the landing, Marine engineers and Seabees went to work on the site, and by the deadline date for flight operations, 1 June, the field went into operation with the arrival of four A-4 'Skyhawks' from Cubi Point in the Philippines.

Several weeks later the VC tested to find out what military difference all this activity might have made in the effectiveness of the ARVN—the Army of the Republic of Vietnam. On 30 May the 1st Battalion, 51st ARVN Regiment, was ambushed by the Viet Cong on Route 5 a short distance from their base at Ba Gia. Only three American advisors and 65 South Vietnamese escaped, of the 400 men in the unit. General Thi sent in his 39th Ranger Battalion and a Vietnamese Marine battalion against the enemy's estimated 5 battalions, with ensuing heavy losses for his units. Thi then asked Saigon for reinforcements, including an American Marine battalion; his request was refused, but he did get air support from US Air Force fighters and from Marine evacuation helicopters. With this aid, a total disaster for the ARVN forces was averted. However, it left a question in the minds of everyone involved: what would it take to bring American fighting men to the aid of their allies, the South Vietnamese?

Other events were at that moment bringing the question closer to being answered. Three months of defensive operations by the III MAF had resulted in almost 200 casualties, including 18 Marines dead; the feeling was growing among the officers and men in I Corps that if this was what constituted a static defensive role, they didn't like it. In fact, this opinion reached as high up the chain of command as the Commandant, Marine Corps, who on 28 April had told the press while on a visit to Da Nang that his Marines were not in Vietnam 'to sit on their ditty boxes,' they were there to 'kill Viet Cong.'

In Washington as well, a movement toward a more aggressive involvement

could be detected between the lines of statements by Administration spokespeople. On 5 June Robert J McClosky of the State Department, speaking with the approval of the highest authorities, said about the role of American troops in Vietnam: 'In establishing and patrolling their defense perimeters, they come into contact with the Viet Cong and at times are fired upon. Our troops naturally return the fire. It should come as no surprise that our troops engage in combat in these and similar circumstances.'

There were then some 51,000 American servicepeople in Vietnam, about 16,500 of them Marines and 3500 Army Airborne troopers performing defensive missions and the rest doing jobs that could be lumped under the general description of 'advisory capacity.'

It was obvious that the White House was seeking a politically acceptable way out of a militarily unacceptable situation in Vietnam. President Johnson met with the soon-to-retire ambassador to South Vietnam, Maxwell D Taylor, and with his top political advisors prior to a meeting of the National Security Council. The consensus regarding prospects in Vietnam was one of concern; hopes were dimming that the ARVN could turn the tide on the Viet Cong, even in those areas where America was providing security troops, training and equipment, and the view was even gloomier regarding the central highlands area of Pleiku-Kontum, where there were as yet no US support troops. At the Washington meetings, the necessity of committing as many as half a million American troops began to be mentioned.

Against such a background, a statement released by the State Department on 8 June stirred up great excitement; it seemed to say that General Westmoreland had been given wider lattitude by the President to use US troops in offensive roles. The next day the White House released a statement that neither confirmed nor denied the previous day's information. It said: 'The President has issued no order of any kind in this regard to General Westmoreland recently or at any other time. . . . If help is requested by the appropriate Vietnamese commander, General Westmoreland also had authority within the assigned mission to employ . . . troops in support of Vietnamese forces faced with aggressive attack. . . .'

Faced with the cautious obliquity of political leaders, the country's press began its own speculation regarding America's military options in Vietnam. Two general viewpoints rose out of this, one the so-called 'Army' strategy and the other the 'Marine' strategy. The 'Army' strategy called for the aggressive employment of US troops on 'search and destroy' missions against the

Below: The Marines' assault landing craft hit the beach at Da Nang. Many of the Marines taking part had expected to have to make an opposed landing and were instead rather embarrassed by the friendly welcome they received.

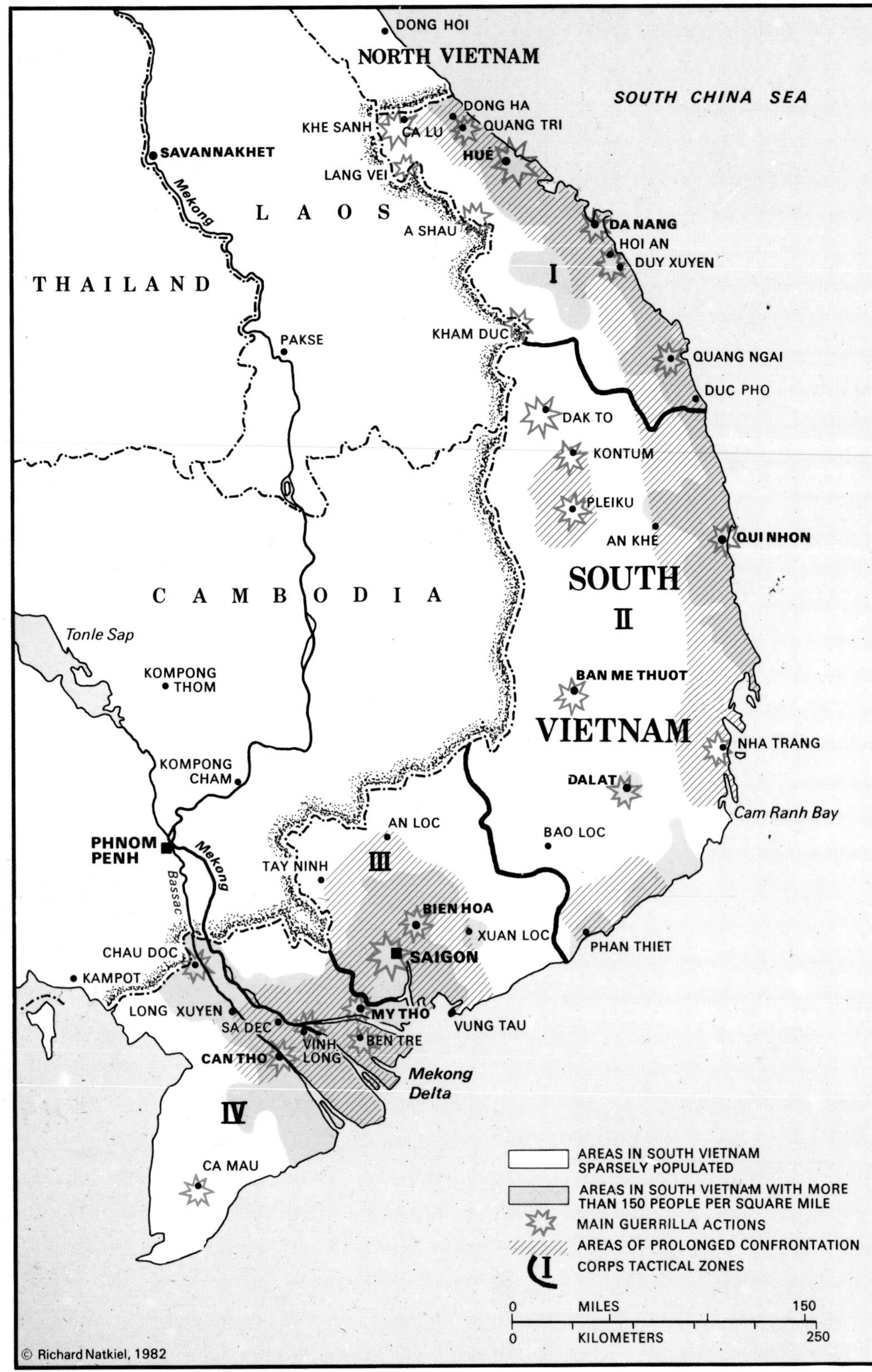

VC, while the 'Marine' strategy affirmed the status quo, giving priority to the establishment of secure coastal positions such as Da Nang from which forces could move out gradually in 'clear and hold' operations. As General Westmoreland had reminded his senior officers, the US government's official policy was then firmly on the side of the 'Marine' strategy.

This policy would gradually erode, in large measure due to the effects on the attitudes of politicians and the general public back in the United States of incidents such as that which occurred just before dawn of 1 July at Da Nang air base. A Viet Cong demolitions team slipped through the ARVN perimeter security south and east of the field and struck the parked aircraft with mortar and rocket fire and explosives, destroying or damaging three C-130s and three F-102s. A hastily-formed Provisional Base Defense Battalion was created out of support and service personnel to strengthen security until additional combat units arrived.

On 8 July Henry Cabot Lodge was sworn in by President Johnson as ambassador to Vietnam to replace the retiring Maxwell D Taylor, and immediately afterwards he and Defense Secretary Robert McNamara flew to Vietnam to inspect the American forces there and gain an up-dated sense of the situation. McNamara's comment on it while in Saigon was that 'In many respects it has deteriorated since 15 months ago, when I was last here.' On his return to Washington, McNamara joined President Johnson and his top advisors and long meetings stretching over several days, planning America's policy for its involvement in Vietnam. On 28 July the president announced that the country's military forces in Vietnam would be increased from 75,000 to 125,000 'almost immediately, that the draft quota would be increased from 17,000 to 35,000 a month, and enlistment programs would be stepped up. The next month, as a consequence of the President's July decisions, an increase of 30,000 Marines, up to 223,100, was authorized.

On 30 July General Westmoreland informed General Walt that he was to have operational control of all US ground elements in I Corps, and that ComUSMACV expected to see his forces undertake larger offensive operations that struck out farther from the protected bases. When Walt mentioned that his mission, as presently defined from Washington, called only for defensive operations, Westmoreland invited him to rewrite the instructions and make those changes he thought necessary to free up his forces for the kind of operations now being considered. This Walt did, and out of the new plan the concept of Tactical Areas of Responsibility was born. The TAORs presented some matters for thoughtful consideration: they made it necessary to work more carefully and closely with the office of General Thi, Vietnamese commander of I Corps, to avoid cross-purposes between his troops and the Americans; the TAORs growth was limited by the shortage of American troops; the Americans would be depending on ARVN troops to secure the territory within each TAOR as the Americans pushed its boundaries outward, and how well the ARVN could do this was an unknown factor.

As of that August the Corps had four regiments in Vietnam, as follows: 3rd Marines, with its 1st and 2nd Battalions at Da Nang and the 3rd Battalion, 4th Marines, attached and stationed at Phu Bai; 9th Marines, with its 2nd and part of the 1st Battalion guarding the area south of Da Nang; the rest of the 1st was on the air base itself; 4th Marines, at Chu Lai with its 1st and 2nd Battalions and 3rd Battalion, 3rd Marines, attached; 7th Marines, also at Chu Lai with its 1st Battalion; the 2nd Battalion was at Qui Nhon and the 3rd was at sea with the Fleet Special Landing Force. Additionally, four Marine Aircraft Groups were in Vietnam, MAG-11, 12, 16 and 36.

On line with the new point of view regarding offensive actions, III MAF Headquarters decided to enage the Viet Cong in a major battle, to take place in the area south of Chu Lai, where intelligence indicated that the 1st Viet Cong Regiment, some 2000 men, was gathering for an attack on the air strip. By chance two large fresh American units were in that area, and they became the basis for Operation Starlite, the first regimental-size American attack force since the Korean War. The attack began on 18 August with a three-pronged assault: a river landing from the north, a helilift on the west and an amphibious landing on the beaches to the southeast. In six days of battle the Marines caused 964 VC killed, broke up a probable attack on Chu Lai, and rendered a VC regiment unfit for combat.

Shortly afterwards Operation Pirhana was launched, beginning 7 September. The mission was a sweep of Batangan Peninsula south of Van Tuong, where reports said remnants of the 1st VC Regiment might be hiding out. This time the Marines coordinated their attack with Vietnamese military units, with a degree of operational success; in three days of fighting the Marines killed 183 Viet Cong and the South Vietnamese another 66.

While these victories took place, setbacks of a sort occurred as well. VC raiders struck on 5 August at an Esso tank farm near Da Nang at Lien Chu, setting afire and destroying two million gallons of fuel. The terminal lay outside the area of the Da Nang TAOR, and the Marines simply could not afford the manpower necessary to provide total security for the fuel depot; instead a rifle platoon was sent to guard the Nam O bridge on the road leading to Lien Chu. At the air base a number of changes were made in the disposition of the security forces which, on 21 August, made it finally possible to dissolve the Provisional Base Defense Battalion and send the clerks and maintenance personnel back to their regular duties.

The changes were not sufficient to keep out the VC however. On the night of 27 October a Viet Cong raiding party arrived at a village on China Beach between Monkey Mountain and Marble Mountain. From there they moved to a point near MAG-16's area of Da Nang air base, close by a Seabee camp, and opened up with mortar fire on the sleeping sailors. Under cover of this diversionary action, four demolition teams slipped onto the flight line and, with grenades and bangalore torpedoes, destroyed or damaged 47 helicopters; a nearby hospital was hit as well. Three Americans were killed and 91 wounded, while the VC suffered 41 dead. That same night 15 VC sappers attacked Chu Lai air base but did little damage, and most of the attackers were killed or captured; west and south of the Da Nang Marines struck and dispersed VC rifle units, one with artillery fire and the other in an ambush set by a Marine squad in which 15 Viet Cong died.

Operation Blue Marlin

The increasing activity was tied to the weather, for the VC were implementing what was called their 'monsoon strategy.' The monsoon season, which arrived a month late in I Corps that year, was an exceptionally heavy one, with rains averaging an inch each day. At III MAF headquarters this was seen as an opportunity to exploit the basic strength of the Corps, its ability to function efficiently in adverse circumstances and particularly those involving amphibious operations. Operation Blue Marlin went into effect on 10 November, the Corps' birthday, when BLT 2/7 and the 3rd Battalion, Vietnamese Marine Brigade, went ashore through storm-tossed surf onto the beach at Tam Ky, a village between Da Nang and Chu Lai. The force moved to Highway One, then turned and swept the area south to Chu Lai, concluding Phase One of Blue Marlin. In Phase Two, 17 November, the 3rd Battalion, 3rd Marines, joined with two Ranger battalions and two ARVN 'strike' forces on a 'search and destroy' movement through the VC-infested fishing villages below Song Gua Dai and 25 miles south of Da Nang. In three days of hit-and-run battles the allied force killed 25 VC and captured 15.

While Phase Two was in operation, the Viet Cong regiment that was badly mauled

Left: Map of South Vietnam showing the tactical zones of each American corps.
Below: A Marine sergeant investigates a Viet Cong tunnel in operations near An Hoa in May 1966.

in Operation Starlite attacked and captured Hiep Duc, a district capital 25 miles to the west of Tam Ky. Hiep Duc was in a mountain-surrounded valley that experienced even worse monsoon weather than the rest of I Corps, making it difficult to aid the town, and probably this was why the VC regiment had withdrawn to that area to regroup. The I Corps Vietnamese command sent two battalions of the 5th ARVN, with helilift support provided by MAG-16 and MAG-36. The Americans lifted in over 1000 ARVN troops and delivered heavy air-support fire on the target area, and after heavy fighting Hiep Duc was retaken, with the enemy slipping away into the mountains. It was subsequently decided by ARVN headquarters that they lacked sufficient manpower to hold the village, and it was abandoned to the VC.

The picture was becoming clearer as to the nature of the Viet Cong 'monsoon strategy;' it was to concentrate on attacking and destroying isolated government outposts with locally stronger VC forces, picking them off one by one, until such time that they might begin applying this strategy to larger communities such as district capitals. The objective was to wear down and exhaust the ARVN, both psychologically and militarily. Against the Americans the strategy was to avoid large-scale battles, but rather to pick away with constant attacks on smaller American units so as to create a climate of defensiveness and caution.

At Thatch Tru, on 22 November, the enemy performed what was for them a rare error in judgement, obviously based on poor military intelligence. They attacked the coastal village's outpost fort, apparently believing it to be garrisoned by poorly-trained and under-motivated Popular Force or Regional Force troops. But the fort was defended instead by part of an ARVN Ranger battalion, with two other Ranger

Below: An M-48 tank gives fire support to the 2nd Battalion 3rd Marines, 4 May 1966.

companies close by. The fight went through the night and into the next day, and by noon the VC had managed to make their way through the barbed wire, over the palisades and into the fort, where savage hand-to-hand fighting began.

Luckily for the defenders, three American warships, the USS *Bache*, *O'Brien* and *Fletcher*, were close by, and during the next 24 hours they delivered pounding fire on the VC forces still outside the fort. The 5-inch guns made the difference; the back of the attack was broken and the VC fled, leaving 175 dead on the ground. Next morning the 3rd Battalion, 7th Marines, flushed and struck units of the fleeing attackers. From prisoners it was learned that this was not a VC unit; these were North Vietnamese soldiers of the PAVN (Peoples' Army of Vietnam) belonging to the 95th Regiment, 325th Alpha Division.

The week after the Thach Tru attack Defense Secretary McNamara arrived back in Saigon, where he said in a press conference that the arrival of PAVN soldiers put a different completion on the war and on America's role in it. In a subsequent meeting of senior American officials it was accepted that there were then seven PAVN regiments in South Vietnam, the presence of an additional one more was considered 'probable' and that of another 'possible.' In ensuing discussions with the senior American military commanders in the area, the major part dealt with considerations of how much of an increase in US forces would be required to deal with the new circumstances.

One topic of discussion was the list of recommendations submitted to ComUSMACV by General Walt at General Westmoreland's request. It called for a strategy in I Corps balanced among the various military tasks facing the allies and the various military tools available to deal with these tasks. Walt proposed an increase in Marine infantry battalions from 12 up to at least 18; the number of fighter-attack squadrons should be increased to eight. He based these numbers on the tasks facing the allies rather than on considerations relating in combat terms to the enemy, the tasks being: first, to maintain secure base areas; second, to provide support for the offensive operations of the Vietnamese I Corps forces; third, to commit American units in offensive operations against the VC; fourth, to ready American forces for supportive roles in other regions of South Vietnam; fifth, to provide personnel and know-how for what came to be called 'pacification' operations.

There was at that time some difference of opinion between the Army and the Marines regarding the value of pacification efforts, with the Corps having more belief in its potential value; this resulted from the experience of Marines in earlier pacification efforts, some of it originating with small Marine units and even individual Marines, but most of it a well-planned product of III MAF headquarters. A particularly successful early example was My Lai, which developed into a model 'protected hamlet.' The techniques developed there were later applied in many villages: the village was liberated from VC occupation or domination, it was made secure, then programs designed to raise the village's quality of life in every way were carefully begun. While the process saw success in the thinly-populated area west of Da Nang, it had much less success in the heavily-populated region of rich ricelands south of the air base, strung along Highway One.

The Viet Cong were in this region in force for a number of reasons: the rich farmland took care of the VC's food needs, the adjacent coastline made resupply from North Vietnam by sea simpler, and the dense population of the area made it easier for the Viet Cong in their anonymous black pajamas to—as their leader, General Giap, was fond of saying—'swim like fish among the people.'

Operation Golden Fleece

To catch some of these 'fish' attempting to exact tribute from the farmers, III MAF ordered the 9th Marines to conduct Operation Golden Fleece between September and October when the rice crop was being gathered. The tactics of the operation involved saturation patrolling by small units, heavy use of night ambushes, and the stationing of Marine guards to protect the working harvesters. The harvest-protection function of 'Golden Fleece' was successful, and the name was used frequently afterwards for similar operations.

The 9th Marines continued their effort into October and succeeded in clearing half of Hoa Vang district of VC, a total of nine villages; then came the more difficult part of the operation, the pacification program. A trained government team of 350 people was ready for the job, but the South Vietnamese did not have the necessary security forces, to be stationed in each of the villages, that would make pacification possible. The Marines' job, as III MAF saw it, was limited to providing the outer perimeter of defense for the villages, some of the materials required to carry out the program and, of equal importance, the appropriate support structures within the American military and diplomatic organizations. To carry out the latter objective, III MAF made significant changes in its staff structure at headquarters; in addition, a Joint Coordinating Council was formed with both civilian and military members from the American and Vietnamese communities to provide contact and coordination among many agencies that dealt with related concerns. Both the concept and the organizational plan were brilliant; however, the abiding failure that worked to the detriment of all the other efforts was the inability of the South Vietnamese to provide Popular Forces of sufficient numbers and caliber to carry out the security job.

Involvement by attrition: counteroffensive campaign

Following the withdrawal of the Vietnamese from Hiep Duc in late November, the Viet Cong infiltrated eastward into the Phuoc Valley, threatening the government outposts at Viet An and Que Son. To relieve this pressure and perhaps entrap the VC, now thought to be the reestablished 1st Viet Cong Regiment with North Vietnamese reinforcements, Operation Harvest Moon was created. It called for a coordinated strike by ARVN and US Marine units that would catch the VC in a pincer action; it would develop into one of the war's turning points.

Units of the 5th ARVN and the 11th Vietnamese Ranger Battalion entered the contested zone the morning of 8 December and, after several uneventful hours of advancing, came under heavy fire. Within a half hour the South Vietnamese units were pinned down, and were relieved only when US helicopters brought in ARVN reinforcements. Next day the VC struck again, this time killing a battalion commander and sending the ARVN unit backwards in retreat.

At this point, Marine units were committed to the battle in force. Helicopters brought in the 2nd Battalion, 7th Marines; the 3rd Battalion, 3rd Marines; and the 2nd Battalion, 1st Marines to relieve ARVN units as well as to press the fight against the enemy. On 12 December the Marines began moving against the high ground at the southern rim of Phuoc Valley while ARVN forces attacked the northern rim. The Marines advanced steadily over the next five days, aided in their fire fights by precision bombing done by B-52s. The VC broke contact, and the Marine battalions moved out of the valley in a sweep of the country to the northeast of the original contact area; small Viet Cong units brought them under fire and were quickly cut down. At dusk of 19 December the Marines reached Highway One and Harvest Moon was completed. The Viet Cong dead totaled 407, and significant numbers of heavy and light weapons had been captured, as well as other supplies taken from a depot uncovered in a hill south of Que Son.

That year saw the first experiment by both sides in the war with a Christmas and Tet holiday truce; 'Tet' is a solemn Far East holiday celebrating the lunar new year. The Marines had no great enthusiasm for the entire idea, presuming that the VC would use the truce as an opportunity for some adventure against an American or South Vietnamese position; however, aside from three small attacks in the Da Nang and Chu Lai TAORs, the Christmas truce held, and the Tet truce was even better observed. However, immediately following the Tet

truce, Da Nang and Marble Mountain air bases were hit with mortar attacks; an ominous aspect of these attacks was the use by the VC of 120mm mortars, only the second time such large weapons had been used in I Corps.

As 1966 began there were 180,000 American military personnel in South Vietnam, 38,000 of them members of the Corps, but these numbers were about to change. As a follow-up on Secretary McNamara's latest visit, American troop strength was to be increased, and for the Marines, this meant the introduction of the 1st Marine Division to Vietnam, along with additional elements of units already in the country. The zones of action assigned to the 1st Division were the two southern provinces of I Corps, Quang Tin and Quanag Ngai.

Operation Double Eagle

Early in January of 1966 the most ambitious attempt yet at coordinated action against the enemy was activated; its name was Double Eagle. It would involve not only I Corps forces but also II Corps and the US Army's Field Force Victor, a special strike force. Their target: the 325A PAVN Division, believed to be encamped in an area adjoining both Quang Ngai province and Binh Dinh province.

The operation began when the 3rd Battalion, 1st Marines, landed near the site of the November battle with the PAVN, close to Thach Tru, in the largest amphibious operation of the war until that time, with three attack transports, an attack cargo ship, three LSTs, two LSDs, an LPH, a cruiser, a destroyer and two auxiliaries. Standing offshore were three other ships carrying the 2nd Battalion, 3rd Marines, as reserves; this unit was helilifted in on the second day of the operation to a site five miles west of the beaches. On D plus Four, the 2nd Battalion, 9th Marines, moved out of Quang Ngai airstrip into the mountains to the northwest of the beaches.

Marine attempts to make strong contact with the enemy were disappointing, and before long reports came in that the major part of the PAVN division had slipped south into Binh Dinh province. There, in Operation Masher (a name later toned down into White Wing), the enemy was engaged

Below: 3rd Regiment Marines during Operation Cormorant, a search and destroy mission conducted north of Da Nang in July 1966.

by the 1st Air Cavalry Division and II Corps troops in a big battle north of Bong Son and on into An Lao Valley. The total count of VC killed there and at later battles near Tam Ky came to 337.

Far from the battlefield, others were trying to shape the course of the war by diplomatic means. A conference was held in Honolulu early in February between President Johnson and the South Vietnamese leader, Premier Ky, out of which came a strong declaration for winning the war through a combination of military strength and expanded civic reforms for the country's peasants; a communique from the conference called the latter 'as important as the military battle itself.'

Efforts in the first so-called 'pacification' area had been disappointing, due as much to shortcomings on the part of the South Vietnamese as to aggressive efforts by the Viet Cong to see that it failed. However, things began to change for the better in February and early March when a concerned and intelligent Vietnamese, Lieutenant Colonel Lap, assumed overall command of security for the area and of the rural pacification program; Lap soon convinced the peasants that he truly cared about their welfare. A second and equally important factor in the turn-around was the invention by the 9th Marines of a new technique they called County Fair.

County Fair

On 24 and 25 February the first County Fair was held at Phong Bhac hamlet, just north of Song Cau Do river. Under cover of darkness the night before, units of the 9th Marines crept up on the hamlet and took up positions to seal it off totally; this was to make sure that any VC in the community could not escape and, of equal importance, no VC outside the cordon could enter later to provide reinforcements. At dawn, the hamlet dwellers were informed over loudspeakers that the hamlet was surrounded and about to be searched, and that the people should leave the hamlet and go to a designated assembly area nearby. There, in an atmosphere that was made as cheerful as possible under the circumstances, the people's identity cards were checked, then they met their district leader (perhaps for the first time) who explained what was going on. Next, the people experienced a 'County Fair' of speeches, events and such

strange foodstuffs as cokes and candy bars, sometimes along with movies, live entertainers and a Marine band. As this went on the hamlet was searched for VC. Some were found—hidden underground in tunnels, from which they had to be blasted out—but the searchers also discovered such evidence of their presence as propaganda leaflets, uniforms and arms.

Following this first County Fair, many more were conducted throughout the III MAF area, with heartening success.

In February and March, fighting in the area stepped up, with a number of vicious battles. Operation New York pitted the 810th Main Force Battalion of the VC against the 2nd Battalion, 1st Marines, who were called into the battle northeast of Phu Bai to support the hard-pressed 1st Battalion, 3rd ARVN Regiment. In a night helilift, the Marines landed in the objective area and moved in line across the Phu Thu Peninsula against well-prepared enemy positions. The battle lasted until 3 March; the final count was 122 Viet Cong killed.

Above: A watchful Marine radio operator on a jungle patrol. He is armed with an M14 rifle, soon to be replaced by the more modern M16. *Left:* The 9th Marine Expeditionary Brigade lands at Da Nang.

It was learned on 3 March that units of the 2nd ARVN had made contact with an enemy force northwest of Quang Ngai city, and that prisoners they had taken were members of the 36th PAVN Regiment, which the prisoners placed in the vicinity of Chau Nhai village. The Americans and South Vietnamese responded to this news the next morning with Operation Utah. Marine helicopters lifted the ARVN 1st Airborne Battalion to a point a short distance southeast of Chau Nhai, where they landed through blistering fire from the ground. The ARVN went into action; within hours they were joined in the battle by 2nd Battalion, 7th Marines on their right flank and the 3rd Battalion, 1st Marines to the north of the combat zone. That evening the trap was completed with the landing to the south of the 2nd Battalion, 4th Marines. The fight, a hard-fought one, lasted 24 hours, and at the end the Marines counted 359 PAVN dead in their sectors and the ARVN another 228 in theirs; almost a third of the enemy regiment had been destroyed.

An even more vicious fight happened on 9–11 March at a Special Forces camp near A Shau on the Laotian border. Three PAVN regiments attacked the camp, which was garrisoned by 17 Green Berets and about 400 Vietnamese irregulars, most of them local Montagnards. In the ensuing battle many of the irregulars refused to fight—in fact, some of them turned their weapons on the defenders, but were shot down. The defense, which lasted two days, was borne mostly by the Americans and a few loyal Vietnamese. Finally, Marine and Air Force helicopters managed to get to the camp through the terrible monsoon weather, land, and carry out a relatively successful evacuation; 12 Special Forces men and 178 irregular troops were airlifted to safety.

On 19 March the Marines of III MAF received a call for help from the Regional Force garrison at An Hoa, 30 kilometers northwest of Quang Ngai. This triggered Operation Texas. The 3rd Battalion, 7th Marines and the ARVN 5th Airborne Battalion were helilifted to within a kilometer north of the besieged outpost while the 2nd Battalion, 4th Marines came down at a point seven kilometers south of it. The enemy force, again the 1st Viet Cong Regiment, was caught between them and, following four days of fierce fighting, 405 VC dead were counted.

Another operation with a state name, Indiana, took place at almost the same spot on 28 March when the 5th ARVN Regiment came under heavy fire. This time the 1st Battalion, 7th Marines, flew in to help and, landing behind the enemy, they killed 69 of the VC in several hard hours of fighting.

While these traditional military missions were taking place, fighting of another sort went on among the South Vietnamese people themselves. A strong movement spearheaded by university students and Buddhists, in each case most particularly those in the city of Hué, called for the ouster of Premier Ky's government in Saigon. All through that spring a series of moves and countermoves by opposing groups kept the country in a turmoil as units loyal to Ky and other units aligned with the anti-government 'Struggle Force' came close to the point of bloody showdown. General Walt repeatedly stepped into the middle of these tense situations and, working skillfully as an arbitrator, prevented a bloodbath. A loser in this situation was the pacification effort as the VC infiltrated back into previously 'sanitized' hamlets.

In March Major General Wood B Kyle arrived in I Corps to assume command of the 3d Marine Division. A top-of-the-list priority for Kyle was to reduce the Viet Cong presence in the area south of Da Nang, and he soon made a number of changes in the disposition of several units in order to accomplish this. Operations Kings, Georgia and Liberty expanded the areas of responsibility of the 9th Marines and more closely connected its flanks with the 3rd and 1st Marines. Operation Jay was a sweep through an area 20 kilometers northwest of Hue by the 2nd Battalion, 4th Marines and the 2nd Battalions, 1st Marines, in a pincer movement that caught and killed 82 Viet Cong soldiers in a nine-day running battle.

Left: Men of the 2nd Marines during a search for Viet Cong suspects in the Mekong Delta area.

Above: Press photographers accompany a Marine patrol. Press and television coverage of the Vietnam War was more widespread than in any previous conflict.

Counteroffensive Phase II

On the 4th of July Operation Macon kicked off what turned out to be a grinding four-months' long series of battles against a particularly tough unit, the Doc Lap battalion, in the area north of An Hoa. Five Marine battalions were alternately involved, and the final kill count was 507 VC.

The next weeks saw a series of actions of a somewhat new and escalated nature. Reports said that a new North Vietnamese division, probably 324th Bravo, had entered the country into northern Quang Tri province. When 2nd Battalion, 1st Marines went into the area to investigate the reports, it precipitated the most savage large-scale fighting of the war to that date, involving 8000 Marines and 3000 South Vietnamese troops. Operation Hastings was the name given the action; other Marine units involved were the 2nd Battalion, 4th Marines; the 3rd Battalion, 4th Marines; the 3rd Battalion, 5th Marines; the 1st Battalion, 1st Marines and the 1st Battalion, 3rd Marines; five ARVN battalions also were involved, and B-52s repeatedly flew precision bombing support missions. The operation finished on 3 August with 824 of the enemy killed and large numbers of weapons captured.

The division had entered the country across the DMZ, or demilitarized zone, which was a 'first.' Speculation regarding the reason for the unusual line of march included it being an experiment to see if the PAVN could avoid the difficult and roungabout route through Laos, or an attempt to off-set the series of gains the allies had been making through the pacification program and the many Marine clean-sweep operations of recent months.

This action evolved into Operations Prairie I and Deckhouse IV. Prairie took place in the same area as Hastings and, in fact, involved the same PAVN unit, the 324B Division. Enemy losses by the end of August were an additional 110 killed. Deckhouse IV involved a landing at Dong Ha by the 1st Battalion, 26th Marines, on 15 September. Over ten days of battling

with units of the 324B Division, these Marines added 254 dead to the count. Prairie I would continue on and off into the following year.

The stepped-up pace of combat the Marines were experiencing required an associated increase in the Corps' strength, and a source for such growth had been set late in 1965 with an authorization for 55,000 additional Marines. The Corps' goal was 278,184 by mid-1967, somewhat more than half its all-time high of 485,113 reached during World War II. The Corps recruited 80,000 volunteers during 1966 and received about 19,000 draftees.

The basic success of America's efforts up to that time in South Vietnam was underscored on 11 September when national elections were held on schedule to elect members of the Constituent Assembly, who would draft a new constitution. The most extravagant guess as to the voter turnout had been 70 percent; in fact 80.8 percent of the electorate went to the polls despite deadly efforts by the Viet Cong to stop them.

Above left: Vietnamese civilians are escorted to a transport helicopter for evacuation from their village.
Below: Men of the 2nd Battalion, 7th Marines during an operation in the Da Nang area in June 1967.

And in Hué, center of student and Buddhist opposition to the central government, 84 percent of the voters cast ballots.

Concrete examples of the III MAF's contribution to this success, if tallied up in the Fall of 1966, would have revealed:

- a steady buildup during a year and a half period of the Marine presence to 60,000 soldiers;
- an expansion of the Corps' zone of responsibility from eight square miles and 1930 local people to 1800 square miles and nearly one million people;
- action in more than 150 operations of battalion or regimental size, resulting in 7300 enemy deaths;
- an additional 4000 enemy deaths resulting from 200,000 Marine patrols, ambushes and other small-unit actions;
- Marine losses in the period of 1700 killed and over 9000 wounded; better than 80 percent of the wounded returned to duty.

Out of the strife of 18 months one thing had become increasingly clear: fully as important as the military effort was the attempt to reach the hearts and minds of the people with the pacification effort, or Ngu Hanh Son as the Vietnamese called it. The government had committed 25,000 trained cadre to the effort, and this number was scheduled to more than double within a year. The number would be barely enough for the task, for there were 11,000 hamlets in South Vietnam, of which only 4500 were considered friendly to the government; the remaining 6500 either were uncommitted or under Viet Cong control.

1967: Heating up

As the year began, General Walt had 67,729 Marines under his command in III MAF. The force's 18 infantry battalions were committed in combat operations that ranged from one end of I Corps to the other, stretching 225 miles from the DMZ in the north down to Binh Dinh province and the border of II Corps in the south. Knowing this made it understandable why some people in Saigon referred to I Corps as 'Marineland.'

Operation Prairie I, which evolved out of Hastings, had continued in northern Quang Tri province since the previous July. This was a major operation; at its height six Marine battalions were engaged with large Viet Cong and North Vietnamese units. But the monsoon season had gradually squeezed the number of clashes down to only a few, and on 31 January Prairie I came to an end after 182 bloody days. Marine casualties were 225 killed 1159 wounded and 1 missing in action, while the enemy (PAVN and VC combined) lost 1397 killed and 29 captured.

On 1 February Prairie II began in the same long-contested area, but it involved a less intense level of combat. The PAVN division had withdrawn back across the DMZ into North Vietnam, and reports indicated they were moving toward the longer route through Laos. Given this, Marine strength in the area was reduced, and the mission was changed from a search-and-destroy one into clear-and-secure. This meant that substantial support could be given once again to providing security for the rural pacification efforts of the 1st ARVN Division.

Operation Chinook had begun the previous 19 December with the 2nd and 3rd Battalions, 26th Marines, assigned to block infiltration routes used by the VC to come down through the mountains toward Hue. The Marines had no sooner disengaged when the Holiday truce went into effect, when they observed a thousand enemy troops moving down the approaches toward Hue. With their intent obvious, General Westmoreland gave permission for artillery and air strikes. These were carried out, but the heavy cloud cover and monsoon rains left the result in doubt. 3rd Battalion, 26th

Right: A Marine sits by his foxhole and camouflages his helmet in preparation for a patrol.

Below: Clearing a helicopter landing zone. Although helicopters undoubtedly conferred greater mobility on Marine and Army combat troops, selecting suitable landing zones in Vietnam was often difficult.

Above: Marine on jungle patrol. Viet Cong booby traps were a continual hazard of all patrolling operations.

Marines, took over the mission but made only light contact with the enemy until 6 February when, in the last hours before the start of the Tet truce, 80 rounds of 81mm mortar fell on their headquarters, wounding five Marines.

The pulse beat of action and reaction by the Marines as well as the Viet Cong and the North Vietnamese accelerated through the winter and into the spring. The III MAF launched numerous operations against the enemy during that period, including Prairie II, III and IV, Tuscaloosa, Sierra, DeSoto, Independence, Stone, Beacon Hill, Newcastle, Union and Beaver Cage, most of which lasted only a few days or weeks while inflicting relatively high casualties on the enemy; down in the south of Vietnam in IV Corps, the 1st Battalion, 9th Marines, landed on 5 January in Operation Deckhouse V, the first use of US combat troops in the Mekong Delta. The results were modest, but in the subsequent Deckhouse VI landing and attack by 1st Battalion, 4th Marines, 204 enemy were left dead in nine days of battle.

The bloodiest fighting of the period began the morning of 24 April in what could be called the First Battle of Khe Sanh, located in the northwest corner of Quang Tri province. A platoon-sized patrol from 1st Battalion, 9th Marines, encountered an enemy force which did not return fire. When another American platoon moved up to join the first, the enemy attacked furiously, forcing the Marines to withdraw carrying their 13 dead with them. The following day, additional contacts indicated that an enemy force of at least battalion strength was entrenched on high ground before the Marines. Two additional Marine battalions were flown in and, over the next 18 days, the deeply dug-in enemy was hammered by artillery, repeated air strikes by the 1st Marine Aircraft Wing and repeated assaults by Marine infantry units. Both sides were badly hurt, with the Marines suffering 155 killed and 424 wounded, the enemy 940 dead and two prisoners.

Counteroffensive Phase III

On 1 June 1967 General Walt stepped down from his two year stint as commander of III MAF and was replaced by Lieutenant General Robert Cushman, holder of the Navy Cross. In his departing remarks, Walt commented on the changes he had seen take place in the individual Marine during his tenure with III MAF. Two years before the Marine infantryman had been armed with the M-14 rifle, actually a modified version of the old M-1 rechambered for the NATO 7.62mm cartridge, but by the time of the Khe Sanh battle the M-14 had been replaced with the M-16, a high-velocity weapon firing a 5.56mm round; after some initial difficulties, the weapon had proven itself to be a fine arm. The Marine combat uniform and footwear, too, had been modified for better service in Vietnam's terrain and climate.

The pace of action through spring into summer was a mixed one, with quiet periods in certain sectors suddenly torn apart by bursts of combat activity. Two Marine operations were directed, for the first time, against the DMZ in force. Operation Hickory, a massive Marine-Navy-Air Force operation, was begun on 19 May when five Marine battalions moved out from positions near Con Thien. In a well-coordinated assault, the enemy was pinned against the Ben Hai river by attacks from air, land and sea, losing a total of 815 dead. Operation Belt Tight followed Hickory, carrying the fight more deeply into the DMZ, and between 20 and 28 May it inflicted 71 deaths on the enemy.

Enemy activity in Quang Tin, Quang Tri, Thua Thien and Quang Nhai provinces was becoming more frequent and involving increasingly larger units. On 26 May the 5th Marines initiated Operation Union II with support from ARVN units. They engaged two PAVN regiments northwest of Tam Ky. After ten days of stiff action the enemy casualties, including those from the earlier Union I, were 1566 dead and 196 captured; Marine casualties for both operations were 220 killed, 714 wounded.

The Quang Tri actions involved three Marine operations, Crockett, Buffalo and Buffalo and Hickory II. Crockett was a response to continuous enemy probing of Marine positions in the Khe Sanh area; units of the 26th Marines took the enemy

Left: Keeping a close watch for approaching Viet Cong troops during Operation Deckhouse 5.

under fire repeatedly during the month of June until they finally broke off contact, with losses of 206 killed; Marine deaths totaled 52. Buffalo, which followed on 2 July, was a short but deadly battle. Five battalions of heavily-entrenched VC at a point northeast of Con Thien engaged what eventually became three battalions of Marines in a series of battles that included some of the most intense artillery fire by the enemy in the war to date, as well as the most intense air strikes by American planes. Between 2 and 10 July air support units dropped over 1066 tons or ordinance on enemy positions; the enemy lost 1301 dead in the operation, the Marines 159.

South of the DMZ, in Quang Tri province, Operation Kingfisher kicked off on 16 July with the objective of blocking enemy entrance into the province. Units of the 9th Marines repeatedly engaged enemy units in fire fights that served to scatter them. On 21 August and again on 7 September, major enemy units attempting ambushes were pounded by air and artillery support fire and fled, leaving a total of 554 dead.

Also on 7 September Secretary McNamara announced a decision to create a security wall below the DMZ running from Con Thien through Go Linh to the coast. Its purpose was to block the entrance into South Vietnam of PAVN forces and supplies for the Viet Cong. The barrier was to consist of barbed wire entanglements laced with land mines and electronic sensors to detect movement. Much of the US press was skeptical regarding the wall—they dubbed the project McNamara's Wall'—and their skepticisms was shared by the Marines in Vietnam.

'With these bastards,' explained one Marine officer, 'you'll have to build the zone all the way to India, and it would take the whole Marine Corps and half the Army to guard it.' And he added, 'Even then they'd probably burrow under it.' Despite

Below: A South Vietnamese patrol advances between rice paddies. Well defined paths were a favorite site for booby traps.

Above: A platoon sergeant consults his map before calling in an artillery strike.
Right: Marine radiomen prepare to set out on a jungle patrol.
Previous page: An M60 machine gun team of the 5th Marines in a firefight in 1968.

such comments, operations began to secure the area in which the wall would go.

Through the balance of the year the enemy pressed the fight at a number of points, all of them familiar targets for attack. For a four week period in September they directed a series of intense infantry and artillery attacks against the outpost at Con Thien, which the press had taken to calling a 'little Dien Bien Phu,' referring to the besieged French fortress of the Indochina War; during one six-day period Con Thien was shelled 24 times. Under intense pressure from B-52 bombings the enemy finally broke off in what General Westmoreland called a 'crushing defeat.' October saw Marine operations in the Hai Lang National Forest south of Quang Tri City, in Thua Thien province, and south of An Hoa near the area of the old Union operations. In each case the Viet Cong showed an undiminished zest for close and vicious fighting; they demonstrated this also with bloody raids against district headquarters and refugee settlements. As the year came to a close, reports suggested that some sort of major offensive was in the immediate offing.

Tet Offensive (1968)

As in previous years, a truce was arranged over the lunar New Year holiday of Tet. But then the North Vietnamese and VC broke the truce with the strongest all-out assault of the war.

It began with a major attack on Khe Sanh; the city had been relatively quiet since the hard fighting of the previous year, but intelligence indicated there now were four enemy regiments within 20 kilometers of the city. Westmoreland ordered reinforcements for the 26th Marine and ARVN troops at the strongpoint, for he considered it an important blocking position against enemy movements from the north.

On 20 January an enemy force of better than 20,000 hurled itself against Khe Sanh; on the second day they took the village itself and crowds of refugees moved for protection into the outpost fortification. The North Vietnamese moved toward the barricades, commencing a seige that would last 71 days. In their assaults the PAVN troops would suffer what were probably the heaviest casualties of the war from combined air and artillery strikes. The enemy in turn delivered intense shelling on the outpost, with the number of rounds numbering in the thousands, and though this continued through February and into March, the Marines held their ground. The defender's particular sense of appreciation went to the artillerymen and airmen who, with their deadly strikes, prevented the enemy from ever mounting a large-unit ground attack. On 6 April friendly ground forces were able to reach Khe Sanh; on 9 April no enemy fire fell on the outpost for the first time in 45 days. The siege was over.

In coordination with their attack against Khe Sanh, the enemy launched attacks against other American and ARVN strongpoints throughout South Vietnam, and against the civilian population as well, striking against undefended villages. In I Corps enemy forces consisting of both VC and PAVN units hit military and civilian targets, starting 30 and 31 January in the middle of the cease-fire. It was fortunate that American and ARVN units were in prime fighting readiness, as well as being alert to the enemy's move beforehand, for they were able to throw back their assaults in most instances. Quang Tri, Da Nang, Hoi An, Tam Ky and Quang Ngai—in these strongholds the Marines and ARVN met the enemy's best effort and threw them back. The only place where the North Vietnamese had success was in Hué. There they infiltrated soldiers dressed as civilians who, at midnight of 30 January, changed into uniforms and joined the attack on the defenders from within. The next day the city was taken, but soon three understrength Marine battalions and 13 ARVN battalions counterattacked, and after weeks of bloody house-to-house fighting, they retook the city on 24 February. Enemy losses at Hué were over 5000.

Above : The Vietnamese climate brought the Marines many problems with skin diseases and insects.

The Tet offensive did not turn out as the Viet Cong and North Vietnamese had hoped. The overriding purpose had been to give the impression of their having overwhelming power and presence in South Vietnam; the enemy presumed that such an impression would weaken the allies' will to continue the fight, particularly the Americans, which might lead to an uprising against the government by the South Vietnamese people. None of this happened—in fact, the American and ARVN forces fought side by side with greater efficiency than ever before.

Immediately following cessation of the Tet attacks, III MAF prepared to strike back in force against the enemy. They were in a stronger position to do so; the 27th Marines were newly arrived in Vietnam, raising the Marine strength there to a record 163,000 as of 1 April. However, diplomatic events taking place in far-off places would effect these plans dramatically. Public enthusiasm for the war had required a number of years before it grew strong; now that enthusiasm had gradually eroded away. President Lyndon Johnson, a strong advocate of pursuing the war, responded to this new general will of the people on 31 March by announcing on national television that he would not seek another term in office. He also said that he had instructed the Defense Department to place specified limitations on the bombing of targets in North Vietnam; on 2 April the 20th Parallel was identified as the line north of which no further bombings by the US would take place. On that day also it was announced from Washington and Hanoi that the two countries would soon commence talks aimed at bringing the war to an end. Paris, France, was selected as the site for these discussions, and on 13 May W Averell Harriman for the United States and Xuan Thuy for North Vietnam held their first meeting.

The existence of the Paris peace talks, rather than diminishing the level of combat, obviously intensified it, as each side aimed at establishing its strength on the battlefield as leverage for establishing its strength in the negotiations. Westmoreland approved a three-pronged plan that included elimination of the enemy's capacity for repeated seiges of Khe Sanh, a major attack on enemy positions within the DMZ, and a raid into the A Shau valley. The relief of Khe Sanh, dubbed Operation Pegasus, was accomplished by means of a brilliant aerial operation that included tactical aircraft of the Air Force, Navy and Marines delivering over 35,000 tons of bombs and rockets on the enemy in a ten week period, and by Marine helicopters that flew in supplies and flew out the wounded. Operation Delaware Valley, a raid to oust the enemy from A Shau Valley, followed on 19 April and lasted a month, causing the enemy huge losses in war materials. A plan for an attack into the DMZ was pre-empted by a major enemy strike against Dong Ha, in the eastern side of the fighting zone below the DMZ, and then by what was referred to a 'mini-Tet,' begun on 5 May, a second major offensive by the enemy that year that included 119 rocket strikes against positions throughout South Vietnam. Though the attacks hurt many civilians, it was militarily of little merit.

Left : As well as the problems of personal hygiene illustrated above, the Vietnam climate required that great care be taken to maintain arms and ammunition. Here machine gun belts are checked over.

The success of Operation Pegasus contributed to an important decision on the part of General Creighton W Abrams, Westmoreland's replacement as ComUSMACV: the base at Khe Sanh would be abandoned, and in the future US ground forces would change from a defensive static-position strategy to one of using strong mobile forces to carry the war constantly to the enemy. The tactical mobility provided the US forces by this new strategy served to blunt the enemy's attacks; in just eight days of fighting, units of the 5th, 26th and 27th Marines in concert with ARVN forces scored 1072 dead. Despite such losses, the enemy continued to press toward their principal target, Da Nang, and on 18 August they began an attack on the air base in the 'Third Offensive' of 1968. By 28 August, when the 38th PAVN Regiment broke off and retreated, they had lost 1072 dead south of Da Nang.

Action during the fall months was widely scattered, and in many instances was fierce, but now the enemy's actions seemed more and more to be the expression of a political rather than a military strategy. Ironically, the coordinated actions of the US and ARVN units went off with previously unmatched success, and the performance of all South Vietnamese troops, including the semi-military Popular Forces and Regional Forces, were lauded by the US command. An outstanding example of this took place late in November in Operation Meade River. During a three-week period of hard fighting against the 36th PAVN Regiment, the 1st Marine Division and attached units, together with ARVN soldiers and Korean Marines, killed a total of 1210 enemy; a key element in the operation's success was

Above: A Marine from the 1st Regiment (3rd Marine Division) returns North Vietnamese fire during fighting in Hué, February 1968.

the carrying out of one of the largest helicopter assaults in Marine history.

But the war was winding down; its ultimate outcome was not to be determined on the battlefield but at the conference table. Early in October the USS *New Jersey* came on station of the DMZ and began pouring the devastating fire of its 16-inch guns into that area; on 31 October President Johnson announced that henceforth there would be no air, artillery or naval bombardment of North Vietnam. In the III MAF, the announcement was not well received, particularly by the men of the 3d Marine Division; located just south of the DMZ, they would bear the brunt of any advantage this decision gave the enemy.

Throughout this period the Marine efforts in the pacification program moved ahead at an accelerating pace; Marine units not immediately involved in combat operations built hospitals, schools and orphanages for the South Vietnamese, as well as homes for families and bridges to connect villages with the rest of the country. The well-proven technique of the County Fair, developed first in I Corps, was used throughout the country as a key part of the pacification effort. At year's end, as the peace talks went on in Paris, the Marines counted their dead—about 10,000 going back to the war's beginning—and made ready to press the war to the enemy.

As in years past, the Tet holiday of 1969 saw the truce violated by the enemy, but the effort was only a pale shadow of its former self. An attack was launched against Da Nang, a 'nut' the enemy had never been able to crack, and once again their effort foundered in the face of fierce Marine resistance that turned into counterstrikes against the retreating Viet Cong.

Marine units remained active throughout 1969, though at a reduced level to match the enemy's reversion from large-scale attacks to small-unit demolition attacks and anti-civilian terrorism. Operation Bold Mariner in January was the largest Marine Special Landing Force operation of the war, sweeping through the area south of Chu Lai in a successful sanitizing search for Viet Cong. Dewey Canyon I was a strike into Da Krong valley in Quang Tri's southwest corner; three battalions of the 9th Marines, over a month-long period of January and February, engaged heavily-entrenched North Vietnamese units and inflicted losses of 1617 dead on them. Other operations named Virginia Ridge, Oklahoma Hills, Utah Mesa, Daring Rebel, Pipestone Canyon, all bloodied the enemy with the same lopsided ratios of killed and wounded that had prevailed throughout the war. Defiant Stand, the last Special Landing Force strike of the war, was unique in being a combined landing of US and Korean Marines; coming ashore at Hoi An, the force killed 293 enemy and processed the documents of 2500 civilians.

1969 saw nearly 60,000 enemy killed by I Corps alone, yet at the end of the year their strength was greater than at the year's outset, almost totally as a result of fresh troops from North Vietnam. On the American side, the process of troop withdrawals had cut into its strength. The year had begun with 79,844 Marines in III MAF; it ended with 54,541.

Shortly after midnight on 6 January 1970, a hundred-member demolition team of the 409th PAVN Sapper Battalion, under cover of mortar fire, got through the wire around the headquarters of the 1st Battalion, 7th Marines, and though they took a loss of 38 killed, they inflicted casualties of 13 killed and 40 wounded on the defenders, which seems to have been an acceptable exchange for the enemy. It was an example of the enemy's will to press the fight even harder than ever despite the peace talks in Paris, probably as a means of hurrying the exit of Americans.

On 20 April a further reduction of 150,000 American troops in Vietnam was announced from Washington, with 41,800 of that number to come from the Marines. With Marine strength significantly reduced, ComUSMACV decided to reduce the Marine's TAOR—Tactical Area of Responsibility—in I Corps, with the ARVN taking over the relinquished area. General Lam, the ARVN commander, decided on a July offensive that he hoped would inflict major damage on the enemy's forces as a means of offsetting the negative effects of the reduced American force. In Operation Pickens Forest, the 7th Marines participated in this offensive, but little contact was made with enemy forces.

Heroic attempts were made to carry on US military operations in a professional manner, but the process of redeployment was accomplishing what years of enemy action had failed to do—hobble and curtail the ability of the Marine Corps to carry out its mission in Vietnam. Air support missions were becoming scarce. Combined action operations were drastically reduced. The burden of carrying out rural pacification programs was largely passed to the hard-pressed South Vietnamese.

But there was another side to the story, and that was the increasing indication that the enemy soldiers were suffering from exhaustion, hunger and sagging morale; a significant sign of this was the rising number of unburied enemy dead being found as well as unprotected caches of supplies, sure signs of a serious morale problem. Typhoon Kate, which struck in Quang Nam in October with the coming of the monsoon rains, added vastly to the enemy's misery.

Above : During the Tet Offensive a Marine fires on Viet Cong positions with an M79 grenade launcher.
Left : A scene from the fighting in Namo village during the Tet Offensive.

1971: The bleeding stops

During 1970 the level of combat for the Marine forces had declined steadily; this pattern continued in 1971. Contributing to this de-escalation was a conceptual change in the definition of Marine responsibility in Vietnam. For 'Tactical Areas of Responsibility' it substituted 'Tactical Areas of *Interest*.' This meant that local Marine commanders did not have primary responsibility for the area in which they operated—that now was passed to the local ARVN commander—and they could involve themselves in combat activities only as they chose to or were ordered to by ComUSMACV. From the point of view of the ordinary Marine rifleman, the difference this meant was that he went out on fewer patrols and ranged shorter distances away from his base.

Marine operations in the early part of the year were few and light. The 1st Marines Upshur Stream operation west of Da Nang in a search for enemy artillery positions turned up little. Marine support of Operation Lam Son 719, an ARVN strike into Laos against enemy bases and supply lines, was minimal on the ground, though Marine aircraft flew better than 500 sorties in support of it. Even a major North Vietnamese attack, the Easter Offensive,

Above : Marines lay down fire on a suspected North Vietnamese position. Because of the difficulty of detecting enemy positions the 'reconnaissance by fire' technique was often used, despite its drawbacks.
Left : Scene during Operation Lancaster II.
Right : Marines aboard an LCM during Deckhouse III. Amphibious operations were disappointingly ineffective in Vietnam.
Below : A typical fire support base with guns sited for all round defense.

saw no involvement by Marines in repulsing it; the enemy's message seemed to be, 'If we can do this while the Americans are here, imagine what we'll do when they are gone.' On 7 April the 1st Marines made one final foray, called Scott Orchard, sweeping the wild country west of An Hoa. There was little contact, and four enemy were killed.

The 14th of April was the day on which the III MAF, after six years of combat, left Vietnam; elsewhere throughout the country, other American units departed almost daily. However, a significant share of the duty of aiding the South Vietnamese military now passed to the guns of the ships of the Seventh Fleet, and to the Marine and Navy pilots operating from the carriers' decks. They seemed to be supporting a losing cause, for North Vietnamese units had for the first time captured a South Vietnamese province, Quang Tri, and were sweeping toward Hué. But by 28 June the South the South Vietnamese forces north of Hué were ready to strike back; an Airborne division and a Marine Division, their east

Above left : Tan Son Nhut Airbase burns in the background from North Vietnamese artillery strikes during the evacuation of Saigon, 29 April 1975.
Right : South Vietnamese refugees hurry off a CH-53 helicopter under the eyes of a watchful Marine aboard the USS *Hancock*.
Below : A Marine observation plane flies low over Hué in February 1968.

Above: Bewildered refugees on the deck of the USS *Hancock* during the evacuation of Saigon. They have been brought to the ship by the helicopters of Marine squadron HMH-463.

flank on the sea, moved north. The fighting was bitter; one month later the Airborne was relieved and the fight was left for the Marines to complete. They battered their way through massive enemy resistance to the walls of the Citadel, Quang Tri city's fortress where, on 16 September, they raised the red-striped yellow flag of South Vietnam above the shell-blasted west gate.

As the year ended a state of military equilibrium had been achieved; it would subsequently be destabilized not by military failures in the field but by decisions made at a far-off conference. Vietnam had been the longest and biggest war in Marine Corps history. At its peak size in 1968, III MAF had had one-quarter of the total Corps strength. Total Marine deaths due to enemy action totaled 12,936, and wounded in action came to 88,589; enemy deaths due to Marine actions came to 86,535.

Perhaps the most poignant footnote-comment on Vietnam was made by combat correspondent Keyes Beech on his departure after ten years of covering the war: 'I would like to offer a salute to that skinny little Viet Cong somewhere out there in the jungle shivering in the monsoon rains. . . . He is one hell of a fighting man.'

On 10 June 1968, General Westmoreland held his final news conference in Saigon as ComUSMACV. Most of his remarks and the queries from correspondents were routine and expected. Then some reporter raised his voice to ask Westmoreland one final question to end the news conference:

'General, can the war be won militarily?'

'Not in a classic sense, because—' Westmoreland paused, then continued in a deliberate, flat voice—'of our national policy of not expanding the war.'

Westmoreland placed his uniform cap on his head, and tugged the peak down at a slight angle. He looked around the room silently for an instant, then said one final word:

'Good-bye.'

The Marines left Vietnam with pride in how well the Corps had performed, but disappointment in how their efforts had been compromised politically. Before many years passed, they would know these feelings again.

The Mayaguez incident: 1975

With American aid gone from South Vietnam, the end was long, painful and inevitable. The ripple effect of the Communist victories in Vietnam spread to neighboring Cambodia where, in April 1975, the Khmer Rouge seized the capital of Phnom Penh. And in Saigon, at 0753 of the morning of 30 April, the last CH-46 helicopter lifted off from the roof of the burning American embassy building with the last 11 Marines.

At 1420 on 12 May, a Cambodian gunboat bearing the Khmer Rouge flag fired across the bow of the American container ship *Mayaguez*, on its way from Hong Kong to Thailand. The unarmed American ship hove to, and a boarding party of of Cambodian sailors ordered the crew to sail the ship to follow the gunboat. They finally dropped anchor off Koh Tang, a small jungle-covered island 34 miles off the Cambodian mainland, where the 39-member American crew was taken ashore. When they were later moved to the mainland on one of a small flotilla of gunboats, they narrowly escaped death at the hands of fellow Americans when the boats were strafed by Air Force jets and five were sunk.

Back in Washington, the National Security Council met the day after the seizing of the *Mayaguez* at President Gerald Ford's orders, and it was decided to retake the ship. Marines would make two assaults: one group would board and capture the

Above : Vietnamese troops during a river operation. Riverine rather than true amphibious operations were widely practiced but the Vietnamese proved uncertain allies in this as in other respects.
Right : Marines from the destroyer *Harold E Holt* board the *Mayaguez* only to find that the ship was deserted.
Below : Marines wearing gas masks and with M16 rifles at the ready during the capture of the *Mayaguez*. Another group of Marines landed on Koh Tang.

Mayaguez, the other group would land on Koh Tang and free the prisoners; it was not yet realized that they had been moved. 2nd Battalion, 9th Marines, reinforced, was airlifted from Okinawa to Utapao airfield in Thailand, over the protests of that neutral government. The attack carrier *Coral Sea*, the guided-missile destroyer *Henry B Wilson* and four destroyer escorts sailed at top speed into the Gulf of Siam.

The raiding party would go in aboard 16 helicopters. Lift-off was at 0415 on Wednesday, 15 May, only three days after seizure of the ship. Marines were helilifted to the destroyer-escort *Harold E Holt* which, at 0830, came alongside the captured ship. The Marines scrambled aboard, found the ship deserted, and took possession of it. Meanwhile, by remarkable good luck, just at that time the crew of the *Mayaguez* was being returned to Koh Tang aboard a captured Thai fishing boat by the Cambodians; the *Wilson* intercepted the boat, freed the captured Americans, took aboard the Cambodian guards and sent the Thai fishermen home to their village.

In the American attacks on Koh Tang and also on Kampong Som, as well as in the rescue operation itself, three helicopters were shot down and ten others damaged by the enemy; 11 Marines, two Navy men and two airmen died, 41 Marines, two Navy men and seven airmen were wounded.

PEACEKEEPING AND OTHER MODERN ROLES

Semper Fi . . .1973-Present

On 10 November 1975 several hundred Marines stood silently in the cold and rain before the Marine Corps War Memorial—the great bronze statue of the Iwo Jima flag-raising on Mount Suribachi—at Arlington National Cemetery. The occasion: the 200th birthday of the United States Marine Corps. President Ford was there and spoke of the Corps as 'a living monument to devotion and self-sacrifice.' The new commandant of the Corps was there, General Louis H Wilson, as was the last surviving Marine portrayed in the statue itself, René A Gagnon. There were prayers for all the dead Marines, a rifle salute, and then Taps. That night there would be dancing and celebrations all around the world, wherever a few Marines or former Marines gathered. It was a momentous occasion, one little dreamed of when the Continental Congress back on 10 November 1775 called for a small unit of 'Continental Marines.'

Yet all thoughtful Marines, like all their fellow Americans, must have been somewhat troubled that day. For the United States was undergoing one of the most traumatic periods since those dark days of 1775. The nation had recently experienced two profound losses. One, the Vietnam War, which—whatever the role of the US military—had to be considered a national loss. The other, the resignation of President Nixon in a swirl of scandals and legal threats. And although the Marines were by no means singled out for any special blame, they undoubtedly shared in the malaise that now gripped the American people.

In particular, many Americans were raising disturbing questions about the performance of their military forces during the Vietnam War. Although far and away most individual Marines and units had performed to the highest standards, there were some few who had been involved in actions that were not. Some Marines had undoubtedly been unnecessarily destructive in their sweeps through Vietnamese villages: young men under stress had often been so. Meanwhile, in 1973, one former American officer who had been a prisoner of war in North Vietnam charged three Marine and five Army enlisted men with 'misconduct while in the prison camp': they had formed a 'Peace Committee.' And in a much publicized event, former Marine Private Robert Garwood returned in 1979 to face charges that he had collaborated with the enemy while in a prison camp and then chosen to stay in North Vietnam ever

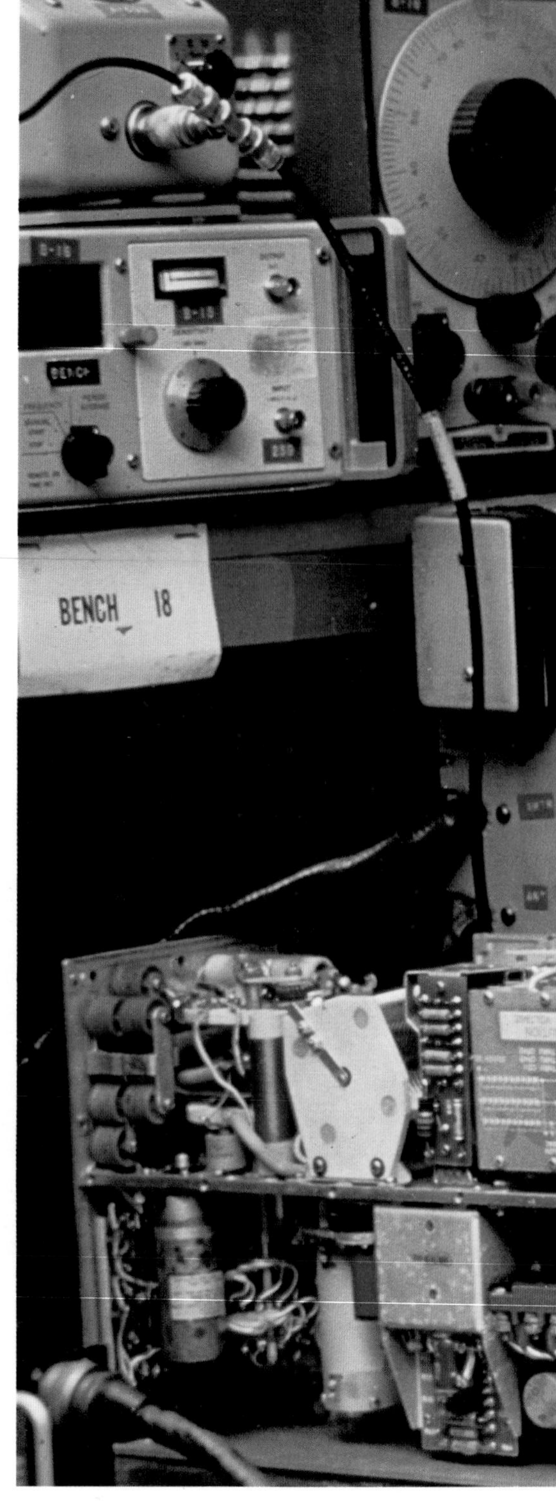

Above : Women are employed in many technical specialties in the modern Marine Corps.
Left : Contemporary recruiting poster.
Previous page : Marines of the 24th Amphibious unit come ashore to join the peacekeeping force in Beirut in November 1982.

since the other prisoners were allowed to return in 1973.

Throughout America, too, Marines—like all veterans of the Vietnam War—were being buffeted from all sides. There was a national debate raging over whether the deserters from the military should be given amnesty or pardon. Meanwhile, many former Vietnam veterans were complaining of ill-treatment from the very citizenry they had thought they were serving—treatment ranging from abusive remarks to just plain avoidance. Individual Marines were also beginning to show the first symptoms of what would become known as the 'Vietnam veterans syndrome,' a complex of psychological and emotional problems caused by the intensity of their experiences in Vietnam now recurring to prevent them from functioning in the civilian world.

The Corps itself was also finding itself experiencing various stresses and strains as it moved into the post-Vietnam world. The use of narcotics, which had undoubtedly been widespread in the military in Vietnam, was not to be tolerated in the peacetime Corps, and there were several well-publicized incidents of Marines being transferred from sensitive assignments. There were the usual cases of unnecessarily harsh Drill Instructors at Marine training camps, incidents that in some cases led to trials of the DIs involved.

There were also many more positive aspects to the Corps in these years. Women were rising in the ranks. In 1973 Colonel Mary E Bane became the first woman to command a unit, a company of some 2150 men and women. In 1977 the first women Marine officers began combat training with male Marines. And in 1978 Colonel Margaret E Brewer was promoted to Brigadier General, the first female general in the history of the Corps. Blacks, too, were rising in the Marines, and in 1979 Colonel Frank E Petersen Jr, became a brigadier general, the first black to achieve that rank in the Corps.

The fact was that the Corps could no longer, if it ever had been, be regarded as apart from American society as a whole. If it had an exceptionally high desertion rate in these years—and in 1976, the Marines reported a rate of 69.2 per 1000 enlistees, versus 31.7 per 1000 for the US Navy and 17.71 for the US Army—it was because young Americans had new attitudes about discipline and authority. And if the Marine Corps had a disproportionately high percentage of blacks—by 1982, 22 percent of the Corps, while they constituted only 12 percent of America's population as a whole—it was undoubtedly

Above: The amphibious assault ship USS *Inchon* and her six *Iwo Jima* class sisters can each carry 30 helicopters and over 2000 Marines.

because young black males were having a hard time finding other employment. Meanwhile, the Corps, like all branches of the US military, was having trouble attracting qualified volunteers now that the United States had eliminated the draft. Except in wartime, of course, the Marine Corps had prided itself on being an all-volunteer unit, but now the Marines found themselves recruiting within a society that was at least temporarily 'down on' the military. General Wilson, the Commandant, was so concerned that in 1978 he recommended the reinstatement of a draft—which would traditionally serve to steer some young men to enlist in the Marines. And in 1979, the new commandant of the Corps, General Robert H Barrow, proposed cutting back on the authorized strength of 190,000 to 179,000 Marines and putting more effort and budget into improving a trimmed-down and advanced Corps.

Below: The assault transport *Spiegel Grove* (LSD.32) operates landing craft (as well as helicopters) to deploy heavy equipment during amphibious operations.

Again, though, the problems and issues that were current in the Corps during these years could not be divorced from those abroad in American society as a whole. Thus, the question of the numbers and qualifications of enlistees in the Marines was part of a national debate over just what role the traditional military would play in the future. Would not the weapons systems and wars of the future call for relatively few but highly trained personnel? Should so much money be budgeted for training, maintaining (and eventually retiring) conventional personnel when the new weapons, ships, planes and advanced technology required such large sums? In particular, were the Marines even required in the the wars of the future?

Now the Marines had often found their function, even existence, questioned, especially after a major war, and once again, in the 1970s, the Corps found its role being scrutinized. Some critics were claiming that if the Marines prime justification was as an amphibious landing force, the last true contested assault had been at Inchon, Korea, in 1950. (The several amphibious landings in Vietnam had been more for demonstration than for real.) In an age of nuclear weapons, missiles, versatile airplanes and advanced weapons of all kinds, would there be any need for Marines to storm ashore? Other critics were pointing out that both in Korea and in Vietnam, the Marines had essentially served as supplements—however valuable and courageous—to the regular army. Meanwhile, the Marines argued that their speciality——amphibious landings—required co-

ordinated air support, while critics claimed it required a disproportionate amount of the Corps' budget to maintain its own air force. Perhaps the debate that raged around the Corps was best summed up in a much-publicized study made by one of the most prestigious 'think tanks,' the Brookings Institution, which in 1976 issued a report, *Where Does the Marine Corps Go From Here?*

The Marines stand by

Yet even as the debate was going on, the role of the Marines was made clear for all who would look. Even in a world of complex geopolitical and military decisions, there were the occasions when the old-fashioned US Marines seemed best suited to fulfilling America's goals. Thus, in the October 1973 war between Israel and Egypt and Syria, when the United States decided to supply planes and other military equipment to the beleagured Israelis, a force of 2000 Marines was sent from the USA to the Sixth Fleet in the Mediterranean—a clear signal to the Egyptians and Syrians, as well as to their patron, the USSR, that the USA 'meant business.' That was what the appearance of the US Marines had always meant.

In a somewhat different incident in 1974, the Marines also carried out their traditional role. The Greeks on Cyprus had overthrown their island's government in July, and the Turkish army had invaded the island to protect the Turkish minority there; a truce was soon arranged that left the island divided, and since the United States was perceived by the Greek Cypriots to have favored the Turks, a mob of Greeks attacked the US Embassy in the capital, Nicosia, on 19 August. Five Marines of the Security Guard Detachment defended the embassy with tear-gas grenades, although bullets fired by the Greek Cypriots killed the American ambassador and a woman secretary. No Marines were killed or wounded in this episode, nor were any in another attack on the embassy in Nicosia in January 1975, but there are times when the US Marines best serve America's interests by not getting killed—or killing.

This is particularly true for the Marines who serve in the Security Guard Battalion in some 125 embassies, consulate generals, and missions around the world (and occasionally with the American delegations to international conferences). This battalion was in fact created only in 1949, and its personnel serve under the arrangements made between the Corps and the US Department of State. Their basic assignment is to protect the official personnel, classified materials and government property at these posts, but on occasion the Marine guards find themselves bearing the brunt of foreigners' anger at the USA in general. Thus, in 1973, President Idi Amin, the violent and anti-American dictator of Uganda, demand that the Marines at the embassy leave—he claimed they were engaged in subversive activities. (The USA countered by closing the whole embassy.) And in 1974 the Communist Chinese government demanded that the six-man Marine unit at the new US liaison office in Peking be removed. And then, in 1978, Chinese Nationalists protesting the US recognition of Communist China attacked the US Embassy and military headquarters in Taipei, Taiwan, and it was the US Marine security guard that had to drive back the mob with tear gas.

The Iranian crisis

But perhaps the most dramatic episode in the Marines' history of service as security guards—and one that demonstrates so well the peculiarly delicate nature of this assignment—is the one that became known as the

Below: During the 1980 Bright Star exercises, Marines advance with support from their LVTP-7 amphibious personnel carriers.

The Marines are looking for a few good men to join them.

Above: A modern recruiting poster but a traditional message.
Main picture: Marine M60 tank. The M60 entered service in the early 1960s but soldiers on today with more modern fire control systems among the many improved items of equipment.

Above : Physical fitness and discipline remain prime objectives of Marine Corps basic training. *Right :* Marines with an M110 8-inch self-propelled howitzer. Such weapons are normally not organic to Marine divisions but are controlled by higher echelons.

Iranian Hostage Crisis. In fact, for the US Marines, this crisis had both a prologue and an epilogue. The former came in February 1979, when in the turmoil that followed the overthrow of the Shah, forces supporting the Ayatollah Khomeini overthrew the government of Premier Shahpur Bakhtiar. President Jimmy Carter made plans to evacuate the 7800 Americans said to be in Iran, and a contingent of 69 Marines and six helicopters was stationed in an undisclosed location near Iran. But before any official evacuation began, leftist guerrillas stormed the US Embassy in Teheran; the compound was guarded by 19 US Marines of the Security Guard, and they fired tear gas grenades at the first attackers; outnumbered, they began to switch to shot guns loaded with birdshot, but they were soon overwhelmed by the sheer numbers of Iranians and were forced to surrender, along with some 100 embassy employees—including the US Ambassador, William Sullivan. Eventually representatives from Khomeini arrived, and after two hours the guerrillas were persuaded to release all the Americans. However, two Marines had been wounded in the attack—they claimed after

Above: The tank landing ship *Fairfax County* (nearest) and the *Inchon*, typical components of a force for Marine landing operations.

surrendering—and when one of them was taken to a Teheran hospital for treatment, he was then kidnapped by supporters of Khomeini. It was a week before US pressure on Khomeini brought about this Marine's release. At that time, it seemed a long while to hold an American hostage.

Following that incident, hundreds of Americans began to leave Iran, and the US government cut back its embassy staff to about 65, with a Marine Security Guard of 13. Some of the more experienced diplomatic personnel were warning the US government that continued support for the Shah would endanger any Americans at the Teheran Embassy, but on 22 October 1979, President Carter went ahead and allowed the Shah to enter the USA for medical treatment for cancer. From that day on, there were daily demonstrations in front of the entrance to the extensive compound where the US Embassy and its associated buildings were located.

So it was on Sunday morning, 4 November, when the embassy personnel saw and heard the usual mob shouting 'Death to America!' and similar slogans, there seemed nothing that different from other recent days. But for whatever reason—whether it was a totally planned and directed move or not—about 10:30 that morning the demonstrators began to force the gate and climb over the compound walls. The Marines on duty at the main gatehouse immediately realized that they would not be able to hold back this mob. As one member of the Marine Security Guard, Sergeant James M Lopez, would later say: 'To put it bluntly, all hell broke loose and we couldn't stop it.'

The Marines who could got inside the main chancery building and bolted its heavy front door. They then began to put on their flak jackets and helmets and to pass out rifles, shotguns, pistols and tear gas grenades. (Several of the 13-man Marine guard were elsewhere around the compound.)

Meanwhile, Bruce Laingen, chargé d'affaires at the US Embassy in Teheran (as there was no ambassador at that time), was at the Iranian Foreign Ministry. Informed by phone of the mob attacking the chancery, he gave orders that no Americans were to fire any weapons: this may have been one of the wisest decisions taken by anyone involved in the entire Iranian Hostage Crisis. And the US Marines there at the chancery deserve equal credit: trained to fight—to shoot—yes, to kill—to protect America's goals, Marines might have found it easy to start shooting. It would have made a heroic tale for the grandchildren—even if it had to be told by a widowed grandmother. For if any Marines had begun to shoot, the whole episode would almost certainly have ended in violence of a different kind, with many Americans equally certainly dead.

Instead, the Marines acted as the professionals they were, and as the civilian staff of the embassy began to retreat to higher floors and start to shred documents, the guards held off the Iranians who had broken in from the basement windows and were now forcing their way up the stairs of the chancery. Sergeant John D McKeel Jr and Corporal Westley Williams were the two Marines last in the stairway, and they were forced to don gas masks when tear gas began to spread. Sergeant McKeel did spray one young Iranian with chemical Mace (and would later be severely beaten for this) but neither Marine fired the shotguns they held. Gradually, all the Americans in the chancery were trapped and taken prisoner.

Other Americans, including some of the Marines, were at other stations in the compound, and one by one they were being captured by the Iranians now roaming free in the compound. One Marine was actually outside the compound on an errand, but when he heard that the mob had broken in, he rushed back into the grounds—only to be taken prisoner. At the consulate building, only one Marine, Sergeant James Lopez, was on duty, and he would later be singled out for praise by other Americans for his

Above: Marine training takes account of the possibility of biological or chemical attack. Practice routines with tear gas are common.

cool courage. Lopez not only took steps to make the consulate as secure as possible—at one point shoving an Iranian out of a second-floor window as he was about to climb in—but he calmly destroyed official consulate property while other Americans were slipping out a side door of the consulate. (Five of those eventually escaped from Iran with the help of Canadian Embassy officials.) Lopez was the last person to leave the consulate—he tried to disguise himself as an Iranian—but was caught as he was locking the door. One of the Americans who escaped would later say: 'By keeping the consulate secure, he made it possible for us to go. He was the one all of us looked to to tell us what to do. He may have been the most junior guy there, but he was certainly up to the occasion. He didn't get excited. He didn't lose his composure.' Marine Sergeant Lopez was 21 years old, and like the other Marines at the compound take-over that day, he may have performed his most courageous act by not firing his pistol.

By about 1:00 that afternoon, all 61 Americans in the compound were taken prisoner; two other Americans would be taken at the offices of the Iran-America Society elsewhere in Teheran, while three were held at the Foreign Ministry. Thus began the Hostage Crisis that would not end for most of them until 20 January 1981—444 days of captivity. (Thirteen of them would be released on 19–20 November 1979—five women secretaries and eight blacks, including five Marines: the Iranian revolutionaries were trying to show the world their support for 'oppressed' groups.) The US Marines held hostage did not suffer any more than the civilians—although, again, that would most certainly not have been the case had they killed even one Iranian. Indeed, in some respects, the individual Marines were less harassed by their Iranian captors than were certain civilians. It is not unreasonable to suggest that this was in tacit recognition that the US Marines were true professionals who carry out the orders of their government but do not make policy. If this was why the Marines were not bothered by the Iranians, it says something for the image—and performance—of the Corps.

But in the epilogue to the hostage crisis, other Marines were less fortunate. Almost immediately after it was clear that the Iranian government was not going to release the hostages, that very November 1979,

Left: Marine in full jungle camouflage aims his M16 rifle.
Right: Marine scout team. As the Vietnam experience proved, intensive patrol operations are vital in jungle terrain.

American military planners began to discuss possible ways of releasing them by force. The Carter administration insisted on using diplomatic and other channels to seek their release, but finally, convinced that all negotiations were at an end, at a secret meeting of his National Security Council on 11 April 1980, President Carter gave the go-ahead to a military rescue plan.

The plan had been rehearsed for some time, so it did not take that long to put it into effect. On 24 April, at 7:30 in the evening (Iranian time), eight Navy helicopters took off from the aircraft carrier *Nimitz* in the Arabian Sea off Iran. They were piloted and crewed by US Marines. About that same time, six US Air Force C-130 Hercules transports took off from an undisclosed base or aircraft carrier. The plan called for all these helicopters and planes to rendezvous at a desert site some 250 miles southeast of Teheran; at that point, troops aboard the transports would transfer to the helicopters, which would carry them to another point some 50 miles outside Teheran; from there they would be trucked into Teheran (the trucks arranged by CIA operatives), release the hostages, and then fly out on the helicopters. The plan called for a minimum of six helicopters to make it operational.

One of the helicopters was forced down only about 80 miles into Iranian airspace by rotorblade trouble. A second helicopter's navigation and flight instruments failed after flying through a dust storm, and the pilot returned to the *Nimitz*. And then, when the remaining six copters were at Desert One, the rendezvous site, a third one was revealed to have hydraulic failure. This meant that only five helicopters were available, so Colonel Charlie Beckwith, the US Army officer in command of the ground rescue team, recommended to the Defense Department in Washington that the mission be abandoned. At 3:15 in the morning of 25 April (Iranian time), President Carter ordered that the mission be canceled.

The helicopters now began to refuel from one of the C-130s, and as one was changing position, it collided with a C-130. As the two aircraft burst into flame, ammunition and shell casings from within the C-130 began to fall on the other helicopters. Colonel Beckwith gave orders for all the helicopters to be abandoned, and all surviving men were put aboard the C-130s, which then took off. But the intense fire had prevented them from carrying away the eight men who had been killed in the initial blast, and the charred bodies would be publicly displayed by Iranians at the embassy compound. (Later they were returned to America.)

Above : A Marine M60 tank comes ashore during joint maneuvers with Australian forces.
Left : Although scrambling nets are now used comparatively seldom in operational conditions they still feature in fitness training programs.

Debate over the mission—its very conception, its planning, its operation, the decisions made along the way—would continue for some time. But one point was undeniable: of the eight servicemen who died, three were US Marines—testifying once more to the prominent role played by the Marines whenever Americans were asked to make the extreme sacrifice.

The invasion of Grenada

In the months that followed the resolution of the Iranian Hostage Crisis, the US Marines, like all Americans, would have plenty of time to think about the cost to the US of its global commitments and of the uses and limits of its vast powers. The greatest test of this commitment—to the US Marines in particular—would come in Beirut, Lebanon, of course, but the nation was usually under some pressure in one part of the world or another. And where the US felt itself pressured, the US Marines were usually to be found. This holds especially, and traditionally, in the Caribbean and Central America, where at least since the Monroe Doctrine of 1823 the US has exerted a special concern. Since the intervention of the Marines in the Dominican Republic in 1965, there had been several incidents involving attacks on the US Embassy in El Salvador, and the Marine security guards had responded with their usual tear gas. But for the most part, the Marines were not involved in the training of the government's troops in El Salvador or of the anti-Sandinista forces in Guatemala. (Marines do train regularly in Panama, however, and they participated in the ongoing training exercises known as Big Pine in Honduras in 1983–84.)

But Marines were called into action once again in the controversial intervention in Grenada in October 1983. The USA's problems with this tiny Caribbean island had been brewing for some time, ever since its Marxist Prime Minister Maurice Bishop had invited Cubans to help construct—with obvious Russian support—a 10,000-foot airfield; Bishop insisted it was simply to handle the large airplanes that would bring tourists, but the USA claimed it was designed to allow Russian airplanes to 'service' Caribbean nations. Then, in an unexpected development, the Prime Minister and about 100 other Grenadians were killed on 19 October by a group of even more radical leftists. They imposed a round-the-clock curfew on the island, yet seemed unable to provide any further leadership that might avoid anarchy. There were about 1000 Americans on Grenada, most of them students at St George's University School of Medicine, and there was genuine concern among some members of the US government that they could become hostages—just as had occurred in Iran during a similar time of turmoil.

So it was that President Ronald Reagan authorized the American military to go into Grenada. Meanwhile, six neighboring Caribbean nations had also asked the USA to intervene, as they feared the threat to their own people should a strong Marxist government take hold on Grenada. And there was no denying that the Reagan administration, aside from this appeal and the threat to the students, had its own determination not to let the USSR get any more of a foothold in the Caribbean.

The first ashore on 25 October 1983, were a small group of US Navy Seals, especially assigned to sneak ashore and rescue the Governor-General, Sir Paul Scoon, held under house arrest by the coup leaders. But at almost the same moment, on the opposite side of the island, some 400 Marines in troop helicopters from the amphibious assault ship *Guam* landed at Pearls Airport, the only really functional airstrip at that time. That was about 5:30 in the morning. About a half hour later, hundreds of Rangers, the Army's special force, parachuted onto the new 10,000-foot airstrip at Point Salines at the southeastern tip of Grenada. The Marines met little resistance and declared their airport secure within two hours. The Rangers, however, met unexpectedly heavy resistance, most of it apparently coming from the area where the Cuban workers lived. (The Pentagon had expected that some of the Cubans might fight but did not know that they were so well armed—including antiaircraft wea-

Below: The *Austin* class amphibious transport USS *Dubuque* can carry 900 Marines and their equipment, 6 transport helicopters and from 4 to 20 landing craft depending on type.

pons.) By 7:15, however, the Rangers had cleared the airstrip so that C-130s could land.

That afternoon, the *Guam*, which had moved around to the west coast, sent ashore 13 amphibious vehicles—with 250 Marines and five tanks—to take Fort Frederick and its Richmond Hill prison, on the high ground outside St George, the island's capital. As the Marines moved down from the north of the fort, Rangers moved from the south. Resistance from Grenadian revolutionaries was again unexpectedly heavy, and when night came that Tuesday, the US military could not really claim to be in control of Grenada. By Wednesday, however, most organized resistance was put down. Early that morning Marines stormed the mansion where the US Navy Seals were now besieged with the Governor-General. That evening, Marines were taking Fort Frederic at about the same time other Marines were relieving the campus of the medical school where hundreds of young Americans had been cut off by Grenadian revolutionaries.

On Thursday, 27 October, the Atlantic Fleet Commander was reporting that 'all major military objectives in the island were secured.' Pockets of resistance remained, however, for some days. By this time, there were some 50 Marines, 500 Rangers, and 5000 paratroopers from the 82nd Airborne Division on Grenada, plus about 400 members of the six-nation Caribbean force that served as a token of their support. The total American casualties for the operation were 18 dead and 67 wounded. A week later, all the US Marines and Rangers had left; and within another six weeks, only about 300 US Military Police and support troops were still on Grenada. As usual where American troops and casualties were involved, many Americans were left to raise many questions about this intervention. But when the large amounts of Russian-made arms and ammunition, not to mention 12 Soviet-built armored personnel carriers, were displayed; when the majority of the students expressed gratitude for being rescued; and when so many of the native Grenadians declared their joy of being freed from the repressive rule of their Marxist military revolutionaries—then most Americans conceded that it was one intervention that had succeeded.

The tragedy of Lebanon

America's involvement in Lebanon would not end so happily. It had begun in August 1982, when an agreement—negotiated by US envoy Philip Habib—called for the Israelis to pull their troops away from west Beirut, where they were besieging the Palestine Liberation Organization's (PLO) army, while an international peace-keeping force moved in to maintain order. On 19 August the Lebanese government formally requested that the USA, France and Italy send troops for such a force, and the USA assigned, quite naturally, 800 Marines. They were to be armed, but were to assume a 'carefully limited non-combat role,' and they were to stay no more than 30 days.

The first US Marines came ashore on 25 August—the French and Italian troops having come several days previously—and they relieved the French troops at the port.

Above: Men of the 6th Marines (2nd Marine Division) pause for orders in front of an M48 tank during the intervention in the Dominican Republic in 1965.
Right: A Marine points out a crate of Soviet AK-47 assault rifles found by the American forces on Grenada.
Below: Marine looks out for snipers near the town of Greenville, Grenada, 25 October 1983.

By 1 September all the Palestinians (and their Syrian supporters) were officially declared to be out of Beirut, and so on 10 September the 800 US Marines went back to their ships offshore. They had never fired a shot in action, and there were no casualties.

But then, on 14 September, the newly elected president of Lebanon, Bashir Gemayel, was assassinated by Moslem extremists opposed to Gemayel and his Christian-Phalangist party. To control the violence that everyone feared would ensue, the Israelis moved back into Beirut, but they made the mistake of allowing Christian-Phalangists into refugee camps housing Palestinians, and sometime between 16 and 18 September, Phalangist extremists massacred several hundred Palestinians in revenge. In the turmoil that followed, President Reagan agreed to send American troops back as part of an international peacekeeping force, and on 29 September, the first detachment of Marines once again came ashore at Beirut to join the French and Italian troops. The Americans were assigned to guard the Beirut International Airport, and they took up their posts around the airport.

As it happened, the first US Marine was killed within 24 hours by an 'accidental detonation' of some undetected explosive around the airport. This turned out to be significant in more ways than one, because the US Marine commander on the scene would later state that the Marines long considered such hidden explosives to be their greatest threat, along with the Israelis, who refused to leave Beirut so long as the Syrians also refused to leave. And in the weeks and then months that followed, several Marines were killed by various explosions, snipers, and shells fired into their midst. Americans began to raise questions about the role of the Marines there in Beirut; by 12 September 1983, there were 1200 Marines on shore and another 2000 in a backup force on ships off Beirut. The next day, President Reagan authorized the Marines to call in US naval artillery and air strikes if deemed

Below: LVTP-7s of the 32nd Marine Amphibious Brigade in Beirut on 15 November 1982. The 32nd Brigade was being relieved at that time by the 24th Marine Amphibious Unit.

Above: A 155mm howitzer of C Battery, 24th Marine Amphibious Unit, serving with the Beirut peacekeeping force in September 1983.

necessary, but the US Marine commander in Lebanon, Colonel Timothy J Geraghty, insisted that there was no change in the Marines' peace-keeping mission.' On 29 September the US Congress passed the War Powers Resolution allowing for US forces to remain in Lebanon only for another 18 months. For too many of the Marines, this would prove to be far too late a deadline.

Left: Amphibious assault ships lie offshore as a Marine M48 tank lands.
Below left: The LVTP-7 is the Marines' standard amphibious assault vehicle.
Below: US Navy minesweeping RH-53 helicopter refuels from a Marine KC-130 tanker.

At daybreak, 23 October, a large yellow Mercedes truck pulled into the parking lot at the south side of the compound where the Marines were headquartered on the edge of the Beirut airport. There was a roll of barbed wire bisecting the parking lot; behind this were two sentry posts, but at that time of morning only one sentry was on duty—and his rifle was not loaded; then there was a wrought-iron, six-foot high fence, with a knee-high cement base, with an iron grillwork gate through which vehicles had to enter; at the far end of a driveway was an 18-inch diameter pipe placed lengthwise as a barrier before the entrance to the headquarters building. All these devices seemed like reasonably adequate protection at the time.

No one noticed the Mercedes truck as it circled the parking lot two times, as most Marines were still asleep in the headquarters building. Suddenly the truck turned straight toward the building and crashed through the barbed wire, ran through the sentry posts, drove through the grillwork gate, and on over the pipe and went straight into the entryway. Later, the one Marine sentry who saw the driver would report that he appeared to be 'smiling.' If so, it was his last act, because his truck's cargo had the explosive force equal to 12,000 pounds of high explosives.

In the tremendous blast that followed, much of the headquarters building simply collapsed, floor by floor, onto itself, killing or trapping most of the 300 Marines inside. Those Marines who were outside began to dig frantically to save as many of their comrades as they could. Meanwhile, almost simultaneously, another truck had crashed

Above: Marines of the 24th MAU employ a MULE utility vehicle to transport communications equipment, Beirut, 15 November 1982.
Right: Fully-equipped Marines come ashore from their landing craft to join the Beirut peacekeeping force.

into the French troops' building and killed 58 of them. The American toll would eventually turn out to be 240 dead Marines. It was one of the worst single days in the entire history of the US Marine Corps. More Marines died in this one incident than had died in any single action in the entire Vietnam War, and on only one day in that bloody war had there been more US military fatalities.

What made it especially tragic to the Marines, at least, was that it seemed so unnecessary and so uncharacteristic. The Marines, who prided themselves on being so alert, so mobile, so combat-ready. To be caught, literally, in bed, with their defenses down. Inevitably there were charges, accusations, blame; inevitably, too, the Marine command—from the colonel in charge of the contingent in Beirut to the Commandant himself—came in for its share of criticism. There was a Congressional hearing, and later there was an official military review board. There seemed to be enough blame to go all around, but the simple conclusion was that there had not been adequate security measures, both in the literal sense of barriers and in the broader sense of alerting the Marines to all the potential threats from terrorists. Ironically, it turned out that it was less a lack of sufficient verbal warnings from intelligence sources but more a case of too many warnings: the Marines in Beirut had been receiving so many warnings of terrorist attacks that they were being disregarded. In the end, President Reagan tried to defuse the situation when in January 1984 he said he would assume final responsibility as Commander in Chief, and even if not all Americans felt this quite answered the charges, few were inclined to continue blaming the Marines who had already suffered more than their share of the sorrow of Lebanon.

Looking to the future

The explosion at the Beirut headquarters marked one of the lowest points in the history of the Marines. And even in the weeks that followed, the killing of the Marines stationed there in Beirut did not stop. In December 1983 one intensive artillery barrage by Syrian-backed Druze militiamen resulted in the deaths of eight US Marines. Questions continued to be asked as to whether this assignment in Beirut was the proper one for the Marines. As the Marine fatalities in Lebanon rose to 260, and all they could look forward to was a slow attrition, there was increasing doubt as to the viability of the US presence there. Eventually, as the situation in Lebanon deteriorated further in the early weeks of 1984, the decision was taken to withdraw the Marines from Beirut.

But through all this agonizing and scrutinizing, there was one noticeable fact: the US Marines were not complaining. They were doing what they had done throughout the 200 years of their existence: they were serving their nation as its first-line troops, wherever and whenever they were needed. The debate over their exact composition

Left : A Marine launches a Redeye antiaircraft missile. This type is now being phased out and replaced by the more modern Stinger.
Above : Marine C-130 Hercules employs a rocket pack to shorten its take-off run. Operating from restricted airfields is a Marine speciality.

and function would undoubtedly continue. There would be discussions over what new weapons and new tactics and new strategies the Marines should adopt. Almost from the moment they had been formed, the Marines had heard—and survived—these debates. There would be new problems, too—challenges brought on by the changing role of America and its Armed Forces and the new weapons. The Marines would come through these, too. Through it all, the Marines would remain on station and alert around the world.

Why could Marines be so sure of this survival and dedication? Perhaps it is best expressed by an incident that followed the Beirut explosion. The Commandant of the Marines had gone to a US military hospital in West Germany to award Purple Hearts to some of the wounded survivors. As General Paul X Kelley was pinning the medal to the gown of Lance Corporal Jeffrey Nashton, the young Marine—who was unable to speak because of all the tubes in his face—signed that he wanted a piece of paper to write on. He then scribbled something and handed it to General Kelley. What he wrote was 'Semper Fi,' the Marines' shorthand for their motto, *Semper Fidelis.* So long as Marines like this remained 'always faithful,' there was little doubt about the future of the Corps.

Below : Three Marine light attack squadrons are equipped with the AV-8A Harrier. The improved AV-8B is shortly to enter service.

INDEX

Page numbers in italics refer to illustrations

Acknowledgments

The publisher would like to thank the following people who have helped in the preparation of this book: Kenneth Anderson, Swafford Johnson, and James M Morris, who contributed to the history. David Eldred designed this book, Ron Watson prepared the index, and the photographs were kindly supplied by the following:

Anne Brown Military Collection, Brown University p 22 (top)
AP Worldwide pp 196 (bottom), 197 (bottom)
Franklin D Roosevelt Library p 20 (top)
Robert Hunt Library pp 142 (top), 143 (top), 146–147
Imperial War Museum p 149 (bottom)
Library of Congress Collection pp 24–25, 28 (top), 29 (bottom), 37 (top), 41 (top)
National Archives pp 6–7, 12, 13 (top), 14 (top and bottom), 15 (top right and bottom), 16 (bottom (bottom), 17 (bottom), 18 (both), 19 (both), 23 (top), 25 (inset), 26 (both), 27 (all three), 28 (bottom), 30 (both), 31 (both), 32 (top), 33 (top), 34–35, 37 (bottom), 38 (bottom), 39 (both), 42 (both), 43 (both), 44 (both), 45 (both), 46, 47 (top), 50 (both), 51 (both), 52 (both), 54 (bottom), 55 (both), 60 (both), 61 (top), 62–63, 68 (both), 69 (both), 70 (both), 71 (bottom), 72, 73 (both), 74, 75 (top left, center and bottom), 76 (both), 77, 79 (bottom), 82 (both), 86–87, 91 (top), 112 (top), 140 (bottom), 165 (both), 166, 167, 1 169, 174, 175, 176, 177, 178 (inset), 180, 181, 182, 183 (both), 184–85, 186, 187, 188, 189, 190 (both), 192–193 (all four), 197 (top), 200, 201, 202 (top), 203, 204 (both), 206 (both), 207, 208 (both), 209, 212 (bottom), 213, 216 (both), 220, 221 (top)
© **Richard Natkiel** (maps) pp 32 (bottom), 115, 119, 132, 168
Naval Historical Photos pp 29 (top), 112 (bottom)
Peter Newark's Western Americana p 40
New York Historical Society p 21 (bottom)
New York Public Library p 38 (bottom)
US Army pp 91 (bottom), 113 (top), 145 (top), 148 (bottom)
US Air Force pp 64, 88, 217 (bottom), 222 (bottom)
US Marine Corps pp 8–9, 13 (bottom), 15 (top left), 16 (top left and right), 33 (bottom), 36 (top), 53, 54 (top), 61 (bottom), 65 (both), 71 (top), 75 (top right), 78, 79 (top), 83, 84, 85, 94, 95 (top), 98–99 (all three), 102 (both), 103 (both), 104–105 (all three), 106–107 (all five), 108–109 (all four), 110–111 (all four), 114, 115 (top), 116–117 (all four), 118–119 (all four), 120, 121, 122–123, 130–131 (all three), 132, 133, 134 (top and bottom), 136–137, 139, 140 (top), 141, 144, 148 (top), 149 (top), 150, 151, 152–53 (all three), 154, 155, 156, 157, 158, 159, 160–161, 163, 170–171, 173, 178–179 (main pic), 191 (right), 194–195 (all three), 196, 198–199, 212 (top), 214–215, 217 (top)
US Signal Corps pp 134 (top right), 138 (top), 145 (bottom)
Valley Forge Historical Society p 10–11
Virginia State Library p 41 (bottom)